A MANUAL OF
HORSE TRAINING
&
MANAGEMENT

A MANUAL OF
HORSE TRAINING
&
MANAGEMENT

Elwyn Hartley Edwards

UNWIN HYMAN
London · Sydney · Wellington

First published in Great Britain by Unwin Hyman,
an imprint of Unwin Hyman Limited, 1989

UNWIN HYMAN LIMITED
15–17 Broadwick Street
London W1V 1FP

Allen & Unwin Australia Pty Ltd
8 Napier Street
North Sydney, NSW 2060
Australia

Allen & Unwin New Zealand Pty Ltd with the
Port Nicholson Press
Compusales Building
75 Ghuznee Street
Wellington
New Zealand

British Library Cataloguing in Publication Data
Hartley Edwards, Elwyn
 A manual of horse training and management.
 1. Live stock: Horses. Training
 I. Title
 636.1′083

 ISBN 0-04-440207-4

Designed by Julian Holland
Typeset by Latimer Trend & Company Ltd
Plymouth
Printed and bound in Great Britain by
Butler & Tanner Ltd., Frome

Contents

Acknowledgements   6
Introduction   7
1   The Horse in Perspective   11
2   The Basic Horse – Physiology and Structure   17
3   Conformation – An Eye for a Horse   30
4   The Nature of the Beast   47
5   The Stress Factor   66
6   The Human Factor – Progressive Mounted and Dismounted
        Exercises   71
7   Stage 1 – Preparation for Work – Early Training   89
8   Stage 2 – Training the Three-year-old   107
9   Stage 3 – Work on the Flat   132
10 Stage 4 – Jumping and Cross-country Riding   158
11 Saddle and Bridle   176
    Bibliography   191

Acknowledgements

My thanks are due to June Abbott, who typed the manuscript so accurately; to Julie Hughes, who acted as a model for the mounted and dismounted exercises and who demonstrated movements so effectively with her horse Friar Tuck; to Jill Roberts, John and Shirley Smith-Jones, who organised photographic sessions; and to my old friend Leslie Lane who took the photographs.

Obviously, I owe a particular debt to Lesley Bruce who provided the unusual and arresting illustrations and, as always, to my wife and to all those horses who have taught me over the years so much more than ever I was able to teach them.

E.H.E.
Chwilog 1988

Introduction

The relationship between man and horse extends over some 5,000 years – not so long as that between man and dog, nor as long as the association with sheep, goats, pigs and cattle, all of which precede the horse in the domestication table by some thousands of years.

We know, of course, that horses provided a more or less convenient source of food long before groups of Asiatic steppe nomads, forebears of the fierce horse cultures of Scythians, Mongols and Huns, forsook the herding of migratory reindeer and applied similar techniques to the husbandry of horse herds.

It may seem strange that although there is indisputable evidence of men hunting horses for their meat and hides at least 15,000 years ago (the cave drawings at Lascaux in France and at Santander in Spain provide vivid proof of the relationship), it was to take as much as 9–10,000 years before even a relatively loose form of domestication was accomplished. One has to assume that so long a delay was occasioned by the physical character of the horse and the unpredictability of the equine temperament. But it is that point in our history, when a primitive people effected the last domestication of the animal kingdom, which represents a watershed in the human development only equalled, 5,000 years later, by a man setting foot upon the moon.

It is almost with a sense of physical shock that one realises that after man himself the greatest contribution to the progress of our world was made by the horse, the last of the animal species to receive the sometimes dubious benefit of the domestic state. Without the horse, the human race would hardly have got so far in so short a space of time.

The balance of benefit accruing from the horse/human partnership is obviously tipped heavily in favour of man. For the horse peoples, the various Asian nomadic races, the horse was central to their culture, providing food, milk, fuel, hides and other necessities of life as well as an essential mobility. Horsepower underpinned the armies and the economies of the world up to and beyond the end of the nineteenth century, whilst in ancient times the Gods were propitiated by the sacrifice of horses and the horses of kings were buried along with their masters. In every imaginable area of endeavour the horse was used – and often most terribly abused.

Despite the exploitation, the cruelty and often shameful abuse, the uncomplaining horse (he could, indeed, hardly be otherwise) fulfilled every demand made of him, displaying an adaptability to which there seems to be no limit. Taking into account the nature of the animal, the ways in which he has adapted, and continues to adapt, to the human requirement is almost beyond understanding.

(There is no doubt that centuries of domestication have reduced the horse's independence; they may, indeed, for all we know have reduced the size of his brain. Is it possible that as the horse became more dependent his ability to adapt – or, perhaps, cooperate – increased?)

What did the horse receive in return for 5,000 years of service? Not much you may think and little, if anything, that did not further the use that could be made of him. To that last end men introduced the practice of selective breeding to fulfil particular purposes.

Very early in history the advantages of hand feeding were discovered, the need to maintain large numbers of horses providing one reason for the continual development of agricultural practice.

It is within the restless character of men to improve upon the natural environment. In the case of the horse, human intervention in the production of breeds and types seems to have been wholly beneficial, even though the reasons were selfish rather than altruistic – the same certainly cannot be said about the breeding of dogs.

When at last the horse was largely superseded in the world economy by the internal combustion engine, the survival of his species was made possible because of his value to mankind as a means of recreation and sport. Unless there were these uses made of horses the equine population would reduce in accordance with the inexorable law of supply and demand. In the end, with no useful purpose to serve in the world which they helped to create, horses might at best be preserved as rare breeds kept in small herds in zoological parks.

Happily, there seems no likelihood of that coming about – once more this tenacious species has adapted to a new circumstance. Horses are now kept purely for recreational use all over the world. In Britain's egalitarian society, and probably elsewhere, they are kept very largely as the property of one- and two-horse owners in both rural and urban situations. Abuse and cruelty, often caused by ignorance, still exists but on the whole the lot of the horse in the closing years of the twentieth century is idyllic in comparison with that endured by the species not much more than a hundred years ago.

Without any doubt the new breed of horse owner is genuinely fond of its horses and ponies, but it is, nonetheless, distanced from them by the environment it has created and the pressures to which in consequence it is subjected.

The early horse-peoples, unhampered by the necessities of our modern society, had an instinctive empathy with their surroundings and the animals which were the co-inhabitants of their environment. They shared the life rhythms of nature in ways which are entirely impossible for people who have to be concerned with the demands of a twentieth-century life; people who have to take children to school, pay mortgages, hold down jobs and attend to the hundred and one tasks involved in running a home and existing acceptably within the society of which they are members.

Indeed, is it really surprising if, surrounded as we are by the appurtenances of the space age – instant light, heat and water, transport at the turn of a key and all those videos, washing machines, calculators and computers – we do sometimes, if unconsciously, treat the horse as a sort of bicycle, often expecting of him a mechanical performance.

Then, also, there is a large, active peripheral horse industry tempting and persuading us to buy its varied wares. That such an industry has grown up around a recreational pursuit is entirely admirable as well as being economically desirable. It provides employment, generates wealth and contributes positively to the enjoyment of leisure time – and for the most part it does so with a sense of responsibility.

However, the range of goods on offer is so wide that it can give rise to an understandable confusion, particularly, for example, in the crowded area of feedstuffs and supplements.

Packaged 'convenience foods' are not to be denigrated; they allow even the veriest tyro to keep a horse in good health by doing no more than following the instructions given on the bag, and they certainly form part of the ration of most modern horses. Even so 'convenience' food does not take the place of horsemastership based on the observation and understanding of an individual's needs.

(It is salutory to reflect that although veterinary science and nutritional research has advanced immeasurably in the space of twenty years, horses do not run faster, jump higher or endure any longer than they ever did. The performance of riders has improved enormously in that time, but not the performance of the horses.)

This book is about human beings relating to an animal being within the context of our modern life and in ways which are relevant to what we require from the relationship.

Some of us may have the gift of a special empathy with animals; for others it is something to be acquired by conscious application. We acquire a sensitivity and establish what amounts to a partnership if we have an understanding of the horse's physical characteristics, and then try to appreciate the effects of the environment in which he is asked to live.

The next stage is to find ways of improving our own physical capacity and extending our ability to communicate on a mental plane – the latter takes longer but it is not impossible. Thereafter, there is the need to have a sound knowledge of equestrian theory. It is quite possible to ride by the light of nature alone, if you are very gifted. If not, it is better to understand what it is that you are trying to achieve and then apply a proven technique.

Once we can communicate both mentally and physically our relationship assumes a quite different and far more satisfying dimension.

On a hyper-hair-splitting level it could be argued that by acquiring skills and knowledge we, too, are in a sense guilty of exploiting the horse just as were the old horse-peoples; but if the horse also obtains pleasure from the relationship that is hardly a matter of consequence.

I

The Horse in Perspective

Comparative skeletons of man and horse.

VERY FEW of the qualities which far too many of us accept as a matter of course are, in fact, natural to the horse. Indeed, it could be argued that the imposition of domestication is in itself unnatural. Certainly, the modern horse is a light age away from those primitive ancestors who were stampeded over cliffs by the hunters and whose bones still lie to bear witness to the act at places like Solutré in the south-east of France and elsewhere.

For horses to accept a man sitting on their backs, in a shrieking defiance of a basic instinct, is in itself remarkable. For the same animal to accept with relative equanimity all the necessary adjuncts of equine life as it must be lived in the final years of the twentieth century is, if anything, even less comprehensible. It has to be seen as an extraordinary feat of adaptation unparalleled in any other association of man with the animals, and it highlights a singular quality which is unique to the species. It is the willingness to please, the ability and the desire to co-operate which in some horses comes close to being a necessary part of their lives. It is a quality not found in quite the same form or degree in other animals, not even in the dog whose motivations are indeed quite different, and it is certainly not present in performing animals. It is possible to train a tiger or a bear to perform tricks and movements – whether they do so willingly is quite another matter and at no point in their lives can they be regarded as reliable. Indeed, the older they get the more likely they are to become unpleasant. Dolphins and elephants – the latter, like the horse, an herbivore – come closer but even they do not approach this outstanding characteristic of the equine and both, in a sense, are more limited in their response.

To survive in the modern horse/man context, horses have to conform to requirements quite foreign to their nature. That they do so might be taken, perhaps, as evidence of yet another highly developed survival technique.

The modern requirements

The base requirements of the horse in today's society, other than his suitability for riding or driving, are:

(1) That he should accept the confines of a stable and behave acceptably within it.

(2) That he submits to being tied without making resistance and permits himself to be handled.

(3) That he allows himself to be shod without protest.

(4) That he is reliable and safe in traffic within normal parameters.

(5) That he enters and leaves a trailer or horsebox quietly.

(6) That he can be clipped with comparative ease – a requirement in most instances.

It is also possible that this herd animal, by nature gregarious, will be expected to live in solitary state, apart from his own kind. Many horses are kept on their own quite satisfactorily, but for an herbivorous animal whose defence mechanism is based on swift and immediate flight from danger, or even the smallest suspicion of possible attack, and whose consequently heightened sensibilities contribute to a naturally highly strung disposition, such a list of requirements is a pretty tall order. To an animal of this nature, confinement, let alone being secured so that he is unable to escape, might be expected to produce panic, but only very rarely does it even occasion unease.

It could be, I suppose, a pattern of compliance which, having been accepted by generations of his predecessors, has become a virtually in-bred characteristic. Labradors, after all, retrieve as to the manner born, and sheepdogs, even as puppies, will round up a flock of sheep instinctively – but they are animals of a different species.

Beyond the force of example, provided by a parent, companions or older horses, and my hesitantly offered hypothesis I can see no reason why the horse should accept these situations as being normal. Nor is there any more reason why we humans should consider them in that light.

It is very probable that when difficulties are experienced in any one of these base requirements the initial fault is with the human, who has failed to appreciate that the horse is being asked to act contrary to his nature and, as a result, has neglected to take the necessary steps to prepare him for the particular situation. Trust between the two parties is of the essence, but it is necessary to take some trouble about introducing the horse to what is to be asked of him and in some cases planning a deliberate training programme so as to make it easy for the horse to comply – teaching a young horse to box, or retraining an older one who has for one reason or another developed a dislike of the conveyance, is an obvious example.

Performance levels

Beyond the basic requirements there lies the question of performance. At one end of the scale a horse who will carry his rider out hacking safely and comfortably will be acceptable to a rider who does not aspire to go beyond that level. At the opposite extreme there is the rider who requires a performance level sufficient to allow entry into advanced horse trials. The realisation of the first should not provide too many difficulties but the whole business becomes increasingly complex as higher standards of performance are demanded.

Temperament is a factor common to every requirement asked of the horse and includes, I think, that necessary spirit of willing co-operation. But we have to remember that the temperament that will suit one person and his/her requirement may be quite unsuitable for another.

There is, I believe, a misunderstanding, or

perhaps it is a general misuse, of the word temperament. The *Oxford Dictionary* defines it at some length, devoting, in my copy, no less than 9 ins (22 cms) to the word and its closest derivatives. Disregarding mediaeval philosophy and physiology, temperament emerges as 'a moderate and proportionable mixture of elements in a compound; the condition in which elements are combined in their due proportion'. The suggestion is of a mental stability, a calmness of mind, and I would not argue with that. The implication, nonetheless, is of a state of perfection. 'A consummation devoutly to be wished', no doubt, but one found about as frequently in either the human or animal condition as the perfectly proportioned body.

When people talk about 'super', 'wonderful' or 'marvellous' temperaments they are saying that the horse has a kindly, willing, trusting disposition. Some do have just that; others may just be placid with a minimal adrenalin flow. Such a horse might do very well for the person who asks no more than to be taken quietly round the summer lanes, but it would be unusual if the same horse was suitable to go eventing. The performance horse at the top level needs to have the spark which ignites the adrenalin if he is to have the courage to do well. Temperamentally he is not unbalanced or immoderate, it is just that the mixture is a bit different.

Extremes of temperament

The two extremes in the spectrum of the equine character are represented by the dominant horse on one hand and his opposite, the recessive one on the other. Many exceptional, talented performers are dominant. Nonetheless, if their potential is to be realised their human partner has to be equally talented, for these dominant horses can just as easily become difficult, unreliable subjects if the human fails to measure up to them.

The recessive horse, unsure of himself and

with little faith in his own ability, is, in a sense, even more reliant. He draws confidence and courage from his human partner. The recessive character not only needs leadership but welcomes it also. Again, the onus is on the human if a successful partnership is to be achieved and the horse realise whatever potential he may have.

The great majority of horses are not, of course, entirely dominant nor wholly recessive, any more than are we humans. They can incline more towards dominance than recessivism, or it can be the other way about. A lot occupy the middle ground, tending, like politicians, to be a few degrees left or right of centre.

Wherever they stand in the character/temperament spectrum, their subsequent development depends very much on the qualities of the human with whom they are associated. (Perhaps we can appreciate the confusion that can be caused when the horse passes through two or three homes, or even more, and has to contend with half a dozen people.)

Like people, horses have their limitations. They are imposed by the individual's temperament and, as I have tried to make clear, by the character and physical abilities and skills of the humans who seek to obtain a partnership with him. Finally, there is the influence of the all-important physical factor.

Obviously, if the horse is going to gallop and jump and be subjected to tests of endurance he has to be made fit for the purpose by exercise, schooling, feeding and so on. Physical condition, therefore, either enhances the performance potential or detracts from it.

To a very large extent, however, physical performance, all else being equal, is concerned with the horse's conformation. The word, much used in the equine context, can be defined as: the formation of the skeletal frame and its accompanying muscle structures in terms of the symmetrical proportion to each other of the individual parts comprising the whole. We can go further. It is about symmetry. It is about the perfection of each

of the component parts, their proportionate relationship and their contribution to an overall perfection of form.

The well-built, proportionate horse is not only more efficient in pure mechanical terms but will also have a natural balance and is, in addition, better equipped to remain sound when subjected to the demands made by competitive sport.

Good conformation results in a corresponding correctness of economical movement and is usually (but not always) accompanied by athleticism and gymnastic ability-both enormously important attributes in the competition horse.

Once more, however, the athletic ability of the horse will only be employed to its full extent by a skilful, athletic rider. To a degree a good horse will take a mediocre rider a bit further than one of lesser ability, and conversely a good rider will produce a corresponding performance from a moderate horse. There have been, however, numerous examples of brilliant horses, or just good horses, being bought by riders whose own abilities were less than evident. Inevitably, the performance level declines in a relatively short space of time, which bears out the truth of the saying that 'the horse is the mirror of his rider'.

There is a final point to be made about conformation. It is that the physical structure has to relate to the purpose for which it is intended.

Clearly, the structure suitable for a draught horse pulling heavy loads at slow paces is not in any way relevant to a horse whose purpose in life is to gallop and jump over a horse trials course.

Although the difference is far less accentuated, a similar division can exist between the conformation that is suitable for dressage – where the horse is not required to display an ability to gallop – and that which fits a horse for the rigours of the three-day event. It is probable, too, that there will be a difference in the mental outlook of the two.

It follows that to choose a compatible equine partner we, too, have basic requirements to meet.

If we are to communicate mentally as well as physically it has to be on the basis of our understanding something about the horse's make-up in both those respects, recognising that our own limitations are a governing factor in his development.

2

The Basic Horse – Physiology and Structure

IT IS not necessary, or even possible, for the majority of riders to have a comprehensive knowledge of physiology and equine structure, but clearly it will be helpful to have a sufficient general understanding of these subjects to be able to relate both to the care and training of the horse – otherwise we are working in the dark.

Cells

At the base of the horse, as with all living creatures, is the cellular structure. The body, bones and all, is comprised of myriads of cells, each of which has its own particular function: the liver cells, for instance, make bile; the muscle cells are responsible for developing the power of contraction which is fundamental to movement. Each one has to be fed and the subsequent waste matter removed. In total these countless cells combine to make up the whole organism, which functions by feeding and then reproducing itself.

The continual process of renewal, upon which depends not only the life continuance but also the quality of that life, is made possible by the division of individual cells. In youth the process is marked and vigorous; in old age there is a natural decline.

Cell multiplication is equally affected by the condition/health of the organism. If it is well nourished and in good health multiplication is encouraged; then it works at peak efficiency having, of course, regard for its age. In opposite circumstances the converse applies and results in a far less efficient body function.

It is, therefore, no more than common sense to maintain the horse in a condition of robust health throughout its life. By doing so we ensure maximum efficiency of the organism and prolong its useful function.

Young horses who are neglected in their formative years by inadequate feeding, subjection to a heavy parasitic worm burden and so on, have their development checked at a critical point in their lives. They may, indeed, suffer damage which will never be entirely repaired.

If, for instance, bones become malformed as a result of a severe dietary deficiency, there is no way in which they will be put right entirely. The result of the malformation goes far beyond the bone structure itself. The associated joints, tendons and ligaments will all become more prone to strain and, in the case of the former, to disease.

Heavy worm burdens have just as insidious an effect. Irreparable damage may be done by the activity of these parasites within the bloodstream, which may not necessarily be made manifest until later in the horse's career.

The advisability of turning horses away for periods of the year, allowing them to lose physical tone and condition, must also be questioned. A few weeks' rest will do no harm, but that apart, horses, like humans, are better for maintaining a reasonably constant level of physical fitness.

Structure and locomotion

The framework of the body is supplied by the variously shaped bones which combine to form the skeleton. They support the body mass and their movement when activated by *joints*, and in concert with the muscles, results in its consequent locomotion.

A *joint* is formed at the juncture of two bones. The ends of such bones, the articular surfaces, are of greater density than elsewhere so as to be better able to withstand the friction which will occur between the two surfaces.

As an additional preventive against wear, the surfaces are separated by a layer of gristle, called *cartilage*.

The whole arrangement is held together by *ligaments*, the tough, fibrous and flexible tissues which are attached to each bone.

To complete a remarkable piece of engineering, the joint is encased within a two-layer capsule. The outer layer gives further support to the joint, whilst the inner one secretes an oily fluid (synovia or joint oil) which allows the joint to work within a vessel of oil and therefore in a state of constant lubrication.

As well as holding the joint together, ligaments serve the purpose of limiting its movement so that it cannot be extended beyond its capability. Damage to a ligament, therefore, will have an effect upon the movement of the joint. Damage or disease in the latter will have a similar effect.

Muscle covers a large part of the body and by being attached to bones produces movement in the joints and thus in the body mass. The movement is produced by the contraction of the muscle, which in consequence draws together the two points of attachment and initiates the action of the joint.

However, muscles, though elastic, would be easily torn and damaged if they were not equipped with *tendons*. Tendons, which are tough and inelastic, run like a rope through the length of the muscle. One end is secured firmly to the bone whilst the other is virtually plaited into the muscle substance.

The sort of activity which we expect of the horse, galloping, often over broken terrain, and jumping what are frequently fences of very sizable proportions, places a particular strain on the tendons. Incorrect shoeing which allows the foot to be too long and the heel too low to the ground, also contributes to tendon problems in the lower leg.

Just as damage to a ligament affects the movement so any damage to the tendon will also impair the action of the joint more or less seriously, depending, of course, upon the damage which has been sustained.

Condition and co-ordination

Horses that are galloped and jumped when in unfit condition will obviously be more susceptible to injury in this respect, particularly if the ground under foot is rough and uneven.

Unfit horses, and very tired ones also, lack that slight tension in the muscles which is called *tonus* or more simply, *muscle tone*. This necessary state of tension in the muscle prevents movement which would cause the joints to flex or extend so violently as to be damaged. Violent movement of this sort, as a result of insufficient muscle tone, leads to inco-ordination of the limbs and places the component parts at risk.

The lesson so far as the unfit or over-tired horse is concerned is obvious. However, inco-ordination, the result of undeveloped muscle tone, is very noticeable in young horses in the early stages of their training programmes. They manage pretty well at liberty even though the domestic state – particularly when it involves confinement and artificial feeding – increases the risk of injury. The combination of youth, strength and good condition leads inevitably and not unnaturally to moments of violent exertion as the youngster lets off steam by galloping, bucking, jumping and generally turning himself inside out. That, of course, is when injuries such as strains and sprains can occur.

Beyond taking commonsense precautions in respect of diet and the safety of the paddock into which the youngster is turned, there is not much else to be done. The situation has to be accepted as one of the hazards that are inseparable from domestication.

Protection – progression

We can do more to safeguard the young horse during his early lessons. The legs, of course, need to be protected by boots lest they should strike into each other. It is essential, however, to appreciate that the discipline of the schooling exercises represent pretty strenuous physical exertion. Initially, the schooling periods must be kept short (*far* shorter than most of us appreciate), and only increased

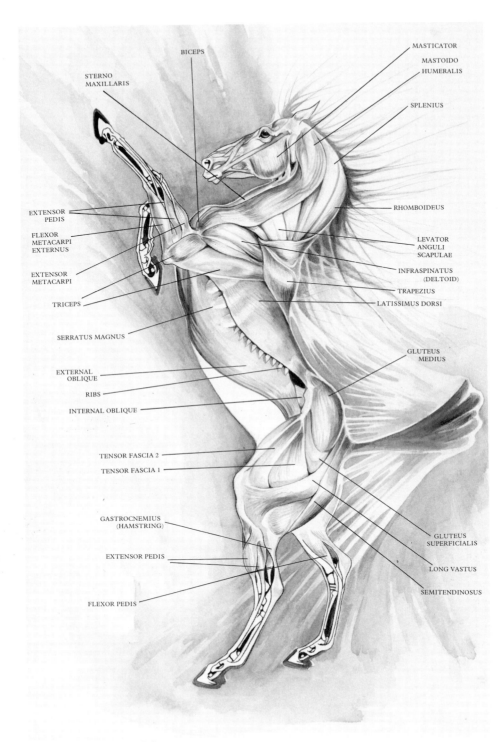

The muscular structure which promotes locomotion.

gradually as the training progresses. Similarly, the exercises can only be made more difficult stage by slow stage. The horse must never be worked until he becomes tired and loses his muscle tone as a result. If the work is hurried and prolonged it becomes a punishment for him instead of a pleasure and increases the likelihood of strain or other injury – not unreasonably, he reacts accordingly.

(To impress the wisdom of hastening slowly upon the mind and to appreciate the physical stress and discomfort which can be caused by injudicious exercise, try at this moment to do fifty press-ups. If you are not in the habit of practising this particular form of physical exertion the point will be made very clearly and quickly.)

Muscle function

A peculiar property of muscles relevant to schooling is that they can be made to contract only to the same extent as they are able to extend, or be stretched. If the training encourages the muscles to first be stretched the power of contraction will, therefore, be increased. It follows that the greater the ability of muscle to extend and contract the nearer the joints, which it controls, will be able to flex to full capacity.

The *voluntary* muscles with which we are concerned when schooling the horse for riding or any other purpose are, in fact, of two kinds. There are *flexors*, which contract to flex the joint, and *extensors*, which extend to allow the opposite effect. The muscles are, therefore, acting in pairs but they also oppose, or compensate.

In achieving that desirable rounding of the top-line, for instance, the big back muscles are stretched, acting as *extensors*, the rounding effect being completed by the greater engagement of the hind legs under the body and the necessary raising of the abdomen. For that to be accomplished three muscles on the side of the abdomen and three others,

running from the fifth and ninth ribs to the pubis, act as *flexors* in opposition to the extending muscles of the back.

The same principle is employed to support the head and neck and permit both to be carried without effort, the muscles on the underside of the neck being matched by the opposing tension of the dorsal muscles lying on the top of the neck.

Lack of development in any of the muscles or an inability to extend and contract fully will clearly make it more difficult and even impossible to obtain the outline, carriage and subsequent movement that results in a strong and mechanically efficient structure.

The carriage of head and neck is a case in point. All too often, an incorrect carriage is achieved too quickly and by artificial means when it really depends:

(a) upon the initial conformation; and

(b) upon the proper development of the muscles.

If the conformation is noticeably deficient, as when a large, heavy head is carried on an overlong weak neck, there is at once an in-built difficulty on account of the former being too heavy for the latter to support. The neck may be strengthened and improved by intelligent schooling to the benefit of the carriage but the defect is fundamental and can never be overcome entirely.

Given that there is no major conformational failing, the carriage of head and neck is governed, largely, by the correct development of the supporting muscles.

Another example of compensatory muscle action is when the horse 'bends' on a circle or on elements of the circle. In fact, the horse does not 'bend', if by that it is meant that his spine is curved to correspond with the arc of the movement. That would be impossible, for the spine, except for a minimal movement in the lumbar vertebrae, is a rigid structure, not a flexible one. In the same way a horse cannot be *bent* round the rider's inside leg', however persuasive are the exhortations of the instructor. What happens is that in turning, the muscles on the inside of the body contract to correspond with the line of the arc, whilst those on the outside allow that contraction and compensate accordingly by being extended. The *appearance* is then of the horse being bent round the inside leg.

Unless the schooling results in the equal development of the muscles on both sides of the body and until both are able, therefore, to contract and expand to the same degree the horse will be 'one-sided' and unable to bend or turn to either hand with equal facility.

In addition to the voluntary muscles there are the *involuntary* ones occurring in the internal organs, like those which cause movement in the bowels, and the independent *cardiac* muscle connected with that function.

Nervous system

It is quite true that movement is the result of muscle contraction and expansion activating joints etc. However, the basis of movement in the body is with the brain and its continuation, the spinal cord.

In very simple terms, signals are sent from muscles or organs to the spinal cord via a nerve. There a response is made unconsciously or the signal is relayed to the principal exchange, the brain, and dealt with consciously.

Nerves are of two kinds: *sensory* nerves, by which the horse feels, sees, hears, smells and tastes without conscious effort and *motor* nerves which are concerned with motion.

It is held that, within limits, the contraction of which the muscle is capable is proportionate to the degree of stimulation provided by its nerves. The strength and the sensitivity of the nervous system in respect of the speed of the reflexes must, therefore, play a considerable part in the selection and training of horses.

Generalisation is a dangerous indulgence, but it seems likely that the more refined, better-bred horse is more receptive and responsive than those of more plebian ancestry because of the former's more efficient nervous system.

Nourishment

The body is nourished by the conversion of ingested food into an absorbable substance. The nutrient, via the liver and lymphatics, enters the bloodstream, is circulated through the organs, taken into the muscle and converted into energy.

The conversion of food into nutrient and the usage made of it for work and exercise produces heat. Heat is regulated to remain practically constant by the actions of the skin and lungs, sweating and breathing respectively, assisted by the bowels and kidneys.

Waste products are excreted by the bowels and kidneys and also by the skin and lungs.

That at any rate is a condensation of an enormously complex subject. The process is discussed in a little more depth under the heading 'Digestive System', but before that we should appreciate the function of the blood, if only in general terms.

Blood

Blood is a light coloured fluid in which is suspended red and white *corpuscles*, the former being the more numerous and giving the blood its colour. The red corpuscles are capable of absorbing oxygen and are therefore an essential factor in respiration. The purpose of the white corpuscles is to combat and destroy germs within the body. Any imbalance of the corpuscles is therefore a serious matter.

Blood conveys oxygen to the tissues and the other life necessities of the individual cells forming the whole structure. Circulating constantly through the *blood vessels*, blood also removes waste including carbon dioxide.

There are three sorts of blood vessel: *arter-*

ies, *capillaries* and *veins*.

Arteries originate in the heart, as strong elastic tubes which run through the whole body and merge finally in the capillaries.

Capillaries are the very thin tubes present in every part of the system. The walls of the capillary, unlike those of the artery are permeable, so as to allow through them the passage of blood cells, together with dissolved gases.

Veins are the continuation of capillaries in which the blood flows towards the heart. To ensure that the flow is maintained in that direction only veins are provided with an arrangement of no-return valves.

At the centre of the circulatory system is the heart, the pump which forces the blood through the body. It is a large organ weighing, on average, about 9 lbs (4 kg), but it may be even bigger than that. Eclipse, the greatest racehorse of the nineteenth century, and the founder of racing's greatest dynasty, had a heart which weighed over 14 lbs (6 kg).

There are four compartments comprising the heart. On the top are the left and right *auricles*, underneath are the left and right *ventricles*. Circulated blood enters the right auricle and is then passed to the right ventricle. From there the blood is pumped into the lungs through the *pulmonary artery*. At that point it comes into contact with inspired air where a significant change takes place. The blood becomes oxygenated and is returned to the left auricle by way of the *pulmonary veins*. It is pushed in that state into the left ventricle and from thence enters the *aorta*, the principal artery of the body, and is distributed around the body.

Respiration

The horse breathes through the nostrils; he cannot breathe as we do through the mouth as well. The inhaled air passes through the larynx, down the windpipe and into the lungs.

It is blood, of course, which plays the major role in respiration. It mixes with the inhaled air in the lungs and once more an exchange takes place. Then, the used air is expelled and the process is repeated.

In respiration the scarlet oxygenated blood pumped out of the heart through the arteries acquires some carbon dioxide and in consequence takes on the characteristic deep colour of arterial blood. It is in this state that it returns by the veins and then back to the lungs, where a change occurs once more, the oxygen going to the blood corpuscles and the carbon dioxide to the lungs. The blood, now once more oxygenised and having regained its scarlet colour is then re-circulated by the heart and the lungs expel the used air.

Unless this continual revivification of the blood is maintained by the passing of oxygen into the red corpuscles and the expulsion of carbonic acid from them, life does not continue, the subject succumbing to suffocation as the blood changes from dark red, through purple to black.

Since inspiration begins at the nostrils, it follows that in an animal frequently expected to operate at speed the nostrils should of necessity be large and capable of great distension so as to obtain the largest possible air supply. Just as important is the need for depth in the chest to accommodate the lungs and allow their full expansion.

Although it may seem to be unrelated at first sight, *muscle* and *muscle development* is also a notable factor in effective respiration. At rest, the natural recoil of the ribs and lungs is sufficient to expel what is sometimes called *tidal* air, i.e. the amount of air changed at each inspiration.

In exertion, however, *forced breathing* demands the additional assistance of muscles. The muscles involved in force expiration are the flank muscles covering the ribs and belly and compressing those parts to push out the used air. They are developed by the effective physical conditioning of the horse which, of course, will include a progression of work at the faster paces.

Lymphatics

Alongside the system of blood cells is the *lymphatic* system. The purpose of the lymphatic vessels is to collect goodness from the digested food in the bowels and to prevent fluid accumulation anywhere in the body, whilst conveying part of the blood back towards the heart.

Lymphangitis is a condition which occurs as a result of a breakdown in the function of waste clearance, the circulation being unable to remove lymph from the limbs. Usually, the lower parts of one or both hind limbs become swollen and in severe cases the leg may swell excessively and the horse will be very lame.

The cause of lymphangitis is usually connected with overfeeding combined with insufficient exercise. In some instances the condition will be produced when constituents of the diet are too high in protein for the individual horse.

Despite the passage of thousands of years, domestication and its attendant human requirements impose an essentially artificial environment on the horse for which his structure and general physiology are not best equipped. Unless we recognise the natural limitations, and operate within them, reactions in the system, like lymphangitis, are inevitable and their effects may detract from the overall efficiency of the body for long periods of time.

Digestive system

An overall understanding of the digestive process is obviously vital to the proper management of the horse.

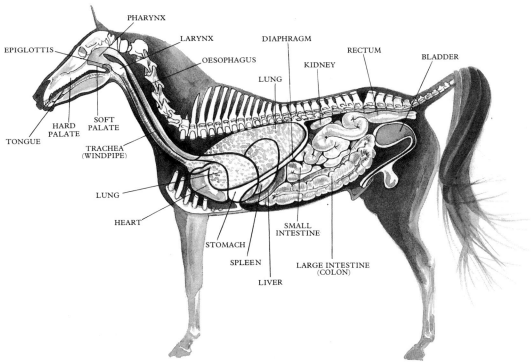

The horse in section showing the principal organs.

Digestion begins in the *mouth* where food is rolled by the tongue and ground by the *molar teeth*. The action of mastication produces quantities of *saliva* from glands under the tongue and in the jaw which reduces the food to a convenient paste.

The mouth, and in particular the teeth, should therefore be subjected to regular inspection as part of the daily routine. After all, if there is a breakdown in the system at the point of the food's entry the process can hardly be said to get under way.

In a 'full mouth', i.e. a mouth of permanent teeth which are *in situ* at about the age of five years, each jaw has a complement of six incisor (biting) teeth and twelve molar (grinding) teeth.

The upper jaw is always larger than the lower and as a result the molars in each grow in opposite ways. Those of the top jaw grow downwards and outwards and those of the lower jaw upwards and inwards. It is, therefore, possible for the·teeth to be worn unevenly so that the outside of the upper molars and the inside of the lower ones become sharp. Clearly, this will cause discomfort in the mouth, sometimes to the point where the cheeks become lacerated, and will interfere with the process of mastication as well as causing bitting difficulties.

Teeth need to be rasped smooth by the veterinary surgeon at least once a year, probably twice, and particular attention should be given to young horses who are in the process of replacing milk teeth with permanent ones.

After the mouth the food mixture is forced into the stomach by the muscles of the *gullet*. In the stomach the powerful involuntary muscles knead the food still further whilst at the same time *gastric juices* are produced. These latter in concert with the muscle action reduce the food to a creamy paste which passes easily into the *bowels*. The horse has two bowels, the small and the large.

The *small bowel*, some 70 ft (21 m) long, receives fluid from the ducts of the *pancreas and liver*, which assist in the breakdown of the food. Bile, from the liver, for instance, plays a large part in preparing the food for use by the muscles and it also acts to disinfect the bowel. As it passes through the bowel the food becomes increasingly liquid and in that form is absorbed into the body.

The *large bowel* (some 30 ft (9 m) long) receives the unabsorbed matter, and the constant motion of the *gut* extracts all the nutriment possible before the waste product is finally excreted.

The process is made possible by the existence of the digestive fluids each of which performs certain functions.

Saliva helps to convert starch into sugar as a preliminary to absorption as well as reducing solid foodstuffs to a form which is easily swallowed.

Gastric juice is acidic. It changes the *proteid* (flesh-forming) element into the more easily absorbed substance called *peptones*. It breaks up fibrous matter and helps in the starch to sugar conversion.

Intestinal secretions act on the peptones and sugars to make them even more easily assimilated substances. In this form they pass through the bowel wall into the lymphatics and the blood vessels.

Bile, as well as acting as a bowel disinfectant, converts fats into an emulsion.

Pancreatic juice is instrumental in the process of converting starches into sugar and proteids into peptones and emulsifying fats.

Worms

Possibly the most important lesson to learn from this necessarily brief and general study, after the paramount requirement of maintaining the horse in overall good condition, is the specific consideration of the worm problem.

Heavy infestations, particularly during foalhood, attack the gut and intestines, enter the walls of blood vessels and seriously damage the arteries, causing aneurisms which obstruct the blood supply. Anaemia, chronic diarrhoea and colic are some of the results and even death cannot be excluded.

Modern worming preparations are effective and simple to administer. Indeed, the only effort required of the horse owner is that of payment for the product. Not to worm regularly is irresponsible and amounts to virtual cruelty by neglect.

The skin

Skin is formed of two layers: the *dermis*, which is deep and sensitive, and the outer, protective insensitive *epidermis*, which is constantly shed and replaced. Apart from protecting the body the skin helps to regulate temperature and to assist in the secretion of waste matter.

The *dermis* contains blood vessels, nerves,

Arrangement of tendons and ligaments in the foreleg and detail of the foot.

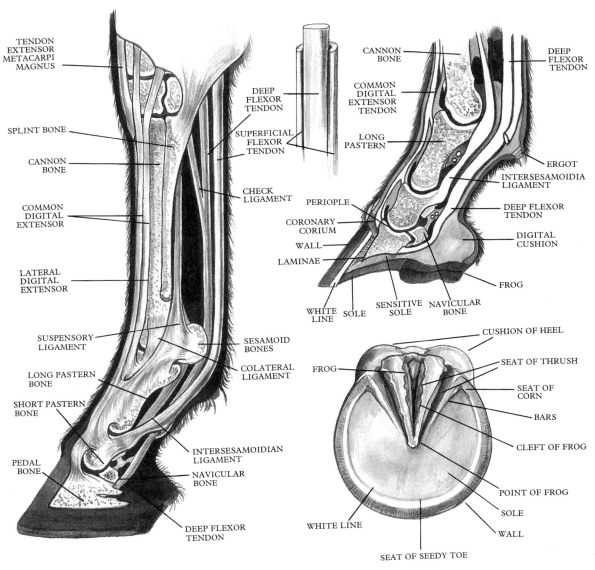

sweat and oil glands and hair roots. The hairs and tubes of the oil and sweat glands pass to the surface through the *epidermis* and their openings form the skin *pores*.

Sweat glands work constantly and sweating is a way by which the temperature is controlled. Furthermore, sweating removes the waste products created by exertion.

Intensive feeding of the stabled horse in hard work produces extra waste products. If they are to be excreted through the pores, it follows that the skin must be kept clean by regular grooming, otherwise the pores will become blocked and will function less effectively.

Hair is produced from hair bulbs deep in the skin, each hair having a muscle allowing it to be pulled into an upright position and each one having an oil gland on each side. The oil glands, by greasing the hairs, give a shine to the coat, a function encouraged by vigorous grooming, and help to render it waterproof.

Horses in poor condition, or suffering from ill-health or exposure, display dry, harsh coats that are said to be 'stary', i.e. the hairs stand on end. This is usually accompanied by a tight skin in contrast to the loose, mobile skin of the healthy horse.

The foot and its function

No part of the horse has been made more vulnerable to disease and injury because of the domestic requirement than the foot, which is central to the horse's performance.

In the feral state the hoof was worn down naturally and was just as naturally replaced by the horn's constant growth. (The feet grow, just like our nails, at the rate of between $\frac{1}{4} - \frac{3}{8}$ in. (6–9 mm) per month.)

Under the domestic condition horses are required to cover greater distances over varying types of ground and usually when carrying weight. If the foot is to stand up to usage of that kind it has, therefore, to be protected by a shoe so that the horse does not become footsore and lame.

Skilfully fitted, the shoe enhances the movement of the horse, can correct the less serious conformational deficiencies, turned in feet etc., and will contribute to the foot's natural function as a shock-absorbing mechanism.

Conversely, neglect of the foot will have the opposite results and will in the end lead to the horse becoming unserviceable. It is altogether too easy for the foot to become out of balance when, for instance, it is allowed to become so long that the weight is shifted onto the heel. The angulation of the joints is then disturbed and the position of the bones in the foot and their relationship to each other is altered. In that situation it is theoretically possible that the initial misplacement of the pedal bone will be continued upwards through all the bones of the lower leg, the possibility of disease in the joints being multiplied half a dozen times or more. (Feet which are allowed to come down on the heel part also stretch the tendons running down the back of the leg and subject them to increased strain as a result.)

A correct *hoof-pastern axis* (HPA) is obtained when a straight line is formed through the phalanges when viewed laterally. In the forefeet this line should relate to the angle of the shoulder (i.e. the line made between the highest part of the wither and the point of the shoulder).

The most effective flight path of the foot and the length and elevation of the stride depend very largely on the observance of the proper HPA. The HPA in the hind feet will be slightly steeper (about 5°) than in the forelimbs.

The maintenance of the HPA together with meticulous care of the feet in all other respects, is a vital element in the schooling of the young horse, and because of its influence on the quality and overall efficiency of the action is critical to the performance.

Feet become too long and the balance altered when the shoes are not removed or replaced with sufficient frequency (once every four weeks is advisable), and when feet are left untrimmed on horses out at grass for relatively long periods of time (again, the feet need attention about once a month). Imbalance will be caused by feet which become unlevel because of faulty preparation or a shoe fitted improperly.

Shock absorption

Work at speed and particularly over fences is very demanding of the structure in all its respects and concussion is a major cause of injury in the foot and lower limbs.

The construction of the well-formed foot is such that it is: (a) able to support the weight of the horse; (b) resistant to wear; and (c) capable of absorbing the concussion caused by it striking the ground and thus limiting the jarring effect throughout the lower leg.

Heavy shoes encourage the leg to be elevated in movement (as, for instance, with the Welsh Cob) and that action will obviously increase the concussion experienced in the foot and lower leg. Light shoes, on the other hand, help to make the action longer and lower, which is preferable in most competitive situations, and will also reduce the concussive effect.

For convenience the foot can be divided into two parts: the outer, non-vascular, *insensitive foot* and the inner, *sensitive foot*. The insensitive foot comprises the *wall* of the hoof, which is made of dense horn, the *bars*, the *sole* and the *frog*. The *wall* is divided into the *toe*, the portion at the front of the foot, which passes into the *quarters* at the sides and thence to the *heels*. The horn of the wall is thickest at the toe, the width of horn being reduced at the quarters and to their rear.

The wall does not, in fact, encircle the hoof. It turns inwards at the heels to form the *bars*, which are joined with both frog and sole. As part of the wall they support the weight. They also give more strength at the heels and provide an extra bearing surface.

The prime function of the bars, however, is that they allow the foot to expand, and expansion is an essential element in the absorption of concussion.

If the bars were to be cut away, one of the more heinous sins of farriery, the foot would lose the support at the heels and would be likely to contract. In consequence its ability to expand would be reduced.

The *periople*, the rim of soft horn at the juncture of the hoof with the coronary band, actually extends rather like a membrane over the wall of the foot, being thicker round the upper part of the hoof. Its function is to provide a protective film which prevents the evaporation of natural oil in the underlying horn. For this reason the farrier must not make too free a use of his rasp and risk its removal. Excessive rasping would result in an increased rate of evaporation which, ultimately, would produce dry and brittle feet.

The moisture content of the hoof is, indeed, critical and whilst it can be lost by too much evaporation, troubles will also arise if the natural evaporation rate is halted. This would result in an accumulation of fluid which would cause a softening of the hoof. The application of impervious dressings – varnishes, polishes, etc. – can give rise to this condition.

On the inside of the wall are layers of *insensitive horny laminae* (leaves). They merge into the inner *sensitive foot* and the layers of fleshy, sensitive leaves. The two are divided by what is called the *white line*, which runs round the inside of the wall and is easily seen when one examines the scrubbed sole of an unshod foot. It is an important feature to the farrier since it indicates very clearly the area of insensitive wall into which nails can be driven safely.

As we know, the wall grows continually, the horn at the toe of the foot being harder than that at the heels. In the unshod foot the hard toe protects the foot against wear whilst the softer horn allows the foot to expand as it takes the weight.

The *sole* forms the ground surface of the foot and the thick outer, insensitive covering is covered with flakes of protective horn, which should not be pared off for the sake of appearance. A healthy sole is notably concave, a shape which affords a better foothold and which is less prone to bruising and better suited to support weight. The horny sole – which like the wall is continually growing, the old growth shelling off to make way for the new – also lies over and protects the inner, sensitive casing, sometimes called the *fleshy sole*, which provides for its nourishment.

The *frog* is the V-shaped structure lying between the bars of the foot. It is made up of soft, elastic horn and contains more fluid than any other part of the foot (40% water content against the horn's 24%), which is why it remains soft and spongy. It plays an important part in the anti-concussion mechanism of the foot and its wedge shape prevents slipping. When the foot comes to the ground the resultant compression causes the frog to expand. At the same time the frog itself is pushed upwards against the digital cushion, situated between it and the under surface of the pedal bone. This in turn expands so as to absorb and reduce concussion and itself brings pressure through the *lateral cartilages* on to the wall, which is compelled to follow suit.

The frog and the digital cushion are also concerned with the circulation. Blood, provided via the arteries, which has fed the tissues of the leg and foot and become de-oxygenated, flows into the cushion. As the frog comes under pressure so that pressure is transmitted to the cushion and forces the blood upwards through the veins on its return journey to the heart.

To function effectively therefore the frog has to come into contact with the ground. This continual contact helps it to remain healthy. If the frog cannot perform its function it will atrophy and the foot, in due course, will become contracted.

The sensitive foot, which is vascular, provides nutrition to the hoof and houses, within its insensitive protective casing: the *third phalanx* or *pedal* (coffin) bone, which is jointed with the *second phalanx* (the short pastern or coronet bone); the *navicular* bone, situated at the back of the pedal bone which acts as a fulcrum for the deep flexor tendon which is connected to the pedal bone; the *lateral cartilages* emanating from the wings of the pedal bone, which function as a shock-absorber to the sensitive foot, and the pedal or digital cushion. To the bones are attached ligaments and the tendons from the muscles of the forearm which create movement.

These are the points to check in newly-shod feet:

(1) That the horse stands square on all four feet and the HPA relates to the slope of the shoulder.
(2) That forefeet and hind feet are pairs in all respects.
(3) Clenches are in line and lie flat. They should be as nearly as possible parallel with the coronary band – not the ground.
(4) The wall of the foot should not show undue rasping.
(5) The foot must not be 'dumped', i.e. the toe cut and rasped excessively in order for it to be aligned with the shoe.
(6) Clips are flat, low and broad.
(7) That the shoe follows the line of the foot, i.e. the shoe fits the foot and not vice-versa.

When the foot is picked up, check these points:

(1) Nails driven right home and not protruding more than a fraction above the shoe.
(2) No heavy paring of sole, frog or bars.
(3) Shoes neither too long nor too short.
(4) No gaps between foot and shoe.
(5) No interference by the shoe with the functions of the frog.
(6) No sharp edges on the shoes.

Finally, have the horse trotted out to ensure that he goes both straight and sound.

3

Conformation – an Eye for a Horse

CONFORMATION

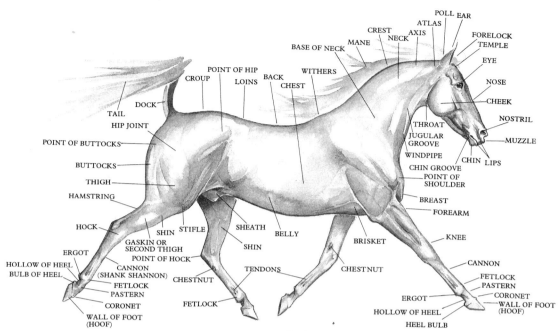

Points of the horse. The nomenclature is that which is in common use.

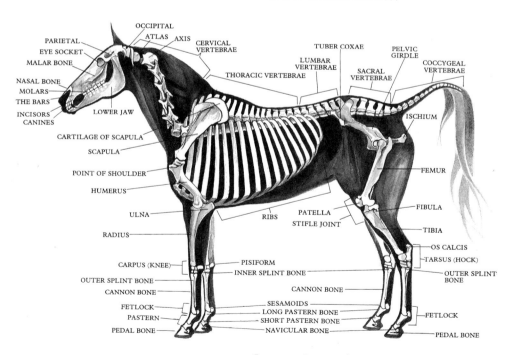

In assessing equine conformation it is useful to have some knowledge of the skeletal framework.

'IT IS by a study of conformation that we assign to a horse the particular place and purpose to which he is best adapted as a living machine and estimate his capacity for work.'

Those words were written by Professor Wortley-Axe, a one-time President of the Royal College of Veterinary Surgeons, a prolific writer and the author of a detailed ten-volume work, *The Horse*, which was published in 1905. He concluded that 'the highest success in this connection' (i.e. a study of conformation) 'will be best attained by the judicious blending of practice with science.'

Wortley-Axe and that group of his distinguished French contemporaries, which included Bourgelat, Duhousset, Goubaux and Barrier, all of whom made exhaustive and authoritative studies of conformation in relation to purpose, enjoyed, however, advantages denied to horsemen and women of our generation.

They lived in an age in which horse-power underpinned the world economy and their day-to-day work was concerned with the practical application of horses in a wide variety of circumstances. Their studies, made a century or more ago, related directly to the purposes to which working horses were put and they were based on comparative measurements and observations made between hundreds and, if necessary, thousands of horses.

It would be impossible to reproduce a similar situation today but we can still benefit from their detailed assessments when selecting horses for the purposes of modern competition.

What follows is intended to provide a general guide to conformation and may be helpful in developing 'an eye for a horse'.

Assessing proportion

Wortley-Axe, using the detailed calculations of the French experts, provided us with a

Professor Wortley-Axe's system of measurement for the ideally proportioned horse is based on two principal units: the length of the head, and the distance between seat-bone and hip (see text).

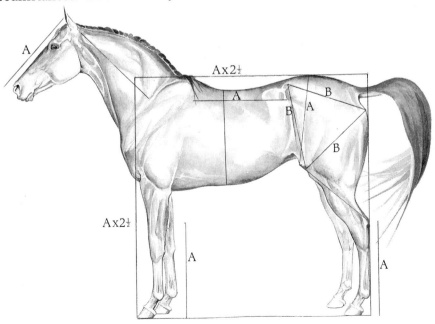

system of measurement by which the ideally proportionate horse might be judged. These were based on two principal units of measurement: the length of the head; and secondly the distance between the seat bone and the point of the hip.

LENGTH OF HEAD = (a) point of hock to ground; (b) point of hock to fold of stifle; (c) chestnut (the horny growth on the inside of the foreleg) to the base of the foot; (d) depth of body at girth; (e) posterior angle of scapula (shoulder blade), i.e. at the rear of its juncture to the wither, to the point of the hip; (f) the fold of the stifle to the croup.

* SEAT BONE – POINT OF HIP = (a) seat bone to stifle; (b) stifle to point of hip.

The length from point of shoulder to seat bone = length of head × $2\frac{1}{2}$.

Height from fetlock to elbow = height from elbow to wither.

A line dropped from the seat bone meets the point of the hock and continues down the back of the cannon bone.

* These measurements govern the placement of the hock. Inequalities in the measurements result in hocks placed behind the normal alignment (seat bone to point of hip and seat bone to point of stifle longer than stifle to seat bone) or in over-straight hocks causing the cannon to be held forward of the normal position. The latter results when the line from hip to seat bone is longer than the remaining two measurements.

A most significant proportion to observe is between the girth measurement, the distance from the top of the wither to the deepest part of the body behind and below the elbow, and the measurement from there to the ground. They should be equal if the horse is to give the desirable appearance of being short-legged. Such an equality between the measurements allows room for the lungs to be expanded without restriction. Horses that look to be long-legged, or 'on the leg', are only rarely so. More usually they lack depth through the girth.

Other useful measurements are these:

The neck, which for speed needs to be relatively long, equals in length approximately $1\frac{1}{2}$ times the measurement from the poll, down the front of the face, to the lower lip.

The back, from the rear of the withers to the highest part of the croup should be short in comparison with the measurement from point of shoulder to the last of the 'false' ribs. The ideal is for the latter measurement to be twice the length of the former.

It is interesting and often highly informative to measure a number of horses employing this formula, and it is also a method of acquiring an eye for a horse. However, do not be too dismayed if the pride of the stable does not measure up exactly. There never was a perfect horse as the French hippotomists admit and, as Goubaux and Barrier observe, 'it frequently happens that a good quality annuls a defect, or that one defect may be counterbalanced by another whose influence is diametrically opposite.'

In fact, those gentlemen went to great lengths to establish in what manner defects in conformation are compensated and produced a long list which they entitled, 'Compensation of defects of Conformation'.

Nonetheless, any notable asymmetrical failures are bound to create schooling problems in relation to balance and they may disturb more or less seriously the centre of gravity. (The latter was determined by the researches made by Professor Colin of London and was confirmed by the experiments of Goubaux and Barrier. The centre, at rest, is around the point of intersection of a line passing horizontally to the rear from the point of the shoulder and that of a vertical line drawn from the wither to the ground – this is accepted generally.)

Speed and to a degree athletic agility are associated with *length* in the overall proportions, in the limbs and muscle structure.

The opposite, short, thick proportions and musculature are indicative of strength and tractive power.

However, there are short, stuffy sorts of horse who, though their capacity for speed is limited, may have outstanding gymnastic ability.

The head

Nothing is more revealing of character than a study of the *head*, which has been termed 'the centre of intelligence and the seat of vice'. We need the former very much but can well do without the latter. In the performance horse one expects to find the lean, refined head with mobile ears and an absence of the coarse, wiry hair which denotes plebian or even cart blood. The desirability of big, generous eyes and large, wide nostrils permitting the maximum inhalation of air goes without saying. To be able to flex easily at the poll the jawbones need to be well spaced and if the horse is to be able to graze satisfactorily the mouth must be neither overshot (parrot mouth) nor undershot. Both conditions can cause bitting problems.

Obviously, the size of the head is important. Used in conjunction with the neck it represents the balancing agent for the body (the head is virtually a 40 lb (18 kg) blob on the end of a pendulum). Raised upwards it lightens the forehand, placing more of the weight over the quarters and vice-versa.

A head that is too big and over-heavy for a weak, narrow neck, for instance, will cause the horse to be overweighted on the forehand and make the transference to the rear of weight and, therefore, balance, a matter of great difficulty. A very small head in relation to the neck and overall body proportions is less usual but it, too, would act against proper balance.

Big, heavyweight horses do have large heads which have, therefore, to be carried on short, strong necks. The structure is indicative of power but not of speed and is not usually associated with outstanding agility.

The neck

The face measurement used in relation to the length of *neck* is a useful way of assessing the proportionate relationship, but of even more importance is the proportion of the neck muscles to the muscles of the forearm. Since the former activate the foreleg muscles causing the limb to be drawn forward the two sets of muscles must be proportionate.

The horse built for speed has a long forearm. Therefore, the neck muscle must also be of corresponding length. In the strength structure, as in the heavy draught horse, the musculature of both neck and forearm is short and thick.

Neck formations to be avoided in the riding horse are the ewe neck and the swan neck. In the former the top-line is concave, instead of curving gracefully, and the underside of the neck bulges outwards. It is possible to correct the fault by remedial schooling which puts muscle on the top-line of the neck and reduces the muscle formation on the underside, but it takes up much valuable time and unless the horse is otherwise something of a world-beater it is hardly worth buying a set of inherent bitting problems.

Swan necks are even less acceptable since they are concerned with the faulty juncture of head and neck. The term describes a neck which is convex in its upper third and gives the appearance of the head having been dropped on vertically. As a result the latter is carried in the horizontal plane and makes bridling an impossibility. Conformation of this sort also causes difficulty with the fitting of the saddle which will continually shift forward so that the girth chafes at the elbow.

Finally, one must consider how the head is joined to the neck at one end and how the latter merges into the shoulder at the other.

Too abrupt a juncture of head and neck is usually found with an excessively thick, short neck which almost as frequently runs into thick, upright shoulders. It results in that unacceptably fleshy throat which inhibits respiration and flexion.

A horse is 'cock-throttled' when the angle of the juncture is over-acute. This compels excessive length from the base of the ear to the throat and is accompanied by a prominent parotid gland. It causes the larynx to be compressed and the breathing is seriously impaired as a result.

The neck should streamline into the shoulders. If it does not seem to do that then the lower end is insufficiently wide, the neck bones themselves are ill-formed and the mastoido-humeralis muscle, at the junction of the neck, will be found to be seriously under-developed.

Necks which come to an end before meeting the withers constitute just as serious a failing. It is caused by the shoulders being too widely spaced. Such shoulders are bound to be upright and the action, so far as the riding horse is concerned, will be uneconomic and uncomfortable.

Shoulders and withers

The shape and position of the *shoulder* is critical to an efficient, comfortable and economical riding action which reduces, so far as possible, the effects of concussion in the lower limbs.

A good shoulder depends upon the shape and relationship of three components: *wither*, *scapula* (shoulder blade) and *humerus*, the bone which forms the shoulder joint at the top end and the point of the elbow at the other, where it meets the radius bone of the foreleg.

The *withers* rise from the superior spines of the third and ninth dorsal vertebrae and they form the essential point of attachment for the muscles supporting the forehand and governing its movement. The suspensory ligament of the head and neck is attached to the withers and passes over them, the latter acting as a fulcrum. Also attached to the withers are the back muscles, those muscles activating the ribs in respiration and those which attach the scapula to the body. It is no exaggeration to say that much of the performance potential is dependent on the formation of this vitally important area.

Relatively high and very well-defined withers provide the best possible attachment for the forehand muscles, allowing them to be activated to their full extent.

The further back the withers are placed the more pronounced will be the obliquity of the scapula. Unless the withers are well back and clearly defined the scapula will not be sufficiently sloped to produce the sort of action needed in the good-class riding horse, nor will it be possible to position the saddle correctly in balance.

The well-made wither allows the shoulder blades to be close together at the top. When the blades are placed wide apart, as they will be when the wither is flat and loaded with muscle, the action deteriorates. Instead of being straight and level the movement degenerates into a rolling one.

The slope of the scapula (the horseman's 'good, sloping shoulder') is, therefore, dependent upon the wither and its position. Thereafter, the concern is with its length. It needs to be long in relation to the length of the humerus. In turn that must be short and positioned well forward if it and the shoulder are to be capable of full and free extension. Given that to be so, the stride is long, low and devouring of the ground. It is economical of effort, reduces concussion, contributes to speed and is comfortable to the rider.

When the opposite structure prevails the foreleg is placed further to the rear, the stride is made shorter, there is an up-and-down movement of the leg and, necessarily in those circumstances, considerable knee action. As well as limiting the length of the stride this will result in a greater expenditure of effort for a less effective return and an increase in the concussive effect upon the lower limbs.

Do not, however, discard the horse with a degree of knee action. It occurs with crosses like the Thoroughbred/Welsh Cob and it often goes with great jumping ability and agility. (The Welsh Cob does not, indeed, or should not, have an up-and-down action. Instead the leg is lifted and then extended fully, which is quite a different thing. A slightly higher action and a structure disposed more to strength than speed is no drawback in the horse required for dressage, although there has to be an ample gymnastic quality.)

Exaggerated Thoroughbred action, exemplified by the very long, low stride, is not desirable in the cross-country or jumping horse. A somewhat shorter stride accompanied by a little knee action is far more easily adjusted to meet the varying requirements of the cross-country or show-jumping course.

Indeed, although Thoroughbred blood is the essential element in the performance horse it has its disadvantages in respect of temperament and soundness. Its presence does, however, provide speed, a unique physical ability, vigorous mental qualities and the inestimable quality of courage.

In my view the ideal eventer has to be at least threequarter bred. The dressage horse, on the other hand, may be better off with a lower percentage of the 'strong stuff'.

Degrees of inclination of the shoulder

The ideal inclinations of the riding shoulder are as follows and they can be easily established by measurement using a piece of string. To develop the eye compare the measurements of half a dozen horses.

(1) Junction of neck with withers to point of shoulder – 60°.

(2) Highest point of wither to point of shoulder – 43°.

(3) Junction of withers with back to point of shoulder – 40°.

The chest and body

The *chest* in a riding horse should not be too broad. Wide chests produce a round, rolling action which is of no consequence in the draught horse but is less than efficient in the horse required to canter and gallop. On the other hand, it should not be too narrow, giving the appearance of 'both legs coming out of the same hole'. When that is the case it is likely that the forelegs will be so close as to brush against each other causing injury to the joints and lower limbs. In extreme instances the horse may even 'plait', i.e. the forelegs cross over one another in movement – a most unnerving and dangerous action.

The *trunk* lies behind the withers and comprises the back, up to the quarters, which is supported by the dorsal and lumbar vertebrae of the spine. On the latter the weight of the thorax and abdomen depend. In addition to the two rule-of-thumb proportional measurements relating to the depth at the girth and the length of back there is also the matter of the ribs to be considered, for they contribute materially to the depth.

There are eight 'true' ribs attached to both vertebrae and sternum bone (hence *sternal* ribs) and these are followed by ten *asternal* or 'false' ribs attached only to vertebrae.

If the horse is to be deep enough in the girth the 'true' ribs must of necessity be long and in the riding horse they have also to be flatter than the 'false' ribs so that the rider's thighs and knees lie flat behind the tricep muscles. The 'false' ribs also need to be 'well-sprung' or rounded, since they lie over the kidneys and other vital organs. If they are short they will not be 'well-sprung' and the animal will be pre-disposed to 'running up light' when put to work. In other words, the horse looks very much like a greyhound in the post-abdominal area leading into the quarters. Such a horse is difficult to keep in condition and is likely to be a little wanting in stamina.

A final tip in this area. The distance

between the last rib and the hip bone should not exceed the breadth of a man's hand. Anything more is termed 'short of a rib' and there will be a noticeable slackness around this point. It is a serious failing and a major structural weakness. Mares, however, are permitted just a little more length in this part.

The back

Of enormous importance in the riding horse is the *back*. If it does not carry a saddle very well there is no point in looking further.

In perfection we need a back strongly muscled on either side of the spine and rising slightly to the croup.

Broad backs are less desirable and width should not be confused with strength. A broad back, apart from the difficulty it presents in relation to the fitting of a saddle, is usually connected with a short, roly-poly action and a singular lack of athleticism. Avoid backs which are dropped (sway) or roach, a convex structure, and do not bother with the so-called 'cold-backed' horse. The back is not so much 'cold' as damaged and the horse may well be suffering from an arthritic condition.

The length of back, although now not so much a controversial subject as in the past, is nonetheless relevant.

A back that is rather longer than shorter is to be preferred and is subject to less damage. Usually a longer back is accompanied by powerful loins and quarters and it is certainly conducive to greater speed, since it allows the hind legs to be brought further under the body to produce greater propulsion and an increased length of stride, all else being equal.

Short backs may represent a theoretically stronger structure but they are conducive neither to speed nor comfort. They are less able to absorb concussion and they may result in an undesirable shortening of the thorax.

In mares, of course, a slightly longer back

is entirely permissible.

Length, however, is not to be encouraged or tolerated in the *loin*, the area between the saddle and croup. The loin must be very strong, the muscles which form it being thick, short and powerful, because upon it depends much of the propulsive force of the quarters. It must also be broad to cover adequately the vital organs. If the loin is too long there is a noticeable space between the last rib and the angle of the haunch, or pin bone, and a prominent hollow in front of the latter. Once more the horse is termed 'slack'.

In the mature riding horse the *croup* is in line with the wither. In draught breeds the croup is often lower, allowing the full weight of the horse to be applied more effectively into the collar. Sometimes, in racehorses, particularly the sprinters, the croup is higher than the wither. This contributes to greater speed, possibly, but the horse is driven downwards on the forehand and the conformation is unsuitable (and uncomfortable) for general riding purposes.

High croups are not to be confused with the formation called a 'goose-rump', a not aesthetically pleasing formation but one that indicates good bone development advantageous for the attachment of muscle. It may give the quarters an unduly sloping appearance, but it usually indicates a particular jumping ability. Too wide a croup is indicative of strength but it gives a rolling action and acts adversely against speed in the gallop.

Low-set tails and a *pronounced* downward slope from the croup usually accompany weak quarters. Slope in the quarters, as in the heavy breeds, can, however, indicate strength. The more horizontal the quarter, the greater in theory is the speed.

The quarters

Clearly, a prime requisite in the riding horse who is going to gallop and jump is a powerful *quarter*. The best way to judge the quarters is

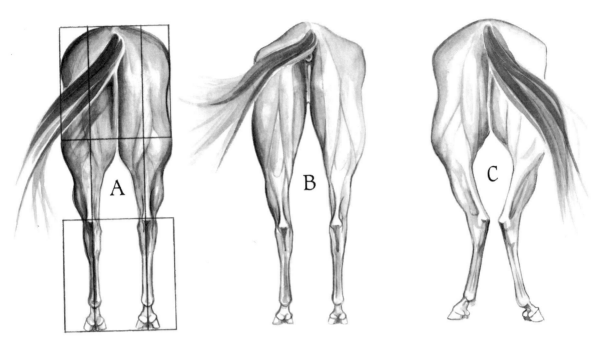

Left: a set of exemplary quarters. In perfection the side of each square should equal the length of the head. The vertical line passes straight upwards from the fetlocks through the points of the hocks. Centre: weak quarters, 'split up behind'. Right: cow hocks, a most ineffective structure.

from behind. They should look rounded and almost pear-shaped, widening into strongly developed *gaskins* or second thighs.

A good way to look at the quarters is in terms of two squares, as in Fig. 00. The sides of each square should, in perfection, equal our old friend, the length of the head. Thereafter, if a vertical line is drawn from the fetlocks upwards through the centre of the hocks the limbs should in no way deviate from that line. Cow hocks or bowed hocks are both signs of weakness and potential sources of trouble since the joints are bound to sustain unequal wear.

Hips should be level and not protrude unduly. A horse that carries a hip lower than

the other is said to have 'a dropped pin'. It is usually the result of some injury, possibly sustained by the hip being banged against a door post or, perhaps, by a bad fall. It rarely has a serious effect upon performance but it is possible for the horse to be a little unlevel in the action of the hind legs.

As bad a fault as any is for the horse to be 'split up behind', a condition in which the juncture of the thighs occurs far up under the tail. It is caused by poor development of the second thigh.

Hocks

Essential to the performance and the athletic ability is the shape and position of the *hock*, the joint which is required to do more work than any other and is subject to a greater number of injuries from strains etc.

A further rule-of-thumb which gives a good indication of a proper placement is

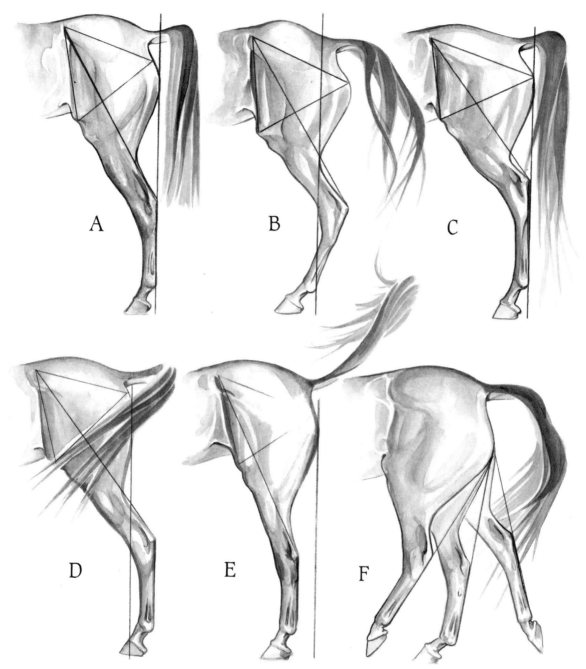

Quarters: (a) Good, straight line from point of buttock down rear of cannon. Good length from hip to hock indicating strong propulsive thrust. (b) Sickle hocks—notably inequality of the guiding triangle. (c) Hocks too high (cannon too long). Again, the triangle is unequal in its proportions. (d) Hocks held too far behind to detriment of propulsive effort. 'Hocks in the next county'. (e) Over-straight hocks with some inequality of the critical triangle. (f) Hock in movement. A straight line is formed from buttock along the cannon.

when the point of the hock is in line with the chestnut that lies just above the knee of the foreleg. If that requirement is fulfilled then almost inevitably the second thigh will be long and the hock joint low because of the shortness of the hind cannon.

For general riding purposes hocks that are high off the ground are best avoided. They do occur occasionally in very fast Thoroughbred horses, usually in conjunction with a croup that is higher than the wither.

Many very good jumpers depart somewhat from the rule which says that a line dropped from the point of the buttock to the ground should touch the hock and continue down the vertical line formed by the rear of the cannon bone, and they do so without detracting from their potential soundness or performance ability. In these instances the hocks and the cannon are placed forward of the vertical line and thus further under the horse. The ability to gallop fast is certainly reduced but the increase in the possible articulation of the joints and the greater strength which is afforded by this arrangement provides additional power and thrust for jumping. Because of the increased articulation of the joints it is, indeed, by no means an unsuitable conformation for the dressage horse.

Hock faults

Apart from bowed and cow hocks, both of which reduce the speed potential and produce uneven wear in the joint mechanisms, other faults which can occur in the hocks are when they are clearly overbent and curved on the *front* surface. This is a 'sickle' hock. When the hocks are carried well behind our useful vertical line from the point of the buttock they are said to be 'in the next county' – yet another highly descriptive horseman's term.

Either condition predisposes the joint to uneven wear and therefore to the possibility of disease. Arthritis is a common occurrence in both formations. Additionally, there is a lack of propulsive power caused by an inability for the hocks to be fully engaged under the body.

Hocks, in company with the stifle, can also be too straight. This will be so when the imaginary line passes behind the edge of the flexor tendon and behind the cannon. Uneven wear is bound to result as well as a loss of propulsive power, but more damaging is the greater concussion to which the limb will be subjected.

The ideal hock

Because of the considerable concussion which must be sustained by the hock joint and because of the weight it carries, the hock has to be large and well formed. Small, mean hocks are an immediate recipe for disaster and cannot be expected to stand up to work.

The larger the joint, within reason, the greater will be the surface area available to absorb the concussive effect which, so long as there is no deviation from an absolutely correct construction, will be spread evenly over the mechanism. Hocks, like feet and knees, must form an identical pair. It may seem an obvious point to make but it is of great importance when assessing the horse's potential. Where one joint is smaller than the other, and thus for that reason alone more prone to strain or disease, it can be as a result of a congenital defect, but it is more likely that it is smaller because of some injury or malfunction.

It is possible for hock joints to be too large. When that condition pertains they appear lumpy, fleshy and generally lymphatic, rather like a pair of over-worked human legs with circulatory problems. Hocks of this sort usually occur in animals carrying a high percentage of carting blood and, like the latter, do nothing to enhance the athletic ability. The effect is to put the whole leg out of balance, restricting the action and limiting the joint's flexion.

The foreleg

Much emphasis is placed in training on the hind legs: their shape, propulsive power and possibility of engagement. They are, of course, enormously important but no more so than the forelegs. Both play an equal part in locomotion and as much use is made of the forehand in jumping as of the opposite end. In the first stage of the leap it is the muscles of the forearm, in conjunction with those of the loin, which lift the body and the burden of the rider, propelling it forward in advance of the thrust from the hind legs.

Once more, it is helpful to make use of that handy vertical line. Viewed from the front a line commencing at the point of the shoulder should pass through the centre of knee, fetlock and foot to the ground. Any deviation from that line throughout the length of the leg indicates a potential vulnerability, since it will cause extra strain to be put on one or other of the limb's components.

Starting at the juncture of the leg with the body, the first concern is with the *elbow*, the position of which depends upon the length of the humerus and will confirm the correctness or otherwise of that bone. If the latter is too long, for instance, the elbow and the foreleg will be placed too far to the rear and the action affected accordingly. When the elbow is positioned in that fashion the spine (and the rider, too) is subjected to greater concussion. Furthermore, extra strain is put on the hocks, which must work harder to compensate for the deficiencies of the front limbs.

Free and unhampered movement of the foreleg will only be allowed, however, if the elbow stands well clear of the ribs. The leg is carried well forward as the whole shoulder is moved. Conversely, should the elbow be 'tied-in', lying hard up against the ribs so that one cannot easily get a fist between the limb and the body, the movement of the shoulder is restricted severely and the leg is moved only from the elbow.

View from the front. (a) Good conformation. Knee and fetlock in line, feet straight. (b) Toes turned out. (c) Pigeon toes.

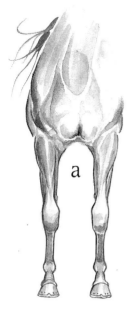 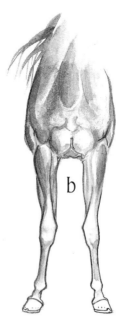 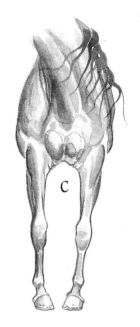

The sketches below show the consequence of conformational failings on the action.

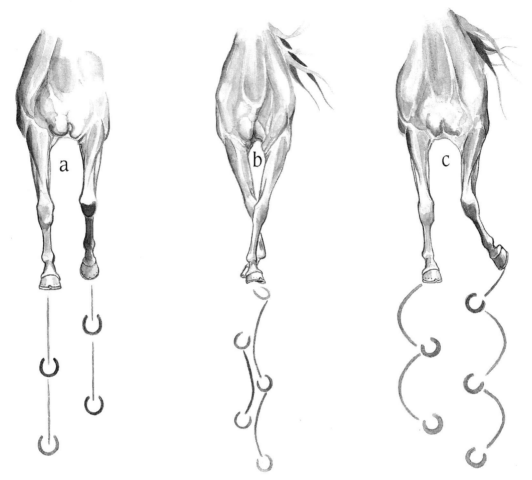

Forearm

Necessarily, the forearm has to be powerfully muscled and long, so as to allow the knee to be carried as low as possible on short cannon bones. Poorly developed forearms detract significantly from jumping ability.

Knees

Whilst being in proportion to the rest of the limb, the knee, like the hock, needs to be large and *flat*, not in any way rounded, and the pisiform bones clearly defined. If the knee meets those requirements the channel formed by the carpal sheath will be broad enough to carry the important flexor tendon without any danger of it being pinched or otherwise restricted. Small, round knees almost invariably accompany chronic tendon troubles.

For the action to be straight the knee has to be perpendicular throughout its length and must obviously be absolutely straight in relation to the rest of the leg.

Like the hocks and for the same reasons,

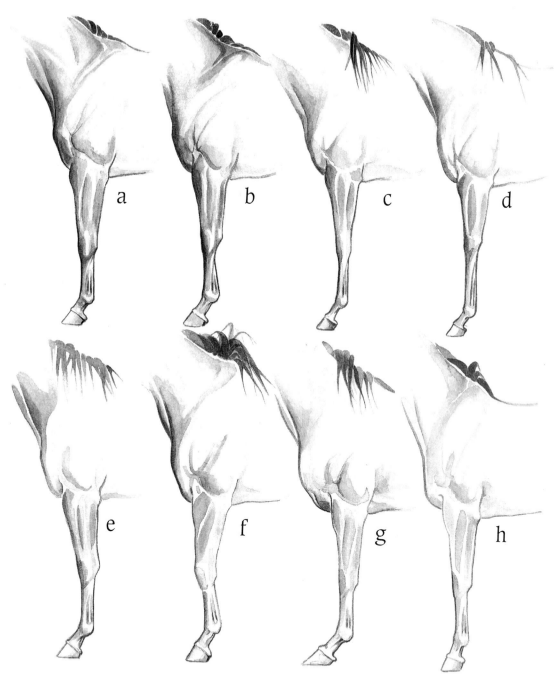

Failings in the lower limb. (a) A good foreleg with strong, short cannon. (b) Tied-in below the knee. (c) Knee too small, cannon too light. Overall impression of weakness. (d) Light of bone with cannon too long. (e) Back at the knee. (f) Over at the knee. (g) Over-long pastern, possible flat feet. Foreleg set too far under body. (h) Upright pastern, boxy foot and straight shoulder.

the knees must be a perfectly matching pair.

Faults of the lower limb

The worst of all failings in the lower limbs is that described, again very graphically, as a 'calf knee'. It is also called 'back at the knee'. A calf knee is when the leg curves inwards below the joint. It does nothing in the cause of concussive absorption and it is an almost certain source of tendon problems.

Nearly as great an abomination is the horse which is 'tied-in below the knee'. This refers to a limb in which the measurement below the knee is less than that taken lower down nearer the fetlock joint. It, too, constricts the passage of the tendons.

The condition of being 'over at the knee' is often attributed to much hard work and that, indeed, is very often the cause. However, it is not always so, because it can occur in young horses who have done very little. 'Over at the knee' is when the cannon slopes back below the knee so that the knee itself seems to project over the cannon and to be inclined forward. Fortunately it seems to have no ill-effect at all and horses having this peculiarity are said to suffer rarely from tendon break-down.

Cannon

The length of the cannon governs the height of the knee from the ground. Long cannons cause the knee to be above a desirable level and their length must be regarded as a serious structural weakness. The strongest construction is one which is both short and thick and that is the ideal for the cannon bone.

Thickness, or rather the measurement taken round the cannon, brings us to the question of 'bone', which combined with the horse's general conformation, determines the capacity to carry weight. (Height has nothing to do with weight-carrying ability.) In fact, of course, there is no way in which the bone can be measured accurately, since any measurement includes a composite structure of surrounding ligaments, tendon and tissue.

It used to be held that a measurement of 8 ins (20 cm) taken below the knee fitted a horse, all else being equal, to carry 11–12 stone (70–75 kg); 9–10 ins (22–25 cm) carried 13–14 stone (80–90 kg) and 10–11 ins (25–27 cm) carried 15 stone (95 kg) and probably a bit more.

It is another useful rule-of-thumb but, of course, neither it nor the measurements on which it is based take any account of the *density* of the bone, and that cannot be decided definitively until after the animal's demise.

Bone is like a tube, the central core being filled with marrow. Its strength depends upon the thickness and density of the surrounding structure, the strongest being that with the smallest core and the thickest and least porous surrounding wall. Arab, Thoroughbred and pony bone has been shown to be denser and stronger relatively than the bone of common-bred animals and that has to be accepted.

Bone, or a lack of sufficient bone, is a notable failing in many areas of modern breeding, for which reason Welsh Cobs, Irish Draughts, etc. are a popular cross with the Thoroughbred which has possibly in some instances degenerated in respect of bone and hereditary soundness.

The cannons themselves should be hard and cool to the touch. They should feel *flat-sided* rather than *round* and there must be absolutely no puffiness.

The same applies to the fetlocks. Like all the joints they need to be large and well-formed and again they should be firm and cool with no hint of their being filled. The condition of the fetlock joints gives an indication of the mileage on the clock and how the mechanism has stood up to work. Puffy, lymphatic fetlocks in young horses are to be treated with much suspicion.

Pastern

Below the fetlock is the pastern, a very important part of the shock-absorbing system. Ones which are short and upright, often found in common-bred horses and in some ponies, are clearly less able to cope with the effects of concussion and very straight ones are almost certain to cause troubles connected with jarring.

Very long pasterns, which are sometimes seen in Arabs and some Thoroughbreds, have to be viewed as a potential weakness if only because they are disproportionate. They do, nonetheless, make for a very comfortable ride.

The ideal is between the two, with the hind pasterns being a bit shorter than the front because of the compensating flexion of the hock joint.

(In cases where the hock is over-straight the failing is frequently compensated by a longer pastern which serves to save the hock from the effects of jarring it would otherwise sustain.)

Feet

Horses, indeed, are as good as their feet and nothing compensates for a poor foot. Once more, the feet must be exactly matching pairs. Indeed, it would be most unwise to buy a horse with odd feet. 'Boxy' feet, which look to be too small for their owner, are a certain reason for rejection – they are too small and are therefore far more prone to disease. Examine, too, the horn forming the wall of the foot and surrounding the 'white line', i.e. the line visible on the underside of the foot which marks the division between the sensitive and insensitive laminae. It has to be strong and thick enough to allow plenty of room for the shoe nails.

Brittle feet, broken ones, ones displaying longitudinal cracks and, in particular, feet with the ringed appearance which denotes a previous attack of laminitis, that most painful of inflammatory hoof conditions, should make us pause and reflect.

An examination of the underside of the foot should show: deep, open heels; strong bars, otherwise the heel will be shallow; and a distinct concavity of the sole – this latter being more pronounced in the hind feet. Flat or dropped soles are obviously more easily bruised and damaged by rough going.

To do its job satisfactorily as an anti-concussion device which also prevents slipping the frog has to be large and prominent. If it is small and shrivelled it cannot come into contact with the ground to fulfil its purpose.

The recommended angle of slope on the feet is generally agreed as being 50° for the forefeet and between 55–60° for the hind.

All four feet should face directly to the front if the action is to be true and efficient.

Toes which turn out result in brushing, i.e. one foot striking into the other. Toes which turn in may cause the horse to dish, i.e. to throw the leg in an outward arc.

Action

Action is the result of conformation and notable defects in the latter or even incipient unsoundnesses will be shown in the movement.

When the horse is trotted out it is easy enough to see whether the limbs are carried in a straight line and whether the feet turn in or out. The following are some additional pointers to the presence of possible defects:

(1) Each joint is flexing properly only when it is possible to see the sole of each foot at some time during every stride.

(2) Faulty hock formation is revealed by the stifle being 'punched' outwards as the joint is flexed. It is caused by the hock being turned inwards.

(3) When viewed from the side the points of the hocks should rise to the same height when the joint is flexed. If one is lifted lower than its partner the presence of a spavin should be suspected.

(A spavin is an inflammation of bones in the hock resulting in a bony enlargement on the inside of the joint. It is caused by strain and, because of the pain it causes, reduces the flexion of the joint.)

(4) One hind shoe showing more wear at the toe than its partner indicates an imperfect joint flexion. Indeed, the shoes tell us a lot about the action (and possibly about the competence of the farrier). In perfection, wear on the shoes should be absolutely even.

There are failings in conformation which may be so amply compensated in some other respect that they can be overlooked, but in the search for a sound horse with good performance potential which will stand up to the work required there are not too many.

Height

It is interesting to note that the horses which have a better natural balance and the greatest athletic ability are those between 15–16 hh. Big horses, 17 hh and perhaps over, are rarely so gymnastic and are, on purely mechanical grounds, less efficient.

Our friend, Professor Wortley-Axe, whose work included an extensive study of height in relation to proportion, pace and overall efficiency, suggested 15.3 hh as being the 'limit of stature' for a riding horse 'within which the greatest usefulness is to be found'.

Sight

An examination of equine sight in relation to performance is included in the following chapter.

4

The Nature of
the Beast

THERE ARE two disciplines involved in the human association with horses. In training, riding or handling horses there is that concerned with the use of our bodies, as well as the over-lying discipline of the mind to which the physical actions must necessarily be subservient. When the two are in balance we have the beginnings of a system of communication between man and horse which becomes increasingly effective as the human develops his technique in both respects and thus becomes better equipped to tune in to his horse.

Such is the arrogance of the human animal, however, that communication, even in the very skilful, is often something of a one-sided affair in which the human gives an order and the horse makes the required response. (There is a book now, happily, not much in evidence, written by a highly qualified establishment figure. In it the use of the word 'must' predominates in every chapter and in almost every paragraph: 'Apply the left leg and act with the right rein and the horse *must* . . .' do this or that.

The book exemplifies the wholly fallacious attitude of the mechanical horseman and highlights, surely, the human arrogance in attempting to impose a rigid domination which, to my mind, is both unattractive, unacceptable and probably unproductive as well.)

This sort of approach to the horse/human partnership is reminiscent of the situation in many British households in the days of the Raj in India. The *memsahib*, in order to run her household, or at least to give the appearance of doing so, acquired a smattering of the vernacular, often termed 'kitchen Urdu'. It amounted to not much more than a number of executive commands – 'Do this . . .,' 'Clean that,' 'Come here . . .,' 'Go there . . .' – supported by a rudimentary vocabulary.

To some extent it served the purpose well enough but it could not be viewed as anything more than a primitive one-way form of communication, since her ability to listen to and understand what her servants were saying was as limited as her command of the language.

On the other hand, members of the Indian Civil Service had not only to speak the language fluently, but also needed to have a deep understanding of the customs and motivations of the people with whom they dealt if they were to appreciate the nuances involved in the unravelling of complicated land disputes, marriage settlements or whatever. The British officer of the Indian Army had to meet exactly the same requirements if he was to fulfil his responsibilities.

In our context there can be no full relationship with the horse until we are sufficiently easy in the language to understand what he is saying to us. That the language is largely physical and to a degree, perhaps, a matter of 'mental feel' and compatibility is of no consequence. He communicates with us just as we attempt to communicate with him, and in the same measure.

In fact, the horse, through a relatively sophisticated body language by which he communicates with his own kind, is probably the better communicator of the two. Certainly, he is far more sensitive to our moods than we are to his.

Of course, the onus to learn the language is upon us. The physical requirements can be acquired, but only by assiduous application and continuous practice. They are no more inherent in the budding equestrian than is the ability on the part of an aspiring pianist to perform a Beethoven sonata without having spent years mastering the scales and five-finger exercises.

Similarly, we can develop a mental discipline and harmony by application and conscious effort. It will, nonetheless, be accomplished more quickly once we have learnt to stop talking (or shouting) to and at the horse through our physical actions and our less than disciplined minds and begin to listen to what he has to say.

Basic to all our efforts is an understanding of the horse in the physical terms already discussed and then, to complete the picture, an appreciation of his nature and those characteristics and instincts which make up the equine personality and govern his behaviour.

It begins, millions of years ago, in the Miocene period (25–10 million years ago) when the process of equine evolution accelerated and changed course dramatically.

Because of extreme climatic changes the swampy, jungle lands gave way to treeless plains and savannah covered in wiry grasses of a relatively high protein content. Faced with the new environment the equine species had either to adapt or become extinct. Many of the numerous strains of *Equus*, including the mammoth *Megahippus*, did just that but those with a greater capacity to adapt to the changing circumstance survived.

From being browsing animals, nourished by a bulk diet of soft plant growth and protected against predators by a striped or blotched coat pattern which acted as an effective camouflage in their forest surroundings, the species took on the characteristics of *Equus*, the grazing horse.

The dentition became compatible with the consumption of abrasive grasses, the molar teeth being used in a grinding action. So as to feed easily at grass level, the neck became longer. The eyes changed to a position more to the sides of the head so as to provide virtual all-round vision, even when the head was lowered in the act of grazing. The lengthening of the legs and the development of a single toe or hoof, together with a heightening of all the senses, stimulated in some respects by a diet of higher protein content, all contributed to a defence mechanism based now on detection and flight rather than concealment. Additional protection and security was afforded by the membership of a herd, or a family group within a herd.

It is probably an over-simplification to suggest the overall dominance of a single herd stallion. In the wild (as in the domestic state) each group quickly establishes an order of precedence and whilst the influence of the stallions is predominant, particularly in the mating season, that of the older mares is by no means insignificant. The old matriarchs play an important role within the group or herd and it would be quite wrong to regard stallions as always being dominant and mares as always being submissive – after all, the female of any species is often far more ferocious in the defence of her young than the male. Interestingly, where horses are kept in large herds, as in the Argentine or in the predominantly Eastern states of the USSR, the herd leader is an old mare with a bell fastened round her neck (the 'bell mare'). The place of honour is not given to some callow colt intent upon impressing the young females of the herd with his virile desirability.

The social arrangement of the herd or group was in itself defensive in a way that would have been quite impossible for an individual operating as a single unit.

In the feral life the prime motivation of the herd was the search for food, the horses moving on slowly from one grazing ground to the next. At certain times of the year the natural urge to reproduce became paramount and sexually orientated behaviour more evident.

Instinctively, the herd avoided the dangers presented by boggy ground and would prefer to find a safer way round rather than attempt to cross stretches of water. In these respects the young horses learnt from the example of their elders.

The seemingly quiet tenor of existence could be disturbed by predatory attacks either from carnivores like mountain lions or wolf packs or, indeed, from the ultimate predator, man himself.

At the first intimation of impending danger whether sensed, heard or observed the horses reacted (and frequently over-reacted) by immediate and unreasoning flight. Should an individual be attacked by a predator close enough to attempt to bring down his quarry by leaping on its back the horse employed violent leaps and bucks in an effort to dislodge the aggressor.

Young horses, like all young things, indulge in play, galloping about and generally letting off steam – 'horseplay', in fact. Obviously, this occurred in the wild herd situation, but when the herd galloped it was because of some threatened danger and must have involved a degree of collective panic. There was no point in galloping aimlessly. That only expended energy unnecessarily and interfered with the business of feeding.

Another relevant observation on the wild or pre-domestic horse is that the weaning of foals took place naturally and gradually. In the domestic horse, forced weaning of foals at around four months is the normal practice and that trauma of separation is probably responsible for the creation of all sorts of behavioural problems.

In the same way selective breeding and gelding could be regarded as being inhibiting to the natural development and might in some instances, as with mares denied a normal sexual life, give rise to difficulties.

We cannot, however, for all sorts of very practical reasons keep horses in the natural way. Nor, I imagine, would the modern horse, conditioned to dependence upon man, be wholly appreciative if we did. What we can do is to try to mitigate the worst effects of domestication and appreciate the limitations imposed by the nature of the horse.

The whole subject of horse psychology and behaviour is enormously complex but a good idea of the horse's make-up can be obtained, and conclusions drawn accordingly, by examining some of the more obvious instincts and characteristics in relation to the domestic condition. Some we are able to use to our advantage, others we shall find less helpful.

Central to any horse study is the *herd instinct* which involves *security* and *leadership*.

Herd instinct

In domestication it is usually impossible to reproduce the feral herd situation. The obvious exceptions are breeding operations involving considerable numbers of horses and ponies. Possibly, in Britain, the native ponies, particularly the Welsh, most resemble the feral herd, the mares and the followers running out with the stallion.

In contrast, the 'domestic' herd situation, as opposed to the near feral, can exist when the composition of the herd is no more than two animals. It is a long way from the natural state but even two animals kept together find *security* in the company of each other and, I believe, in the surroundings with which they are familiar.

Larger domestic herds are exemplified by police and army horses and by those kept in riding schools.

Such horses, enjoying a settled, orderly lifestyle, being well managed and accustomed to a regular routine, undoubtedly gain in their feelings of security. On the other hand, the very cosiness of the herd condition exerts a gravitational pull that can certainly work to the human advantage, but may also do just the opposite. There is the authenticated instance of an embarrassing situation experienced by a British cavalry regiment during the South African War (1900–1902). A trooper was ordered out of the ranks to carry a message but his horse, knowing nothing of military regulations, declined very firmly to leave his troop companions, who represented his herd and in whose company he felt secure. Similar situations arise in all sorts of circumstances.

Such, however, is the horse's ability to adapt to the human requirement that this very basic instinct can be subdued and virtually overcome by training which inculcates the habit of obedience to messages (requests) made physically by the rider. That at any rate is one side of it; the rest depends upon the *rapport* and the consequent degree of trust which exists between man and horse.

Horses, for instance, reject a temporary herd condition when they leave the collecting ring to jump a course of fences in a show-jumping arena. Event horses perform in isolation without the stimulation of companions. A horse in the hunting field, which is certainly a simulation of a herd situation, may be asked to jump out of a crowded lane and away from his herd and will do so if he has been schooled intelligently, trusts his rider and, importantly, recognises the latter's resolution.

Without doubt, racing and hunting are examples of a possibly unconscious exploitation of the herd instinct. The excitement of galloping in company encourages horses to jump obstacles which they might well decline in cold blood and young horses gain confidence as a result.

An event horse or a show jumper, or even a show horse, who has lost his enthusiasm and become soured will often change his views radically if he is sent hunting for a season.

Wise horsemasters aver that there is nothing so good for a horse's system as a little 'Dr Green' (by which is meant fresh, young grass – the natural food). It could be said that there is nothing so good for the horse's mental outlook as a bit of 'Dr Hunt'.

In the context of our own requirement we can use the pull of the herd in the teaching of the early jumping lessons. If an experienced horse jumps a fence in front of the novice the latter will usually follow. He does so because, certainly, of the example set by his companion but also because he does not wish to be separated from him. To encourage the young horse to jump independently and with proper enthusiasm it is helpful and, indeed, advisable to ask him to jump towards his companions, so as to rejoin the herd, rather than risk a stop at this early stage by jumping away from the group.

Security

The herd certainly exerts an almost magnetic influence but so, too, does the basic need for security. In the domestic horse, the influence of the herd apart, the familiar surroundings become very largely the focal centre supplying that need. To a degree this is because of the association with food, a matter close to the equine heart and never far from the horse's thoughts.

The stable – or in the absence of one, the paddock – should be a place which the horse connects with pleasurable experiences: comfort, shelter, relaxation and safety as well as food. They are, after all, the places in which we have the opportunity to create a relationship and to make friends with our horses. To preserve the desirable settled state of mind it follows that to *punish* a horse or subject him to unpleasant or frightening experiences in his immediate surroundings will be to risk destroying his sense of security and all that it entails.

There may be occasions, of course, when horses, like our children, have to be corrected for some misdemeanour or lack of good manners. In those circumstances it would be foolish and most inadvisable to withhold measured retribution for fear of causing a momentary wobble in the animal's feelings of security. It would, indeed, be just as stupid as to refrain from decisive action with a child who behaves unacceptably in the home.

Indeed, if the climate created by sensible management and training is the right one it will be quite sufficient to survive intact the occasional behavioural hiccups and the correction they must inevitably provoke. With his own kind the horse expects and accepts retaliation if he is too rough in play or otherwise makes a nuisance of himself – there need be no difference in his domestic relationship with man.

We need, however, to be able to relate the punishment to the offence. A fit horse on a high-protein diet is naturally sharper and more disposed on occasions to be irritable than dear, old fat Dobbin who lives out on hay and pony nuts.

He may be ticklish and raise a leg to tell you so; he may nip in irritation as you fumble with his rugs and he will probably tell you to get out of the way with bared teeth and flattened ears when you put his feed in the manger, but then that is exactly how he would behave with another horse – in effect, therefore, is he not paying you a compliment?

These minor lapses can best be checked by a sharp word and a determination not to overreact and blow the matter up out of its true proportion.

If he bites at you when being groomed it is better to tie him up short and ignore the face-pulling rather than be bitten and be forced into physical reaction.

Of course, one cannot tolerate the deliberate kick or bad-tempered bite and the offender must be shown the error of his ways swiftly but with a quiet firmness.

Because of its association with food and relaxation it is not advisable to site schooling areas in close proximity to the stable. No horse will concentrate on his work in those circumstances; his mind, indeed, will be in his manger and he will hang continually towards his box.

On the other hand, use can be made of the stable's attraction when introducing horses to traffic. It is noticeable that all horses lighten their steps and generally perk up when they are turned for home, so the wise trainer plans the exercise route so that he makes use of quiet lanes on the way out and returns on the busier roads carrying a heavier traffic flow. By then the horse's mind is more concerned with getting home and back to the feed which he knows will be waiting for him, and he is less likely to be worried by lorries, buses and so on.

So important is this centre of security that a change of ownership and home can be a disturbing experience. For young horses this is certainly so, and it can also have a disor-ienting effect on older horses who may have been in one home for a long period and are possibly less resilient.

The result may be seen in a display of uncharacteristic behaviour. There may be a reluctance to leave the box or the stable yard, an occasional tantrum may be thrown, or the horse may even become dull and listless and go off his food.

Given sympathetic handling, food and a regular routine, almost every horse will settle down quite happily within a couple of days or so. Any rough treatment or bullying will, on the other hand, only confirm his feelings of insecurity and create further problems.

Travelling to showgrounds, living in temporary stabling and so on might also be expected to upset this highly strung and routine-loving animal. In fact, and this is further evidence of the species' remarkable adaptability, horses cope very well with a peripatetic existence. Show jumpers, for example, accept habitual travel with complete equanimity, and one has to conclude that so long as they are fed and watered regularly and have their own people handling them they suffer neither undue stress nor any other ill-effect.

Leadership

In fact, although security certainly has much to do with routine and familiarity with a particular environment, it is also inexorably involved with the quality of leadership.

In the wild the majority of horses accepted the authority of the group leader, a statement which is probably more accurate than attributing the overall dominance of the herd to a single stallion.

This points to the division between naturally dominant 'boss' horses, who can be of either sex, and those that are naturally of an opposite inclination. (It would be unusual to find a stallion in the last category, but it is by no means unknown – after all, in the human species there are men who are more or less dominant or more or less submissive.)

For the domestic horse the matter is complicated by the presence of members of a different species on whom he is to all intents entirely dependent. There will still be a pecking order amongst his own kind but the dominance and the onus to provide leadership belongs to the human.

The horse is most certainly a dependant and just as certainly he has to have human leadership if he is to perform satisfactorily within the parameters set for him by humans. But that does not mean that human authority is accepted automatically.

All horses, dominant or submissive, test that authority just as naturally as they do with their own kind. For the most part the solution lies in quick, firm action but should the horse 'get away with it' the behavioural problems begin to snowball and the performance level certainly deteriorates.

Performance, after all, is as much a reflection of leadership as of riding skills. A rider may be technically competent but still fail to realise a horse's potential for want of what we can term leadership skills.

We are reminded constantly that horses have to be fed according to their individual needs. A blanket approach to feeding is just not practical. In the same way our approach and relationship with a horse needs to be based on the individual character–there is no pattern of management which can be neatly defined beyond general principles which will suit them all.

Dominant and vice-versa

A lot depends on the dominant/recessive factor and that too, as we have seen, is far from being clear-cut.

The temptation with the dominant horse is to react in the same terms, seeking to assert one's authority and attempting to defeat the horse by being even more dominant. The running battle of wills which then ensues rarely allows either party to emerge as the victor and matters for both sides go from bad to worse. In the end the only solution open to such an owner is to sell the horse to someone more sympathetic and more skilful.

To come to terms with the dominant animal the human, whilst retaining the senior partnership, has to meet the horse half way. In fact, we kid the horse into doing what we want, even to the point of allowing him to think that the initiative is with him. If he goes too fast, we let him believe that is what is wanted; if he jumps too extravagantly for comfort then we will go along with that, too. It is from that base that we can begin to contain his courage and enthusiasm within acceptable bounds. If we fight him we only provoke an even more forceful response and in a running battle on physical terms the horse is always the winner.

The recessive horse is to varying degrees unsure of himself and lacking in confidence. With him we may be tempted to be less than positive when we should be giving the strong, dominant leadership which he needs and which leaves him in no doubt as to what is required of him.

Nervous factor

For all his size and strength the horse is essentially highly strung and nervous, which is understandable in an animal that (unlike the carnivores) is non-aggressive, relying for his defence on instant flight.

Any unexpected movement in a hedgerow, a sudden noise or some unfamiliar object will trigger the defence mechanism, alerting all his basic instincts. He may shy, more or less violently; sometimes he may attempt to turn and make off.

It can be an irritating failing but it would be most unwise to express our displeasure by using a whip or shouting at him or, which is just as bad, jabbing him in the mouth as a result of the insecurity of our seat. If the horse is punished it only serves to confirm his fear and make him even more nervous.

The Greek general, Xenophon, whose works became the inspiration for the classical riding masters of the Renaissance period, understood this very well:

'When the horse suspects some object and is unwilling to approach, you must make it clear that there is nothing to be afraid of ... and if this fails you must yourself touch the object and lead him up gently. Those who compel the horse with blows make him more frightened than ever.'

It could not be better said.

Consider this too: 'Never lose your temper in dealing with horses; this is the one best precept and custom in horsemanship.'

There could not be better advice.

Shying can never be eliminated but it can be reduced by quiet firm riding and by the person who is able to transmit to the horse his own quiet confidence.

High feeding and peak fitness, of course, act to heighten the senses, accentuating the natural defensive instincts, and one must expect to sit tight on fit, fresh horses first thing on a frosty morning.

Pain tolerance

If we accept that aggression plays little or no part in the make-up of the horse, it is not unreasonable to suggest that animals without predatory instincts will also be more sensitive to pain and will, in consequence, have a lower pain tolerance.

The instant reaction of the horse to the sudden rustle in the hedgerow is to take immediate evasive action. To him, the rustle represents a potential enemy, something which he has no intention of investigating further.

A dog, on the other hand, a natural hunter and predator though far smaller than the horse and not nearly so powerful, reacts in opposite fashion. To him the same rustle suggests the existence of what might be legitimate prey. His response is to attack with hackles raised and teeth, developed for just such a purpose, bared in readiness.

In days past, fighting dogs were matched against each other and even against bears and bulls, frequently fighting to the death. Even today terriers will go down an earth to bolt a fox and may get mauled in the process. They come out, scarred and bleeding, but screaming defiance and impatient to be at their adversary again.

In a casual dog-fight, provoked perhaps by possession of a bone, a dog may suffer what appear to be considerable injuries, but given a day or two to lick his wounds he will return to another fray undeterred and with his aggression in no way diminished.

Everything points to the dog being less sensitive to pain and with a higher tolerance level than the non-predators, like the horse.

Very occasionally, a pair of stallions will fight in earnest. The wild primitive, the Asiatic Wild Horse (*Equus Przewalskii*) is notably aggressive, far more so than domestic stock, and there is the instance of the Godolphin Arabian, one of the three root sires of the Thoroughbred, establishing his authority by fighting the stud stallion (the Godolphin was then employed as 'a teaser' at Gog Magog) for the favours of the mare Roxana.

For the most part, serious fighting is uncommon, aggression being more confined to the threatening display. Only very rarely, indeed, will a stallion attack a man.

So deeply ingrained is the flight instinct that it can be provoked by a rider whose handling of the reins results in an unedifying tug-of-war between himself and his unfortunate horse.

Such riders may talk about horses 'fighting' the bit, or even about their 'bolting'. *Far from 'fighting' the bit the horse is running away from it and from the discomfort which he experiences*. The more the rider pulls and saws, the more urgent becomes the horse's need to escape the pain. The horse reacts to forceful hands by pulling even harder and galloping faster. To us it may seem to be an act of stupidity but viewed within the nature of the horse it is far from illogical.

Pulling, in short, provokes a similar response in the horse and force exerted by the rider or handler, in this or other circumstances, is always met by a stronger force on the part of the horse, whose far greater weight and strength make him the favourite to win the unequal contest.

There are occasions when the horse seems to act in contradiction to his nature, but they arise because of particular domestic situations which may cause a temporary reversion to the feral state. We have mentioned the horse becoming possessive about his food, threatening the human with laid-back ears and so on.

Kicking in the stable, unless it is habitual and deliberate, is usually for the reason that the horse is startled by a sudden movement and feeling trapped in a confined space reacts in the only way open to him.

Sensitivity

What emerges uncontrovertibly, even from this superficial study of the horse, is that the characteristic non-predatory instincts result in a high degree of sensitivity which will respond easily to external stimuli.

It is largely, though by no means entirely, because of this innate quality that we are able to command the obedience and control the actions of an animal ten times our size and immeasurably more powerful. Recognising this facility, and if we can become sufficiently proficient physically, it is possible to obtain an easy obedience to the indications which we make through the controlling aids of our hands and legs.

As a beginning we teach the horse obedience to the whip. If, for example, we stand at his head and tap his flank lightly with a long whip, thereby imposing the most minimal degree of discomfort imaginable and conveying no more than the veriest suggestion of a threat, the horse will move his quarters *away* from the tapping whip, not towards it. In time he learns to shift his quarters to one side or another from the action of a single leg applied, of course, in the critical position and in proper measure. In the same way he moves forward and *away* from the lunge whip which encourages (*threatens*) from behind even though there is no question of his ever being struck by the implement. In the same fashion we teach him to go forward from the legs, and because of this acute sensitivity we can teach him to respond to the pressure of the bit.

The watershed

There is, however, a watershed dividing submission from induced resistance.

The stimulus provided by the *very lightest* application of the bit on the mouth produces submission, the horse withdrawing, or giving, in his mouth to the pressure.

However, there is a point in the scale of the intensity of applied pressure when the horse instead of submitting acts oppositely and resists. He does so because the use of the hand is insufficiently refined. Instead of making a polite suggestion the hand forgets its manners and resorts to vulgar force and we return to the destructive 'you-pull-me-and-I'll-pull-you' syndrome arising from the horse's natural inclination to escape discomfort.

It works in the same way when riders are insufficiently sensitive to align the use of seat and legs to correspond with the sensitivity of the horse. Riders who employ the deadening influence of a heavy seat provoke resistance in the back, which is either stiffened in retaliation or hollowed under the ungiving pressure. In the same sense, the strong application of the legs, especially when they descend to kicking the horse, is just as unproductive. The horse stiffens against the action throughout his body. The flow and relaxed freedom of his movement is restricted commensurately and there will be an unavoidable stiffening in the mouth.

A lightly brushing leg, applied in the lower scale of intensity, is far more effective, but the horse has to be schooled to respond to it and the rider sufficiently expert to grade the intensity of its application.

The response of the horse to aids sensitively applied has much to do with the quality of the initial training, but it is also much concerned with the animal's level of physical fitness.

Physical well-being and a high-protein diet produce an increased – if you like, an induced – level of sensitivity and a heightened responsive reflex.

Take a fat, unfit horse from his field of lush grazing after he has been allowed to run to seed over a period of months and his reactions will be nothing other than lethargic. Indeed, his full, distended belly will have done nothing for his balance and on the account of imbalance alone it would be unreasonable to expect anything but a sluggish response.

Co-operation

The innate sensitivity is of primary importance but it would be almost entirely negated without the horse's extraordinary ability to *adapt* and his very evident desire to *co-operate*. Indeed, horses seem to obtain pleasure from correctly made movements and responses. When resistances arise it is either because of the human inadequacy or because of some prohibiting physical condition.

If the rider cannot communicate clearly the horse becomes confused and then resentful.

If some physical injury is causing pain then, clearly, the horse will be inhibited in his response. Many jumping problems, for example, arise from a painful back condition. Obviously, if the rider fails to appreciate the difficulty and persists in his demands, the relationship between the two becomes dangerously at risk.

Such is the desire to please, however, that the horse's eagerness can become an embarrassment. With one very good horse of mine I found the lateral work awkward and stiff. Probably it was my fault but one day as we came out of the corner of the school furthest away from the exit (and the stable) the horse felt to be positioned exactly right. I asked for a half-pass and he executed it quite beautifully. I made more than sure that he understood how well he had done and took him back to his stable and his feed – for him the ultimate reward and accolade of approval.

For weeks, thereafter, as he entered that particular corner he attempted to go into half-pass whether it was asked for or not and whether at the beginning of the lesson or at its close.

Possibly, he associated the movement with the return to his box and his feed but there was, nonetheless, an obvious pleasure in having mastered the movement and overcome a difficulty. For ever after, indeed, his impulsion increased and his action became more extravagant whenever he made lateral movements.

Indeed, once in a while we should consider how well the horse responds to the demands made of him and how contrary to his nature some of them can be. It is a good antidote against taking him too much for granted.

We ask him to jump fences which may be sited in the middle of a field – from his viewpoint it can hardly be considered a sensible exercise; it would be far easier, whilst conserving energy, to go round such fences. That, indeed, is often the course taken by young, untrained horses. As the schooling progresses, however, and the horse begins to understand what is wanted he will jump an island fence happily enough.

Sometimes, he is asked to jump fences when he cannot see what is on the landing side. In nature there is no way in which a horse would put himself at such risk, but he does it time and time again at the behest of a rider in whom he trusts.

We even ask horses to jump into water, and to jump fences sited in water, in complete defiance of the animal's atavistic sense of survival. Almost every horse is suspicious of water and displays an initial reluctance about entering it. It is certainly necessary to introduce them quietly and gradually to what in their minds is a potentially dangerous element but thereafter the majority cope with it amazingly well, if treating it with some respect.

Memory, crime and punishment

We come then to the matter of memory, the prime factor in schooling. In the horse it is extraordinarily retentive. Indeed, a lesson once learnt is never forgotten. It is, nonetheless, a two-edged sword for the horse remembers the bad experience with the same ability of recall as he remembers the good ones. 'In our dealings with him, we write on stone and what is written remains, for better or worse, forever.' (How many horsemen and women appreciate how great is that responsibility?)

We use the memory in every aspect of the horse's training alongside a system of repetition and reward. Very, very occasionally it may be necessary to punish the horse, but we have to be absolutely sure firstly that the horse's misdemeanour was not the result of a faulty action on our part or because he became confused on account of our inability to communicate clearly; secondly, we have to be certain that punishment is as nearly simultaneous with the execution of the crime as it can be.

The horse's memory is long and retentive

but he is only able to associate cause and result which are closely related in terms of time. He cannot possibly comprehend delayed punishment.

It is no good at all to take the horse back to his box after a disastrous jumping round and thump him for his behaviour of ten minutes ago. That would be a certain way of making the horse fearful, resentful, sour and confused, but it would do absolutely nothing to improve his jumping. He could not associate the beating with jumping a bad round.

Should he, however, in the hunting field commit that most heinous crime of kicking a hound, he will certainly understand why he gets a couple of thwacks on either side, *so long* as they are delivered almost before the offending leg has returned to the ground. He then associates the action of kicking with an unpleasant and painful experience and will be unlikely to repeat the performance.

Possibly the most frequent disobedience which attracts punishment is when the horse refuses at a fence. I am myself very chary of hitting a horse when this happens. There are all too many reasons why the stop could have been my fault rather than his. I prefer, when schooling, to circle the horse, applying the legs actively, and to re-present him at the obstacle. Usually, the horse jumps at this second attempt, after which, to make the point abundantly clear to him (and just in case it was his fault and not mine), he will jump it twice more.

There are occasions when the horse who begins to have second thoughts a stride or two before the fence can be persuaded to change his mind by a swift reminder from the whip, and there are times when a stop is deserving of punishment.

All too often, however, and particularly with the less expert, riders lose their heads and their calm in these situations and either punish too much or fail to punish the actual disobedience which is in need of correction.

If the horse stops hit him, if you must, at that moment. You are then punishing him for stopping and reinforcing the lesson that he should go forward from the legs.

If the horse stops, is turned away and then punished he has been hit not for the stop but for turning away – which is what he was asked to do. He has, in fact, been punished for an obedience and that must cause confusion in his mind.

Horses may also be punished for that reason, i.e. obedience, without the rider even being conscious that he has inflicted any chastisement.

The rider who puts on his legs, or perhaps his spurs, too strongly, causing the horse to move forward more quickly than expected may just be that sort of horseman. To retain his balance he catches hold of the reins and jabs his horse in the mouth. The horse, having obeyed the legs has been punished for doing what was asked of him. Oh, dear!

There is still a school of thought that trains a horse on the principle of submission and the fear of punishment. One would like to say categorically that it doesn't work but sadly, perhaps because horses are so easily exploited, it does. At least it does to a degree but the performance, although possibly accurate and effective, loses any natural brilliance and gaiety. The horse, as it were, performs with his body but not with any spirit.

Reward

The system in which reward plays the major part is far more satisfying, and far more satisfactory, too, in terms of the quality of performance. As with punishment, reward has to be closely connected in time with the particular action. The horse then associates the movement with something pleasant, knows that he has earned our approval and remembers when he is asked to do the same work again.

There is no reason why, in certain circumstances, the reward should not be a titbit but it need not necessarily be so nor, of course, is it practical or even desirable to be continually feeding the horse.

The voice can be used to reward the horse and so can a pat, whilst at a more advanced level recompense is made by the yielding of the activating aid.

Initially, as an example, we encourage the horse to go forward from the whip. As a preliminary to lungeing we teach him to walk in-hand, when he learns obedience to both whip and voice. In that instance the leader, standing at the horse's shoulder, gives the command 'Walk on'. Simultaneously, the assistant, holding the long whip, point to the ground, walks forward to reinforce the verbal command. The horse is then rewarded with a word and a pat.

In the early mounted lessons the leg and hand aids can be taught in just the same association. The rider applies the legs and at the same time the trainer gives the command 'Walk on' and makes a gesture with his whip. Then the horse is rewarded again.

Very quickly, for horses are by no means slow to learn, the horse associates the squeeze of the legs with the voice and whip with which he is already familiar and in no more than a brief lesson or two he will move forward from the legs without the reinforcement provided by voice and whip. The halt is just as easily taught if the horse has first learnt obedience to the voice and has been rewarded for his compliance.

Once the elementary obediences have been obtained the reward can be less tangible and infinitely more refined. From halt the rider, having prepared the horse for the command about to be made, applies the legs. The horse responds by moving forward and the legs cease to act – in fact, they *yield* to *reward* the horse for his obedience. Similarly, if we want to halt we apply the reins; the horse stops and is immediately rewarded by the hand ceasing to act and thus acknowledging the submission.

The aim is to produce a conditioned reflex

to the point where the horse responds immediately and willingly to the slight pressures made by hand, leg, and, ultimately, as those aids are used, with the disposition of weight and the influence of the seat.

To attain that sort of standard reward, which the horse understands, is essential and *some* repetition is necessary.

It is possible, however, to practise too much and the constant repetition can then dull the movement to the point where it deteriorates in quality. Too much practice only serves to defeat the object.

Whilst reward is integral to the training it, too, can be misused.

It is unwise to give youngstock titbits habitually lest they come to expect them and begin to bully unless they are forthcoming. The indiscriminate feeding of titbits devalues their use as a reward. They should instead be reserved for specific obediences.

Even with mature horses titbits should not be given in the stable. They only encourage pushing and nipping. A bedtime carrot or sugar lump is, however, permissible and it helps to strengthen the good relationship between man and horse.

One area in which food used as a reward may produce complications is in teaching horses to load into trailers, or even into boxes – which are usually more acceptable to them.

Almost every trainer of horses uses a bowl of food in order to encourage horses to enter a vehicle, and every training manual advocates the practice. The horse is tempted by the prospect of food to go into the trailer and is then given the feed as a reward. From then on the trailer is associated with food and the feed bowl is in danger of becoming a virtual condition of compliant behaviour.

Should, one day, the food not be available the horse may think twice about entering and may have to be persuaded by more forceful means. This is a critical point and to re-establish the horse's co-operation and get the relationship back to its former standing, one has to make very sure that the reward is always to hand. Another behavioural eruption which compels the use of force may, indeed, make the animal a confirmed non-loader. The situation may be remedied by patient, skilled handling over a period but habits once acquired can be difficult to eradicate entirely. It is much easier to train correctly from the start and stick to the established methods.

Excitability

There is another characteristic which can never be eliminated and which can interfere with the progression of training at every level. It is the horse's propensity to become *excited*. In the light of the horse's nature it is understandable and forgivable but it can be less than helpful.

All sorts of situations cause excitement. The presence of other horses (the herd) is one and, conversely the disappearance, even very temporarily, of a familiar companion may produce the same effect. Galloping in company, a herd simulation circumstance, certainly excites horses. In fact, some horses will come to the boil when asked to do no more than canter round an arena, and even jumping a small fence will produce a similar reaction.

Fortunately, most of them respond to quiet, progressive training and learn to perform potentially exciting movements in a state of relative calm.

Obviously, in competitive sports involving jumping and galloping there has to be an element of excitement to set the adrenalin flowing, otherwise the horse is reduced to a robot.

The senses

Finally, there are the five senses, plus that enigmatic sixth sense which is apparent in the horse but rare in our own species. It can best be described as a heightened perception.

Taste

Surprisingly little is known about taste in the horse and to my knowledge no work has been done to show what foods are preferred by them. There is a general assumption that horses like sweet things but I suspect that to be a taste acquired by early conditioning. Many feed manufacturers add sweet substances, like molasses, to their products on the grounds of palatibility.

On the whole horses do seem to appreciate sweet tastes and succulent items like apples and carrots. My own horses appear to relish herbs they find in our hedges and in corners of our old pastures, chicory being a particular favourite. One of them, however, rejects anything containing molasses and politely declines sugar lumps!

Touch

If taste is not particularly relevant to our understanding of the horse, that is not quite the case with the sense of touch.

Horses gain confidence by touching strange items with the nose (when the sense of smell is also involved) and they will often in early training over ground poles touch the pole with a foot before crossing it. Touch is used as a means of communication between horses and we, of course, by touching the horse in the process of grooming, are in a sense communicating and establishing a relationship. (I am inclined to think that grooming for both horse and groom creates a closer bond between the two when the physical contact is not interrupted by a brush or rubber curry comb. Indian *saises*, who often develop a particular rapport with their horse, groom and strap their charges with their forearms. I have no evidence to show that the

practice has any advantage over the European method but it's a nice thought.)

Horses, from foalhood onwards, appear to gain much pleasure from being nibbled by their dams or companions on the sensitive withers. They appreciate it just as much when humans perform the same service for them and it is a not illogical way of ingratiating oneself with one's horse.

Touch, of course, is also involved in riding the horse, the pressure of the legs activating groups of receptor cells on the horse's side, which are situated, conveniently for us, in the girth area.

Without scientific training, but from observation and experience, I have long understood, and tried to teach, that it is a fallacy to think that repeating or intensifying the aid when there is no response to the first touch of the legs will produce the required result. It won't. The more pressure that is applied and the greater the frequency with which the aid is applied the more deadened become the receptor cells. The lighter the aid and the shorter the time in which it is active, the more effective it becomes. Continual kicking with the legs and heels is the surest way to make the horse wholly unresponsive.

Dr Marthe Kiley-Worthington (*The Behaviour of Horses*) confirmed my understanding when she wrote of the receptor cells (which I learnt were properly termed *nocioceptors*) that they became '*less responsive if the stimulus*', i.e. the legs, '*is repeated at intervals of less than about 30 seconds*'.

We are less helpful to the horse in respect of his sense of touch when we shut him in a stable which does not allow him to touch (or even see) his next-door neighbour in a sort of arbitrary 'no talking in the dormitory' rule.

Even less sensible is the ridiculous practice of cutting off a horse's whiskers. He uses them to touch and evaluate objects, which he may not be able to see, particularly the contents of his manger, and they relay messages to the brain. To deprive him of that facility, particularly for no more than a cosmetic reason, is hardly acceptable.

Smell

The sense of smell is acute and it seems probable that this is one way in which horses recognise each other and probably areas around their home with which they are familiar. It is suggested also that their pronounced homing instinct may be connected with the sense of smell in some way. Obviously, too, it plays an important part in the equine defensive system.

Quite certainly horses smell us and without doubt, I think, they are able to detect nervousness or fear by the scent given off by our bodies in those circumstances. They then react accordingly, usually by becoming tense and nervous themselves. (I have been assured by a Dyak tracker, who could trail a man in thick jungle by scent, that the human being does give off a distinctive fear odour. Old horsemen, men who belonged to the Horseman's Society, a sort of freemasonry confined to waggoners, carters and so on, used various aromatic oils to calm and tame vicious horses and to make them submissive – but then they used toads' spawn, collected at midnight, the milt of the new-born foal, dried and well ground, and other things both mentionable and otherwise.)

Hearing

Although no scientific evidence exists relative to the range of hearing, it must be presumed that it is sensitive and far more so than our own.

The ears are, indeed, enormously mobile and can be rotated at will to pick up sounds from any direction. They are controlled by no less than thirteen pairs of muscles and their range of movement not only gives expression to the face but tells us a great deal about the horse's state of mind at any particu-

lar moment. Pricked firmly forward they denote an interest in some object that has caught the horse's attention and, if we are working the horse, a corresponding lack of attention to the job in hand. When relaxed or dozing the ears are lowered and are more flaccid. They are laid back in displeasure, temper or aggression. When one is stuck out sideways it is probably checking on the presence of a buzzing wasp or gadfly.

Mobile ears, flicking back and forth as we ride, assure us that the horse is attentive and listening. Horses are exceptionally responsive to the voice and are able to interpret the tone employed.

It is probably the first and most important of the natural aids through which we can soothe the flighty, command the attention of the inattentive, liven the sluggard and rebuke the wrongdoer.

Sight

Equine sight, which is unusual in all sorts of respects and quite different from human vision, is only rarely studied by riders and the subject is certainly not included in any examination syllabus or training curricula.

This is surprising because the position of the eyes on the head and the method of focussing are very relevant to purchase, management and performance.

The eye itself is very large in comparison, for example, with those of a pig or an elephant. This suggests that the horse relies heavily upon the sense of sight, far more so than the two animals mentioned. The large eye increases the acuity as well as the field of vision.

It is interesting to reflect that large eyes are usually associated with nocturnal animals or those that live in conditions of much reduced light, like thick jungle. The horse is hardly nocturnal but there is plenty of evidence to show that he sees very well in the dark, far better than humans. It is possible to ride fast

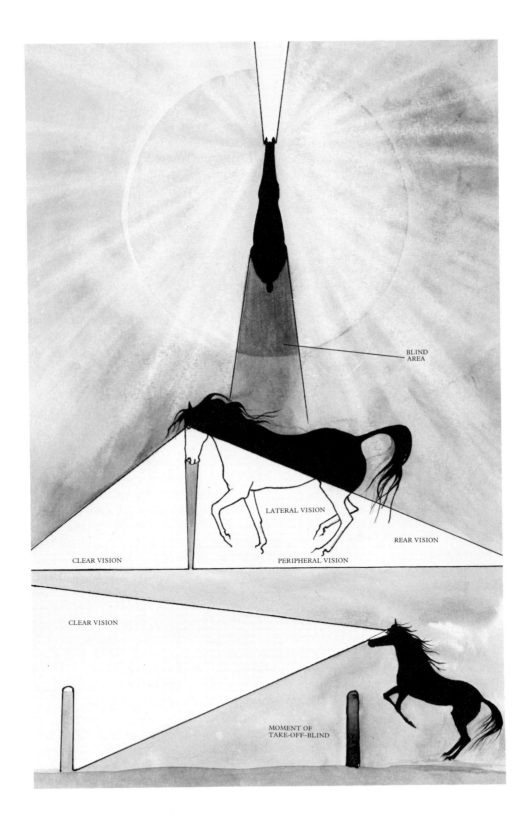

BLIND AREA

LATERAL VISION

REAR VISION

CLEAR VISION

PERIPHERAL VISION

CLEAR VISION

MOMENT OF TAKE-OFF–BLIND

'Equine sight . . . unusual in all sorts of respects and quite different from human vision.'

in perfect safety in the dark and even to jump small fences, if one's nerve allows. (The consensus of opinion is that small eyes in a horse are a sign of bad temper and as such are to be avoided. However, it is also very possible that they afford less efficient vision.)

The majority of animals make use of the ciliary muscle in order to focus upon an object, the latter altering the shape of the eye lens. The horse's ciliary muscle, however, is insufficiently developed for this purpose and a different method of focussing has to be employed.

It depends upon the horse raising the head according to the distance away from the eyes of the object he wishes to bring into focus. The further away it is the greater will be the degree of elevation required. That in itself is an important consideration when the horse is being schooled to jump, but the efficiency of the focussing mechanism is dependent upon more than just the freedom of the head and neck to be raised and lowered.

To a very large extent it is concerned, so far as objects to the front are involved, with the placement of the eyes on the head and, in particular, upon the width of the forehead. Other contributory factors to sight are the width and length of the face and the manner in which the head is joined (or 'set on') to the neck. In general it is supposed that the width and length of the face prevent the horse from seeing the contents of a manger set at chest height and almost certainly prohibit a view of his own feet, at least when standing square.

Heavy, cold-blood horses and 'primitives' like the Asiatic Wild Horse are broad across the forehead with the eyes placed more on the side of the head than otherwise. This arrangement allows wide lateral vision but comparatively poor frontal vision. The same, of course, applies to a riding horse who inclines towards that type of facial conforma-tion. For the purpose of riding, the facility for extreme lateral vision, occurring at the expense of frontal vision, is a serious disadvantage.

The riding horse, as exemplified by Thoroughbred conformation, enjoys far better frontal vision because his forehead is so much narrower than that of the draught breeds and his eyes are placed more to the front than on the side of the head. In the horse that is required to jump conformation of this type is an essential requirement.

(In the beautiful and very distinctive Arabian horse, a broad forehead is a desirable feature and the enormous eyes are, indeed, set more to the sides than otherwise. A recent book on Arab type and conformation gives this description: 'Seen from the front the head appears broad across the forehead, the eyes set well out . . .' The result is to allow extensive all-round vision and may have a bearing on the unique carriage of the Arabian. On the other hand it may well contribute to what is sometimes called the 'awareness' of the breed, an Arab horse always being very conscious of everything going on around him. It would be quite wrong to say that Arab horses do not jump well. They can perform over fences quite adequately, if not to the standard of the Thoroughbred types. However, it is not unreasonable to suggest that the sight mechanism, together with the distinctive carriage, perfect though it be within the context of the 'desert horse', falls short of the ideal required for high-level jumping.)

The eyes and ears of the horse operate in conjunction. When the ear is pricked forward the eye also looks to the front to focus on the object of interest. It follows that the closer the ears are placed to each other the more efficient will be the forward vision.

Horses are able to move the eyes independently and each eye, whatever its placement, is capable of lateral vision quite beyond that of the human being. It is a part of the defensive equipment enabling the horse to detect movements to the side of him and, also, of course those odd flutters of paper in the hedge.

However, the protective mechanism goes further than that, for the horse has the ability to see behind him as a result of the size and position of his eyes. When grazing, the horse has all-round vision without needing to raise or turn the head. It seems likely that horses can see the rider on their backs in certain circumstances and if the conformation of the face in relation to the eye is conducive to that facility. (Personally, I prefer my horse to look to the front rather than to spend time attempting to look at me.)

To focus on objects to his front, however, is a different matter and as we have seen involves adjusting the head position in order to get a clear sight.

Obviously, this will be made more difficult if the head is restricted by the use of martingales and so on *or by the rider's hand*.

Given freedom of his head, the horse can see a fence 45 ft (13.5 m) away quite clearly with *both* eyes (45 ft (13.5 m) is three strides). However, at about 4 ft (120 cm) from the fence the shape and size of his own head prevent him from having a clear view with *both* eyes. Indeed, unless the head has enough freedom for it to be tilted slightly to one side so that the fence is visible to *one* eye or the other the horse actually 'jumps blind'. At least this is so over a show-jumping type of fence. A low hurdle taken at speed is not at all the same since the horse makes his leap well before he gets into the 4 ft (120 cm) zone.

It seems very likely that over a 5 ft (150 cm) fence most horses do jump blind at the last moment, learning by experience and training how to judge the approach and take-off to the obstacle.

This peculiarity of equine sight emphasises the importance of employing a progressive system of jumping training and, perhaps, appreciating the unnecessary difficulties with which the horse is made to contend when use is made of restrictive items of restraint –

which include the human hand.

The sixth sense

The possession of what I have called a heightened perception in the domestic equine is well developed, and that it exists is beyond doubt.

The horse is certainly far better able to read the human than the other way round. He senses instantly timidity, hesitation, irritability, courage, confidence and a whole lot more. Furthermore he reacts to those human strengths and frailties and reflects them in his own behaviour. (Just occasionally it can work the other way. Bold riders make bold horses, but I can affirm from experience that bold horses can give their riders at least the reputation for boldness.) It is said with great truth that the horse is the mirror of his rider. It can also be said that there are no problem horses, only problem people.

Years ago I had a young lady on my staff who viewed the world in terms of black and white. She had no time for the intermediate shades of grey. She had, probably as a result, sterling qualities – unflinching devotion to the projects in hand and an unwavering loyalty strong as new-forged steel.

As a humanising counterbalance she had failings in the same measure. She could be unpredictable, with the most unreasonable of tempers, and she was tactless to the extreme. Physically she was heavy-handed and had a talent for getting in one's way. To walk down a street with her compelled an expenditure of energy altogether out of proportion to the exercise and was moreover demanding of Christian tolerance. The problem was that she could not steer a straight passage, continually crossing from one side of the pavement to the other.

Her horse was an exact counterpart of her own character – or the worst parts of it. He was moody, quite unpredictable in his behaviour, often bloody-minded and was always in the way. What is more, just like his mistress, he could not walk in a straight line!

Whether extra-sensory perception in horses can extend to their being telepathic has never been established scientifically. From my own experience I believe it is possible within limitations. What is absolutely certain is that the horse can respond very accurately to subliminal movement, i.e. very slight changes in muscular tension.

My daughter's first pony was a little Welshman, very bright and quick to learn. So quick was he and so evident was the enjoyment he took in his lessons that I used to give demonstrations of lungeing and loose schooling over fences with him. He learnt, as all horses can, a vocabulary to cover our activities together. He would, indeed, obey my voice whilst being ridden by the children, which was at times most useful.

Our *pièce de résistance*, however, was when I allowed him to circle the school loose before an audience. I would ask the spectators to picture in their minds the pony coming to halt from canter at a particular point on the circle and at the same time to will him to halt there, thinking hard on the single word 'Whoah'.

The pony always halted exactly where I had said he would. It had, however, nothing to do with the audience. He halted because ever so slightly I relaxed my body. He was sensitive enough to pick up that minimal movement (which had, of course, been made previously in his training in conjunction with the vocal command) and he responded to it.

Sex and the single horse

It is possible that horses kept singly may develop behavioural problems as a result of not being in contact with their own kind. However, many horses kept in this way seem to manage quite well although they may initially be expected to evince a fairly high degree of excitement when in company. They are, of course, and in general again, that much more reliant upon the human and the quality of leadership he provides. Sex, too, can cause behavioural problems outside the common run.

Geldings are usually exempt from sexually oriented difficulties but mares, when in season, can suffer temporary changes of character which can interfere with schooling or competitive riding. They may become tetchy, unwilling, inattentive and sometimes very bad-tempered. Or they may become for all the world like a broody hen.

(Having said that, I still prefer a mare. I find them more genuine and interesting and the good ones are courageous and willing to a degree. Unfortunately, in this country, the riding of stallions in company is not encouraged, otherwise I would have one tomorrow.)

5

The Stress Factor

STRESS IN the modern society is both endemic and inevitable. As an antidote we perform aerobics, attend yoga classes or play squash, and quite a lot of us find relaxation in the owning and riding of horses. The difference with riding is that it involves another sentient being of a different species. Paradoxically, in some circumstances the human obtains relief from stress at the expense of the horse, who may be subjected to situations which are at least potentially stressful.

Immediately one thinks of the highly competitive activities as being the prime stress areas. Competition, in the case of particular individuals, may certainly be stressful, but stress arising from poor management or schooling techniques can occur all the way down the line. The neglected child's pony, or the one that is abused through ignorance, is just as much exposed to stress as the eventer or the racehorse – indeed, probably more so.

In an imperfect world we have to accept that stress will be present in most of the activities in which the horse is involved. It will never be eliminated any more than it will in the human society, nor is it desirable that it should be. Without some tension being present the performance in any field loses the essential spark and we descend to the level of the cabbage or the automaton.

What is important in the context of the horse relationship is that stress should not be imposed thoughtlessly, and unnecessarily. If the horse is to live happily and work willingly for us his management must seek to establish acceptable stress levels, appreciating that continued stress at a high level is conducive only to a decline in the animal's well-being, an increase in behavioural problems and a lowered standard of performance.

Stress may be either *physical* or *mental*. Sometimes it is a combination of both, since stress of an initially physical origin can well lead to a similar mental state.

Physical stress

Physical stress occurs in any form of exertion. It becomes unacceptable and is cruel when the horse is compelled to continue the activity beyond the limits imposed by his preparation, conditioning and natural capacity, or when courses are built beyond the possible optimum.

Nor is it any better to allow a worm-ridden pony, ill-fed, if fed at all, to be belted about by an enthusiastic but inexperienced and probably uncaring child during the holidays. (Children, in general, are more rough and more unthinking in their treatment of animals than adults. Except, of course, those adults concerned with the markets and the meat trade or, you may think, the experienced horseman who rides his horse into the ground for the sake of fame and a silver pot.)

Physical stress, which will undoubtedly have an adverse mental effect, may be imposed by reason of an individual's conformation being unsuitable for the rider's purpose. Animals with serious conformational defects, such as pronounced cow hocks, will experience pain and discomfort if forced to jump. Ultimately the exertion will result in disease and unsoundness. Horses with ewe necks, swan necks, or 'cock-throttled' horses all have difficulty in bridling in accordance with the required convention. It is quite impossible for them to flex at the poll, carrying their heads a little in advance of the vertical. If they are compelled to do so by draw reins, balancing reins or some other form of coercive device they experience serious physical discomfort, which if persisted in, will have an adverse effect upon their temperament.

Poorly fitting saddlery can, indeed, be a cause of stress. Something as simple as a browband which is too small and which in consequence pulls the headpiece against the back of the ears can result in problems which are quite disproportionate to the minor nature of the offence. The pressure exerted on the ears could hardly be considered painful but it is a constant irritation to the horse who will often express his resentment by continual shaking of the head. Head-shaking caused in this way as well as others quickly becomes habitual and is difficult if not impossible to cure. For the rider, head-shaking is a frustrating habit and his reaction may well in itself contribute to a stress situation involving both parties.

A throatlatch fastened too tightly restricts the breathing if the horse is made to bridle and flex at the poll. Too large a jointed snaffle fitted with a drop noseband, preventing the horse from opening his mouth, is quickly converted into an instrument of torture. Since the mouth cannot be opened it is possible for the joint of the snaffle to press uncomfortably against the roof. Too small a bit chafes the corners of the lips and quickly makes them sore and tender.

Neglected teeth which have become diseased or so sharp that they lacerate the inside of the cheeks or the tongue cause understandable unease. In young horses the eruption of permanent teeth inflames the gums and makes the mouth uncomfortable. If the young horse, already perhaps fractious, is worked in a bit which exacerbates the condition he becomes resentful and prone to misbehaviour.

In all these cases stress is caused which may have long-term effects upon the horse's progress.

The fitting of the saddle can cause almost as many problems. If the stuffing is allowed to flatten so that the front arch presses on the withers, or if the channel dividing the panel should become closed and so put pressure on the spine, the movement of the horse is restricted and the back may hollow in an effort to escape the discomfort. Jumping, of course, exaggerates the condition. The horse will be more or less seriously pinched on the wither as his back is rounded during the leap. To avoid the pain he soon learns to hollow his back rather than round it. The less-than-bold horse will in the end begin to refuse, declining to have anything further to do with an exercise which causes him pain. The bold horse may not do that, but he is very likely to become a tearaway, launching himself at his fences with a hollowed back in an effort to get the business over with as quickly as he can.

A serious stress situation has then developed which will have a positive effect on the horse's performance and well-being. Furthermore, matters may be made even worse by the reaction of the rider who, in the first instance, may resort to punishing the horse with his whip, and in the second may do the same thing with his hands and the bit.

Mental stress

Mental stress is often the result of interruptions in the normal *routine* when it is for the most part not of major importance. It occurs at a low level if feeds are not forthcoming at the usual time, for instance. Young horses, and older ones, too may become disturbed when first they go to a show or even to a hunt meet, but this is no more than a natural excitement and becomes less noticeable as the animals become accustomed to the experience.

Markets are an obvious source of serious stress, particularly when mares and foals are involved. Weaning, also, produces very great stress for both mare and foal and it may have a long-term effect on the youngster. For most people the only solution is to recognise the trauma and take sensible precautions to mitigate its effects. The matter is discussed in Chapter 7.

Temperamental unsuitability to a particular pursuit can cause tensions which are manifested in behavioural abnormalities and, possibly, in physical disturbances. Too demanding a programme of competitive events, the result, of course, of mistaken management, will sicken some horses and produce a variety of reactions. Then there are the specialists who concentrate on a specific discipline. Clearly they have to be temperamentally suited to the chosen sport if they are to be successful. They must, indeed, enjoy their work. The selection of a dressage horse, for instance, is a matter for very serious deliberation. The rigorous discipline of the manège makes great mental demands as well as physical ones and not all horses, however brilliant they may be in other respects, are able to cope with the pressures involved.

For some horses *travelling* is a prime reason for mental distress. Usually it is the trailer rather than the horsebox which presents the difficulties. We have to assume that some horses, like some dogs, some children and some adults, too, suffer ill-effects from travelling. Dogs and humans are usually sick but the horse has no ability to vomit. Unhappily, there is no blanket solution, it is rather more a matter for experiment with the individual.

Basic precautions include a thorough schooling in entering and leaving the vehicle and taking great care that the horse is never given anything approaching a rough ride. Some horses travel better on one side than the other. There are horses that like to travel facing the rear and some that cannot keep their balance unless they can brace themselves on legs held wide apart.

There are calming food additives now available and there is an increase in the availability of homoeopathic products as well, of course, as the more ordinary sedatives. They can all be helpful in reducing tension but, of course, sedatives should only be given on veterinary advice and one must be careful not to break the rules regarding the use of prohibited substances in competition.

Food may very well be a contributory factor in stress. Heating, high-protein rations produce a change in behaviour patterns and act to heighten the natural reactions. Furthermore, it has been shown that a diet too rich in protein can produce a positive deterioration in performance. Many of the food mixes do not produce the characteristic behaviour of the conventional heating food elements and they do so without impairing the performance potential.

Horses have, of course, managed very well in the past on conventional foods, but under modern farming systems these may vary very much in consistency and quality. They should by no means be ignored, but it behoves the responsible owner to examine other forms of food and feeding methods. It is said of man that he is what he eats; there seems no reason why that should not be applied to horses.

A final contributory stress factor is concerned with stabling which is frequently planned and executed with little thought being given to an area which exerts a powerful influence on the horse's life and outlook. In most instances it would be impractical to house two horses in one box, even though that arrangement might in many respects be ideal. But surely there is no good reason for putting a horse in prison for the better part of the day. Horses are happier and more relaxed when they can see and even touch each other and there is no reason at all why this should not be allowed by leaving the top of the division between two boxes open with perhaps a rail above the partition for one's peace of mind.

6

The Human Factor

KEEPING, TRAINING and riding horses is about communication between two species and is initiated by the human. Often we think of it as being a set of signals based on the physical application of limbs and body-weight.

For that system to work, however, it is not sufficient for riders to learn a set of prescribed aids, parrot fashion from a manual. To obtain the required response it is necessary also for the horse to understand their meaning – and he does not even read the book. The horse has, therefore, to be taught what responses are being requested by the pressures exerted by the limbs, and the rider has to learn how to apply them in a manner that makes their meaning crystal clear to the horse.

In fact this language of the aids, which has evolved in relatively recent times so far as the written word is concerned, is by no means definitive and whilst there is some overall agreement in general terms, there is no such unanimity on the details.

Communication in three parts

Physical contact represents one part of the communication. The second part is concerned with the rider's ability to project a *mental influence*. The third and very essential requirement, and perhaps the most difficult to acquire, is to learn how to *listen* to the horse's response through both mind and body. To become sufficiently receptive in both respects involves subjugating the natural human urge to dominate.

Since communication is so closely linked with physical contact and mental discipline it follows that it will be more or less effective according to the development of those qualities and the rider's ability to use both sympathetically and reciprocally.

Physical fitness

Riding is an athletic exercise in which great emphasis is placed on the physical and gymnastic conditioning of the horse. If that is to be used to the full extent then obviously the rider must have attained a standard of fitness which is at least commensurate with that of his horse, and that applies just as much to the 'weekend' rider, which so many of us are, as to anyone else. Anything less, indeed, is a negation of all the effort required to bring a horse into condition for specific purposes.

Indeed, for anything beyond gentle hacking, the process involved in conditioning the horse and schooling him to the levels required in competition demands physical fitness in the rider of a high order. From the fit body comes the alert, receptive, disciplined mind.

For the young the possession of the sound (fit) body should present little difficulty, but it is sometimes harder for them to acquire the fluency of the calm and disciplined mind. As 'Time's winged chariot' comes closer the opposite may apply.

Physical fitness combines regular exercise – in this instance relevant to the chosen pursuit – and a *sensible diet*.

To be physically fit, whatever the level of our riding, we must be *supple, strong* and have *stamina*, then we can begin to ride with decreasing tension and we will not suffer from aches and pains after taking the exercise.

Tension is the arch-enemy in every sort of athletic pursuit, but it is particularly damaging to the rider because his 'equipment', unlike that of the golfer or tennis player, is an animate being, the horse, who, in the wink of an eyelid, reflects the rider's tension in the stiffening of his own body and movement.

To be able to apply the physical aids harmoniously the rider needs to be *supple* from neck, to shoulder, through the arm and right down to the fingers. Supple, too, in the ankle and the knee to permit the independent use of the lower leg, and, very importantly, supple in the waist so as to allow movement in the pelvis and legs without disturbing the posture of the upper body.

Strength is equally important. The *strong* rider has an obvious advantage over the one who is physically weak and, therefore, becomes insecure so much more easily. Losses of security and balance result in a commensurate loss of co-ordination and in every instance cause an over-reaction, which is usually made through the reins. Gentleness, feel and sympathy in our physical communication with the horse can only be developed through strength.

Stamina, too, has to be developed in order that physical effort can be maintained consistently.

At the centre of any programme of fitness are an efficient heart and lungs and some really strong abdominal muscles.

The first two are virtually inter-dependent and to extend their efficiency the concern is simply with an improved oxygen intake. By exercising we use up oxygen and the more we use regularly the better we exercise, and the more efficient become our lungs and our heart (which is just as much a muscle as the calf and in the same way needs exercise if it is to be kept in good order).

The development of the abdominal muscles has a lot to do with our *posture*. Sagging tummies, the mark of twentieth-century man, are at the root of postural faults. They are accompanied, in the saddle, by that objectionable protruding bottom, slouching shoulders and terrible stiffness in the spine and waist. Harmony between horse and rider is then impossible. To develop and maintain firm stomach muscles is thus of enormous importance and plays a considerable part in riders' exercise programmes.

This chapter includes exercises in the suppleness, strength and stamina categories and suggests how many times each one should be done each day.

However, do start gradually and do consult a doctor if you have any history of heart trouble etc., or if you are over forty or overweight. (If you are over forty (or even fifty)

remember that the stiffness of advancing years is a nasty rumour being spread about by a lot of older people who can't move.)

Mounted exercises on the lunge

Physical fitness achieved through sensible eating and regular exercising provides a sure base for future work in the progression towards the complete rider. It is, however, no more than the first stage.

The second stage is to relate the physically fit rider to the movement of the horse. By being physically fit balance, co-ordination and the ability to sit in a relaxed and effective posture is only made easier. Fitness does not automatically confer the attributes necessary for riding horses but it provides the means by which they can be acquired. The next stage in the development of the rider are the exercises to be practised on the lunge.

These mounted lessons represent the foundation of the rider's training, they are the equitational equivalent of the three Rs. For their full potential to be realised, however, a horse well schooled on the lunge is an essential and he must have, in addition, smooth, easy paces. Probably, this is one of the reasons why mounted lunge lessons are so neglected in the general system of training practised in Britain, although their inherent value in establishing the rider's seat and posture is well recognised in the countries of the European mainland.

Lunge exercises are hard work for the horse; if not performed correctly they can be inhibiting to the movement. Furthermore the horse has to be temperamentally suited to going round in endless circles.

Indeed, the lunge horse requires careful, intelligent management if he is not to become fed up with the whole operation.

As a result, one imagines, few schools train and keep these invaluable schoolmaster horses. (If they did, their pupils might ride better than they do.)

The second requirement is an experienced and skilled instructor, able to derive the most benefit for his pupil from the lessons.

The lunge exercises should be carried out in parallel with regular ground exercises, the latter being performed as part of daily routine.

In a perfect world where time is of no consequence the lunge lesson should also be on a daily basis and over a period of twelve months its duration should be extended to some 40–45 minutes – but that presupposes in addition that we have a horse capable of working on the circle for that length of time.

For most of us, two lessons each week is a more possible objective. For the first lessons 15 minutes is sufficient, the duration being increased over a week or so to a full half-hour.

The progressive lessons on the lunge are detailed within this chapter.

Mental projection

The third, penultimate, stage in the development of the rider's communication skills is the acquisition of a sound knowledge of equestrian theory coupled with the ability to influence the horse through the medium of the aid combination, a facility much encouraged by the physical preparation. By combination is meant the legs, hands, seat and disposition of the bodyweight, to which might be added the *head* aid – one that is all too frequently used insufficiently.

The theory and the use of the aids, to that point where they can be applied and co-ordinated as automatically as the actions of hand and foot which produce a gear change in a car, are discussed in more depth in the subsequent chapters on riding and training.

Here, however, we can examine the final requirement of the rider, which is concerned with the ability to project a mental influence, an ability which is dependent, when mounted, upon the efficiency of the physical system. Until that is at a high level, mental communication is haphazard, momentary imbalance in the body and occasional stiffnesses causing similar interruptions in the mind.

There is no way of teaching riders communication on a mental plane – they can only be encouraged to develop an attitude of mind and increase their powers of concentration, whilst being conscious that, with application, it is possible to obtain the facility to a degree dependent upon their own personality.

As a start it may be helpful to reflect on the sort of qualities necessary in the make-up of a horseman or woman.

My list includes these five words: INTELLIGENCE – SENSITIVITY – SELF-DISCIPLINE – PATIENCE – POSITIVE ATTITUDE.

The first varies in quality between one person and another and, indeed, normally intelligent people in one field can be very unintelligent in another. A lot of otherwise intelligent people, for example, can be extraordinarily stupid when it comes to dealing with horses. It arises, I believe, from thoughtlessness, unfamiliarity and an ignorance about the animal with which they are dealing. In consequence there are a lot of mistaken ideas and attitudes.

As people acquire more knowledge they begin to treat horses more intelligently.

To be *sensitive*, in the way that one can be appreciative of the moods and feelings of people as well as animals relies, perhaps, as much on being considerate to others as on anything else. It is without doubt a quality which can be cultivated and horsemen need very much to increase their sensitivity to their equine partners.

Self-discipline is a more obvious requirement. Without it we cannot expect to exert discipline, or command the respect of either men or horses. Those unable to control their tempers or their irritation have no place with horses – at least, not until they have applied themselves to the problem and learnt self-discipline. It is by no means impossible.

Patience, may indeed stem, in part, from

our ability to discipline our minds and feelings. It is, in any case, a prime requirement.

Finally, there is that *positive attitude* – the core of steel which makes actions decisive. The negative approach (I call it pussy-footing) is always non-productive with horses, who become unsure of themselves and of their handlers, too, when they discern a less than positive state of mind. There is, however, no need to take a course in Pelmanism in order to think positively – with conscious practice it becomes habitual. But there is another side. It is possible that in developing our positive, dynamic personality we do so at the expense of sensitivity and become so dominant that we can no longer be receptive.

Once, of course, we acquire the skills which enable us to communicate through our minds as well as our bodies we approach the ultimate requirement of the complete horseman – the ability to *listen* to what the horse is saying.

A very great horseman, possibly one imagines a nearly complete one, wrote this:

'The first great attribute of the horseman is humility, the second flexibility.' He also wrote: 'We only begin to learn about horses when we begin to understand how much there is to learn.'

Progressive ground exercises

This is a recommended progression of exercises over a six-week period. It can, of course, be modified or extended according to individual circumstances. *(If you have any history of heart or other physical trouble consult your doctor before starting the exercises.)* Never exercise so strenuously that you feel exhausted. If you find the recommended frequency of the exercise too much, reduce it to a comfortable number.

Suppleness

1. *Arm circling – Fig. 1*
   Stand with feet apart, arms loose at the sides. Swing arms forward, up and back and down in one smooth movement allowing them to brush the ears at each rotation. Then reverse the rotation. Frequency: 8 backwards, 8 forwards.

2. *Knee bending – Fig. 2*
   Take this one steadily and aim for a nice, smooth rhythm. Stand with feet together. Raise left knee with the cupped hand assisting and bring the head down to meet it. Then do the same with the right knee. Frequency: 8 times with each leg.

3. *Side flexing the trunk – Fig. 3*
   Feet apart, hands on hips. Bend to left and right alternately keeping the trunk upright. Frequency: 8 times to each side.

Strength

1. *Push-ups – Fig. 4*

   Do this against a firm table. Bend arms
   whilst keeping the body straight until the
   chest touches the table, then push up to
   the start position. Frequency: 8 times
   (progressing to 15).

2. *Tummy strengtheners – Fig. 5*

   Sit on a plain kitchen chair with legs
   outstretched, heels on ground. Hold the
   edges of the seat. Raise legs to press thighs
   against chest and return slowly to start
   position. Frequency: 4 times (progressing
   to 8).

   After one week go on to this more testing
   exercise: Sit in the same start position.
   Bring thighs to chest and then push out
   the legs in front of you. Hold the position
   to the count of three and lower slowly to
   the ground. Frequency: 3 times (progressing to 6).

Stamina

3. *Squats – Fig. 6*
   Feet slightly apart, hands on hips. Bend knees and assume squat position keeping back upright. Straighten legs to stand on tiptoe and repeat. Frequency: 5 times (progressing to 8).

1. *Bench steps – Fig. 7*
   You need a stout box or stool about 12 ins (30 cm) high. Stand in front of it, about 12 ins (30 cm) away and with hands on hips. With left leg leading, step up and step down. Repeat with right leg leading. Frequency: 15 steps with each leg (progressing to 20).

2. *Running on the spot*
   Very hard work so start by running for 30 seconds and work up to 2–3 minutes.

   Carry out this programme for two weeks then add these exercises:

Suppling

1. *Trunk rotating – Fig. 8*
   Stand with feet apart, arms raised straight out to the front. Swing both arms round to the left and as far behind as you can. Repeat to the right. Keep the hips and legs as still as you can. Frequency: 10 times to each side.

2. *Hamstrings – Fig. 9*
   Stand with feet apart, arms to the sides. Bend forward and slide both hands as far down the left leg as you can. Come upright and slide the hands down the right leg. Frequency: 10 times.

Strength

1. *Tummy strengthener – Fig. 10*

   Lie on your back, arms outstretched be-hind the head, knees slightly bent and feet under the open bottom drawer of a chest or something similar. Sit up, pressing chest to thighs and lie back. Frequency: 5 times (progressing to 8).

Stamina

Increase your running on the spot or do a few minutes on an exercise bicycle.

In the final fortnight you should be able to increase the frequency of each exercise and if you are feeling very supple you might vary your exercise period with these suppling ex-ercises, all of which should be done *slowly* and *smoothly*.

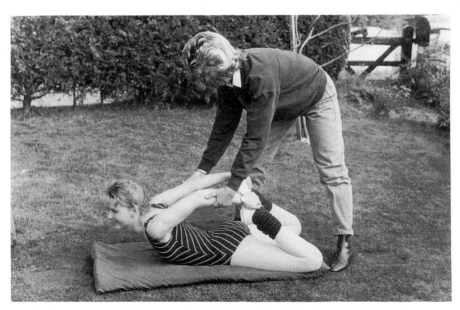

The bow – Fig. 11
Lie face down on the floor. Bend the knees and point the toes. Slowly raise chest and head, reach back and grasp your feet. Now bring the knees off the floor and lift the chin and chest. Do this exercise very slowly and just once.

Elbow to knee – Fig. 12
Sit cross-legged, hands clasped behind your head. Bend forward to touch your right knee with your left elbow, or get as near as you can to doing that. Keep the right elbow pointing upwards. Hold for 5 seconds and return slowly to the start position. Repeat with the right elbow to the left knee. Frequency: once each way.

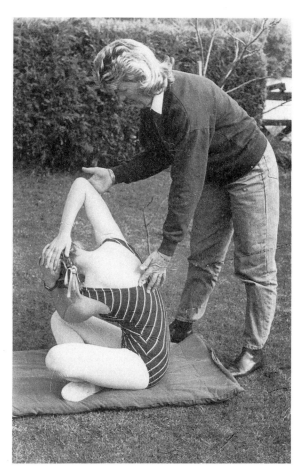

Progressive mounted exercises

1. The first essential· is to establish a correct seat at halt, the trunk upright and the seat deep in the saddle. The leg is stretched down and the lower part is held lightly in contact with the horse. The toe points to the front without there being any constriction in the ankle joint. The

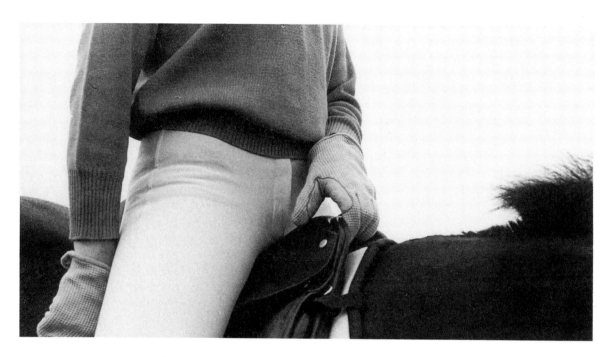

heel is held a little lower than the toe. If the heel rises and the toe points down the whole seat is affected through the knee, thigh, hip and trunk. It becomes insecure and out of balance. However, the extreme of pushing down with the heel is to be discouraged. It causes the lower leg to stiffen in the calf and locks the knee joint.

2. It helps to maintain the position if the rider holds the head of the saddle lightly in the fingers of the *outside* hand because she can then turn the trunk to accord with the direction of the movement.

3. The position well retained at walk. The rider is sitting squarely and in pleasing balance. There is a temptation at this pace to stiffen the back so as to maintain the upright position. The rider has to be encouraged to keep the small of the back supple, allowing it to move in time with the stride of the horse.

4. The position from the rear. Shoulders and hips square and in line with the vertical position of the horse. Shoulders and hips are aligned with the horse's hips. The inside leg is stretched a little to prevent its moving outwards and away from the horse.

   Common faults are: (a) rounding the shoulders bringing the trunk behind the movement; (b) straightening the knee; (c) gripping with the calf causing the toe to turn out.

7. An easy deep seat at trot. Head inclined towards the movement. Right shoulder and right hip a little in advance of the left.

6. The position at canter with the rider in balance with the movement. However, her toe has dropped a little.

7. Working at walk and trot with the hands on the hips steadies and deepens the seat. Each hand must be cupped over the hip bones with the thumbs on the loins and facing inwards. This is a good exercise to combat any 'slackness' in the body posture and good for the rider's confidence, too. (The pressure exerted by the hands pushes the seat downwards.)

8. Folding the arms behind the back helps straighten rounded shoulders and braces collapsing tummies. To brace the back naturally and effectively the rider has to grasp each elbow. This exercise also contributes to the deepening of the seat. Practise at walk and trot.

9. Arm circling upwards and backwards form the basic suppling exercises which teach the rhythmical movement of the limbs. It can be practised first with just one arm, then with both in unison and finally with the arms being swung alternately.

These are the points to be watched: (a) the seat must remain in the saddle – the natural tendency is for it to be raised as the arms are lifted; (b) the exercise must

be carried out slowly and smoothly without any jerkiness; (c) the arms swing only from the shoulders. Practise at walk and trot.

10. Arms outstretched. A difficult position to maintain for more than one or two circuits. It opens the chest, straightens the back and reveals quite unmistakably whether the rider is sitting squarely on the seat bones. Practise at walk and trot.

11. Arms held at chest height and then swung backwards vigorously. Very good for opening the chest and exercising the shoulder joints. Best executed at walk.

12. Probably the most difficult exercise. This swinging of the arms backwards and forwards alternately is best left until the rider has become very proficient. The body needs to remain upright with the seat firmly in the saddle. It is all too easy for the rider to be pitched on too the fork as she swings the arms forward. Practise at walk and then at trot.

13. When the seat is established the hands can be held in the riding position. It helps the rider to hold the hands correctly (i.e. neither turned knuckles upwards nor the wrist 'broken' outwards or inwards) if she holds a stick under the thumbs. It helps her, too, to check her body position on the circle, i.e. outside hand, elbow, shoulder and hip a little in

advance of the inside of the body. The outside end of the stick should be in front of the inside end.

Here is the position at trot. Note how the body is in line with the inclined position of the horse and shoulders and hips parallel with those of the horse.

On the circle the inside leg should always be stretched slightly down so as to keep the weight in balance (over the inside seat bone) and to keep the leg lightly in position.

Finally, at every lesson go through the neck relaxing exercises at halt, walk, and then at trot. Move the head as far to the left as possible and then rotate it slowly to the right.

Notes

It is of no value attempting to work the rider with hands in the riding position until she has established her seat and balance.

The general rule is to get pupils who are stiff in the body to practise active exercises. Those who are slack will be helped by riding in the still positions.

7

Stage 1 –
Preparation for
Work –
The Early Training

GENERAL ALEXIS L'Hotte (1825–1904) was a member of that elite group of French horsemen who extended the teachings of the greatest of the classical Masters, François Robichon de la Guérinière (1688–1751), whilst making their own original and often innovatory contribution to the expansion of equestrian thought. Along with Baucher, de Kerbrech, Raabe, d'Aure and a dozen more, L'Hotte has to be regarded as one of the latter-day Masters and he has left us, through his writings, maxims of the stature of equestrian commandments.

To him belongs the definitive trinity at the base of all equestrian endeavour – CALM, FORWARD, STRAIGHT – upon which all the practical schooling of the horse depends.

His definition of equitation is typically succinct: 'the art of managing the powers of the horse'.

Using that base it follows that the first requirement is to *develop* the powers and then to *direct* them towards the purposes to which the horse is to be put.

Both will be realised by a system of progressive training and management which begins early in life and continues until the required level is reached or, which is more likely, the horse has gone as far as his limitations (or perhaps those of his trainer) will allow.

The schooling of the horse has much in common with the human system. It can, for instance, be divided into stages corresponding to our educational divisions.

Stage 1 (from foalhood to three years) can be compared to the 'nursery school'. *Stage 2* (in the horse's third year) is the equivalent of the 'primary' school, and *Stage 3* (the schooling which begins when the horse is four years old) corresponds to 'secondary' education.

From that point the talented horse, like his human counterpart, can go on to higher education, specialising in the discipline to which he seems best suited, i.e. dressage, eventing, show jumping, etc.

Obviously, both children and horses benefit from an education at least up to the secondary level. It prepares them to fulfil a useful role in society, and in the case of the horse, whose schooling is of a more physical nature, it will contribute to a longer, healthier working life.

There, of course, the parallel ends. Equine schooling has, by the dictates of nature, to be condensed into a shorter period. Necessarily, it is concerned more with physical development than human education. Of equal importance, however, is the conditioning of the mind and the extension of the powers of concentration. In those respects it is not dissimilar to the schooling of the child.

Stage 1, the subject of this chapter, is relatively undemanding in terms of either physical or mental effort. Its purpose is to allow and encourage the natural physical development and to provide a firm foundation for the subsequent stages of schooling.

Whilst it is convenient to make divisions in the training syllabus there has to be a certain degree of overlap between the three. Furthermore, as each stage is a preparation for the next, the success of any one depends upon the establishment of the objectives contained in the syllabus of its predecessor. Stage 1, therefore, is of prime importance – a fact which is not always sufficiently recognised.

Weaning

Although this introductory period is not, like play school, demanding in terms of work, it includes an event whose effect is to cause confusion and distress – conditions which are quite contrary to the trusting relationship we want to establish.

This is the practice of weaning, when the elemental foal/mother relationship with all the comfort and security obtained from physical contact and 'breast' feeding, is arbitrarily terminated by the foal being separated from its dam.

In practical terms it may be unavoidable,

but inevitably it puts the second relationship, that between equine and human, under great strain and initially there is the possibility of a temporary breakdown. Upon how well the 'damage' can be repaired thereafter depends the future outlook, behaviour and response of the young horse, and to an extent beyond what most of us appreciate.

At many studs foals are weaned at between $4\frac{1}{2}$ – 6 months when the 'milk hairs' have darkened and when the foal has been accustomed to feeding on its own account. Usually it is considered advisable for colt foals to be gelded while they are on the mare and before weaning takes place, but a perfectly good case can be made for castration to be delayed until the animal is a yearling on the grounds that the retention of the male hormone testosterone encourages its development. Yearling colts may, however, become unacceptably cheeky and boisterous for the owner operating largely on his/her own.

On the whole, animals gelded as foals seem to suffer no immediate or appreciable setback.

The generally accepted practice at weaning time is to ensure that the foal has been wormed prior to the event – an essential measure at this point in the development. Many stud owners then take the precaution of separating the mare and foal for short periods of time. The foal remains in a box with a companion and with feed available whilst the dam is ridden or otherwise exercised. In this way the foal is prepared to a degree for the final parting.

When this takes place the ideal is for the mare to be moved away out of sight and earshot, even to the extent of being sent off the property for some weeks. The foals are then confined to a box which will have been deeply bedded and ample hay will be put down for them. The top door has to be closed to prevent the foals trying to escape but, as they settle, it can be replaced by a wire grille.

At the end of a week or so the foals should have quietened sufficiently to be led out for exercise and then later to be turned loose in their paddock. In the interim it is probable that the youngsters will go off their food and spend a lot of the time rushing about their box, calling and generally getting themselves upset at the loss of their mothers.

Much distress is involved, as most stud owners will admit, and I cannot agree with those who state that weaning will not cause the slightest worry or set-back, however much I respect their opinions on other equestrian matters.

The procedure I have described is based on the foal having constant companionship, and at studs where this is practised every effort will be made to increase the human contact and supervision so that the stress is mitigated as far as possible.

Consider, on the other hand, the single foal, deprived of the companionship of its own kind and separated from its mother, who may well be similarly imprisoned in a box across the yard and within earshot. Such a situation falls little short of cruelty and the long-term effect on the youngster may be incalculable.

On balance I am in favour of buying young, unbroken horses. They cost less money than a 'made' horse and one avoids the frustration of putting someone else's mistakes to rights. That does not mean that you will not make mistakes yourself, but they will be the ones of your own making and it will do no harm to live with them. However, the purchase of a young horse, like the contemplation of marriage, should be taken advisedly and every effort made to find out about the youngster's early background and handling. No young horse, and certainly not a foal, should be bought unless it can be provided with a companion, either of its own age or alternatively a steady gelding who has reached the age of discretion.

In some parts of the world, where horsemastership is generally considered to be of a lower standard than in this 'sceptred isle', foals are not subjected to the traumatic process of weaning. Instead they are weaned naturally at between 9–12 months when the mare's milk supply dries up. The mare is ridden during this period and the foal runs alongside, often being led from a lead rein attached to its headcollar. The ridden sessions, mostly conducted at the walk, need not exceed 20–30 minutes but they can include very short periods of trotting and perhaps a few strides at canter. It is even possible for mare and foal to jump a low fence together.

What an enormous advantage this early experience represents for the trainer and how much easier it makes all the subsequent schooling lessons. The foal learns from the example of its dam, the very best of teachers. It observes her confidence in humans, and that goes a long way to consolidate the relationship of trust between the foal and the trainer.

Obviously, to be able to manage the foal in this way the mare herself must be a pleasant, equable character and have received proper training – it would, indeed, be unwise to breed from a mare other than one of this sort.

The only drawback in this natural and eminently sensible handling of the young foal is that private facilities, away from public roads etc., must be available.

Objectives

To be successful, any sort of teaching, at whatever level, has to be based on a syllabus which provides for the attainment of a set of objectives.

The objectives in Stage 1 which we will want to achieve between birth and the foal becoming a yearling are these:

(1) To accustom the foal to the presence and acceptance of human beings and to establish a trusting relationship between the two. This will involve handling the foal regularly and frequently and will include lifting the feet.

(2) To fit a halter and to teach the foal to lead in-hand. This is the first introduction to an elementary form of discipline and it teaches the foal the first simple lessons in obedience.

These two objectives are, indeed, concerned with the two basic requirements essential to the schooling of the horse – *submission* and *obedience*. In addition and in parallel with both objectives is:

(3) The teaching of a simple vocabulary. Horses, like dogs, can be taught to understand words and phrases which are given in a more or less consistent tone of voice. They can, in time, acquire quite an extended vocabulary and will respond to words like 'come here', 'stand still', 'lift' (for feet), 'open' (for the inspection of the mouth), 'stand up' (to obtain a square halt), 'back', as well as the usual 'walk-on', 'terrott', 'canter' and 'whoah'.

(4) Preparation for the outside world by taking mare and foal to the occasional show. This, of course, requires both to enter either a trailer or horsebox and is for that reason, as well as for the exposure to potentially exciting conditions, a very important experience.

(5) On the purely physical side, the foal's natural growth is encouraged by good feeding and management. As a guide a foal, in addition to ample grazing of good quality, will require approximately 1 lb (450 g) of concentrate food per day for every month of its age up to 5–6 months. The feeds will comprise oats; a *little* bran for the purpose of regulating the bowel action (fed damp the effect is laxative and vice-versa); boiled linseed and barley, carrots, apples, etc.

Diets with a high bran content are *not* to be recommended. The high phosphate level causes a calcium deficiency affecting the bones which may then become brittle. In extreme cases foals may develop osteofibrosis or 'big head' disease, characterised by the swelling of the lower jaw bones.

Nuts are not usually appreciated by young foals because they find them difficult to eat, particularly the larger varieties. They can, however, be added to the diet as the foal grows.

To the above diet should be added powdered milk (2 oz (50 g) per day rising to 8 oz (200 g)) and cod-liver oil in one form or another to promote healthy bone.

In the winter months the foal needs to be fed as much soft, meadow hay (soft on account of his immature dentition) as he will eat.

An ample, constant supply of fresh, clean water, available from clean drinking containers is a critical requirement for foals. Dirty and stagnant water quickly produces an upset tummy which causes the foal to scour.

On no account should foals be fed titbits. It only encourages them to become cheeky and demanding, and distracts them from the business in hand – nor should they be allowed to play with humans. It is all very well to have a foal put his feet on your shoulders, or box at you while standing on his hind legs, but it is neither sensible, in respect of his future behaviour, nor is it safe.

Foals and youngstock in general need space in which to stretch themselves and let off steam without risk of damaging themselves. This is a necessary part of their physical development and it will not be provided by a back-garden patch deep in mud the year round.

early in the foal's life and by the time he is nine days old he should be accustomed to being held and handled.

It is much easier to begin handling the foal in the confines of the stable rather than outside where it will naturally be shy and more difficult to catch.

To this end the mare is brought in for a short period each day (her foal following as surely as night follows day) when the youngster is about three days old and has had a chance to come to terms with the strange world in which he finds himself.

An assistant is really essential. A good one who is knowledgeable in the ways of horses, quiet, strong, unflappable and able to anticipate possible and probable actions is a jewel beyond price and few difficulties will arise with such a paragon. A bad one, with none of those qualities, is worse than useless.

The assistant places the mare against the stable wall and the foal is encouraged to come up along the near-side of his mother. He will, indeed, need very little encouragement to do so. The trainer approaches the foal with arms partially out-stretched, placing the right arm around the quarters, just below the rump, and the left round the front of his chest. Almost certainly the foal will jump about but one must persist, holding on firmly and trying to calm the little animal with the voice.

Within a few days the foal will be confident enough to stand quietly within the embrace of the cradling arms, so long as he can stay close to his mother. His right flank should be allowed to touch his mother's side. This physical contact is necessary for his peace of mind and he gains confidence from it. He becomes upset when he is separated from the mare and if her baby is distressed she begins to worry and the situation is likely to deteriorate pretty rapidly.

Early handling

Submission and obedience training start

Leading

The next step in the progress towards leading

the foal independently is for the mare to be led round the outside of the box. Instinctively, the foal will want to follow and he can be encouraged to do so by being pushed gently forward with the right arm; the left arm, encircling his chest, being ready to restrain any attempt to plunge forward.

Even at this initial point in the education of the youngster the over-riding first principle of back-to-front is being observed. The right arm, from behind, asks for forward movement; the left hand, in front, receives, allows and, as necessary, contains the movement. Later, when the horse is being schooled under saddle, the same principle will apply, the horse being sent forward from the legs into contact with the bit and the rider's hand.

Once the youngster accepts the arms and follows the mare, a soft stable rubber round the foal's neck can be substituted for the left arm. The right arm, however, continues to push the foal forward from behind, but this time into the light control exerted by the rubber round his neck.

The foal is then ready to be led back to the paddock, the stable rubber being placed higher or lower round his neck according to how he behaves. In time the foal will be sufficiently quiet to be led both to and from paddock and stable.

During these short journeys matters are made easier if the foal is always kept close to the mare – she acts as a magnet to the baby.

The lessons in the stable have to be kept very short indeed, since small minds cannot absorb more than very little at a time. One has, also, to take particular care in acting in accord with that first principle. The left hand has always to relax and give immediately before the right arm pushes the foal forward, otherwise if the arms push and restrain at the same time the foal becomes confused and may panic, possibly attempting to throw himself down. Always before releasing the foal make a fuss of him so that he understands that he has done well and that there is no reason to be frightened.

The best way of rewarding him, and the one he understands most easily, is to simulate the reassuring maternal actions made by the mare. The mare gives her foal affectionate 'love-nibbles' at the chest, in front of the withers and on his quarters, just in front of the tail.

I do not suggest that the human attendant should go so far as to nibble the foal, but a good scratch with the fingers will be just as much appreciated and just as reassuring.

These caring actions mean so much to the foal that eventually it will stand to be scratched without the influence of the restraining arms.

The halter

The above lessons should take about a week or so and it is then time for the stable rubber to be replaced by a leather foal slip. This latter should have been made very soft by continued applications of oil and similar softening preparations long before it is put into use.

Leather, in my view, is preferable to any other material, in particular nylon. Nylon has no advantage beyond tensile strength. It can develop sharp edges which cut, and the material does not have the substance which makes it easy to handle.

The haltering of the foal is an educational watershed and as such the business should be approached with care.

It is always better done in company with a helper but if singlehanded then the foal has to be positioned with his quarters in a corner so that he cannot run backwards. The only way out of the situation is for him to go forward and *into* the slip rather than backwards with the trainer struggling to get the slip over the foal's nose.

Here, again, the method corresponds with one of equitation's first principles – 'always the horse must go forward'.

With a helper positioned at the foal's rear

the trainer places himself at the foal's left shoulder facing the front. He holds the slip by the left cheekpiece, it having been adjusted previously to a size which seems appropriate. It is not necessary to unfasten the buckle at the nose.

The right hand can then hold the slip open at the juncture of the cheekpiece with the head strap. The slip is held in front of the foal, below the level of the muzzle and with the right arm under the neck.

The trick is then to raise the slip slowly bringing both hands slightly to the rear. Simultaneously the assistant urges the foal forward and *into* the slip. When the foal feels the slip round his nose he may well be a little frightened but it should not be too difficult to bring the headstrap over and behind the ears and fasten it to the near-side buckle.

There is a danger that during the haltering the foal will attempt to rear and to frustrate that intention the assistant has to be ready to push him forward with some vigour. Once the slip is in place make a fuss of the foal before asking him to walk forwards. He will probably resist initially by shaking his head, but once he is calm the request has to be repeated.

The method which is likely to be most successful is to give the command 'walk-on' (part of the basic vocabulary), give a little pull downwards and forwards on the slip strap whilst the quarters are pushed forward. As soon as a step is taken relax the pressure on the slip. The foal then associates moving forward with the gentle pull which puts a little pressure on the area behind his ears. (Once more we are complying with the classical precept which runs through the whole of the educational process. The aid 'acts' and at the moment the horse responds correctly it 'yields' to reward the movement.)

If the foal attempts to evade the slip pressure by going on to his hind legs or attempting to run backwards, the quarters must be pushed quickly over to one side away from the handler.

Never pull on the slip at this stage without the right arm or the assistant urging the foal forward from behind. Initially when you relax the feel on the slip strap and cease to push actively from behind the foal will stop. It doesn't matter, you just start the exercise all over again.

In a very short time the foal associates the push-and-pull actions with the command 'walk-on' and will respond to the verbal command backed up by the lightest of reminding hand pressures.

Make sure that the slip is properly fitted. If it is too tight it will chafe; if too loose there is a danger that a scratching hind foot could become caught up. One should be able to insert two fingers between the noseband and the jawbones if the foal is to be able to feed comfortably. The nosepiece should be adjusted so that it lies just under the cheek bones.

So far the foal has been led from the near-side and close up to the mare's flank, now it has to learn to be led from the opposite side. If this is done as early as possible in the foal's life it will accept being led from either side as a matter of course. The only reason why horses may display resistance to being led from the off-side, or for that matter being mounted from that side, is that nobody ever bothered to teach them.

The advantage of leading alternately from left to right is that it prevents the horse becoming one-sided.

The majority of horses turn and circle more easily to the left than the right because from birth they have been encouraged to bend to the left by being led and handled from that side. The result is that the muscles on the near-side of the horse – the dorsal, neck and abdominal muscles – are held in a state of contraction, whilst those on the outside are extended to permit the bend. In time a block of muscle is produced on the off-side which makes it almost impossible for the horse to turn to the right with a facility equal to that displayed in turning to the left.

If you don't believe me measure the backs of half a dozen mature horses by laying an 18 ins. (45 cm) piece of heavy-duty cable over the back behind the withers, shaping it to the outline of the body. The resultant template, instead of being identical on both sides, will show a distinct bulge on the right side of the body.

When turning, the foal should turn *inside* the leader. This method not only permits a judge to have an uninterrupted view of the animal but it is safer and gives more control. Turned in this way the horse is compelled to engage the hocks to make the turn and the likelihood of the animal swinging round to kick out is much reduced.

Extend the leading lessons so that the foal is made to stand whilst the mare is led away and vice-versa, but commence by asking for no more than a very short distance.

Every day mare and foal should be brought into the stable to be fed and for the foal to continue his lessons.

From the second week, or even earlier, the foal has to be accustomed to being handled all over his body. Start by placing the left hand on the neck and running it down the shoulder and foreleg until the foal allows the rubbing hand to reach the fetlock. Do the same with the rear leg and then move over to the opposite side. The same rubbing motion can be applied to back, flanks and then to the underpart of the belly and between the hind legs. A little later it should be possible to use a soft body brush on the body and the mane and tail.

Feet

The object is to get the foal to stand absolutely quiet under this intensive handling. Soon it will be possible to pick up the feet (saying 'lift' as you do so). At first the foot may be held up for no more than a second but as time goes on the foal will allow the foot to be held up for longer periods.

This sort of training is vital against the time when the farrier is called upon to trim the feet. It is, after all, the responsibility of the owner to train the horse to stand quietly whilst the farrier attends to the feet. It is not the farrier's job to school the horse and if he has to cope with an unruly one he can hardly be blamed if he does not make as good a job as he might.

Feet need attention after about three months and thereafter should be dressed monthly. Feet which turn in or out, putting uneven strains on the leg components, can be corrected over a period by the farrier. A toe turning out will be straightened gradually by rasping the outside of the foot a little lower than the inside, whilst the opposite will apply when the toe is turned inwards.

Boxing

Loading the mare and foal into a box or trailer should not present any difficulty if the owner/trainer is willing to spend time practising the operation.

A lot of the trouble experienced is caused by people attempting to load the mare first and expecting the foal to follow on. Of course, it doesn't work. The foal is frightened and won't go in and the mare, concerned for her offspring, tries to get out. A thoroughly bad example has then been set.

The answer is to load the foal first. No mare, or very few of them, will leave their babies and she will follow her foal.

Two people are needed to load the foal. They join hands in front of the chest and below the tail and thus cradled the foal is easily propelled up the ramp. The mare can be led in by one of the helpers holding her lead rope in the same hand that is behind the foal's quarters.

Taking a foal to a show is a broadening experience for the little animal but it is very tiring for him and should not be practised too frequently.

Mare and foal should be taken to the show-ground with plenty of time in hand so that they can rest before being introduced to the excitement of showing.

The foal, of course, will need to be led with a full-length lead rein rather than by the short strap on the slip collar.

Yearling and two-year-old

Once the youngster enters the yearling stage, and more particularly as he grows into a big, strong two-year-old, there is an increasing temptation to do something with him. More horses are probably spoilt at this age through being worked too early than by anything which is done subsequently.

It is quite true that Thoroughbred horses mature early. They were bred to do so and are conditioned and fed to race at two. They do so, however, purely for commercial considerations and as long as prize money is offered for two-year-old races that state of affairs will continue. They are not, however, sufficiently mature in their development to carry weight at this age, much less to carry it at speed. As a result the wastage rate in two-year-old racing is high and horses that survive two-year-old racing may well develop unsoundnesses later on that will limit their useful working life.

Half-bred horses, a term which becomes increasingly synonymous with the Continental nomenclature 'warmblood', take longer to mature. Indeed, as a very general rule of thumb it could be said that the smaller the percentage of Thoroughbred blood the slower they are to reach maturity. On the other hand, horses that are encouraged to develop naturally and do not begin to work until they are in their third year may very well, with good management, continue in service well into their teens and beyond.

One may talk generally, and not incorrectly, about 'green' bones in young horses, about musculature, tendons and ligaments which are insufficiently developed and thus more likely to sustain damage. Weight on immature backs may cause actual fusion of the spinal vertebrae and will predispose the spinal structure to the onset of arthritic complaints in future years. Similarly, it can be argued that the young mind is no more mature than the young body. Its ability to concentrate is limited and it is easily confused.

There is, however, one indisputable fact about the young horse's development to support the case for not working horses before their third year. It has to do with the closure of the epiphyses (or growth plates) on the long bones of the legs. The extent to which they have or have not closed can be ascertained by X-ray. *Until the growth plates have closed, the leg is not ready to sustain the effects of constant work, particularly under weight, without being damaged.* Such damage may result in mis-shapen limbs predisposed to disease in later life.

The epiphysis at the end of the cannon bone, above the fetlock joint, is usually closed at between 9–12 months. That at the end of the radius, immediately above the knee joint, closes at some time between 2–$2\frac{1}{2}$ years.

The epiphyses are the last points of growth in the horse and are therefore the ultimate guide to the animal's overall maturity.

Inflammation of the growing plates results in a disease called 'round joints' (epiphysitis) and it can be recognised by swellings in the immediate joint area which are sometimes, but not always, hot and tender. In foals the swellings occur more usually in the fetlocks; in yearlings in the knee and hock joints. In both cases lameness occurs.

The principal cause, other than being worked prematurely, is dietary, usually an imbalance between the phosphorus/calcium content, the former being much in excess of the latter, or a deficiency in Vitamin D (sunlight vitamin). Such a deficiency can be caused by the inclusion of too much bran in the feed or by a high-protein ration fed without a corresponding increase in the calcium intake.

Animals particularly prone to this condition are youngsters in 'show condition' (a mistaken one) who are allowed or encouraged to develop heavy tops which are, in truth, too heavy for their still-growing legs. The combination of diet, hard ground and excessive weight constitutes a recipe for disaster. Few such animals appear later on under saddle. (Surprisingly little emphasis is given to the significance of the growth plates and the disease of epiphysitis in veterinary manuals directed at a lay market. Four published recently make no reference to the subject at all – very strange.)

This brings us inexorably to consider the feeding of the yearling and two-year-old. It should be generous, without being overgenerous; and it should be simple and balanced (particularly in respect of the energy/protein/fibre relationship and that troublesome calcium/phosphorus balance). Today, apart from the tried and proven methods based on conventional feeds, the matter of balanced feeding is simplified by the various proprietary mixes etc. which are available. Whichever is chosen the responsibility for the welfare of the horse still lies with the owner – it is 'the eye of the master which makes the horse fat', but not, please, too fat.

As a guide a yearling should be in receipt of a 7 lb (3.1 kg) concentrate ration (either on the lines indicated or the equivalent thereof). At two the ration is increased gradually by 1 lb (0.45 kg) and at three the horse should receive at least 9 lb (4 kg). The ration can be given in two feeds per day for yearlings and two-year-olds and in three for the three-year-old.

The remainder of the feed intake is made up of hay and, of course, grass when it is available and in growth.

The total food requirement (concentrates + hay) is reckoned as being 3% of the total bodyweight for youngstock, which is a shade on the generous side, and between $2-2\frac{1}{2}\%$ for

mature stock.

The weight of the horse is easily calculated by using a calibrated tape measure (sometimes wildly inaccurate) or by using the following more reliable formula:

$$\frac{girth^2 \times length}{300} = weight\ in\ lbs$$

The girth measurement is taken in inches round the *largest* part of the barrel. The square of the girth, i.e. $girth^2$, is found by multiplying the figure by itself (e.g. 76 ins × 76 ins). Length is taken (also in inches) from the point of the shoulder *upwards* to the point of the *buttock*.

If it is more convenient to calculate in kilograms use this formula:

$$\frac{girth\ (cm)^2 \times length\ (cm)}{8700} = weight\ in\ kg$$

(This has to be one more reason against going metric.)

The following chart gives an indication of the average daily intake based on height:

	approx.
up to 12.2 hh	—14–16 lbs (6.3–7.2 kg)
12.2–13 hh	—16–18 lbs (7.2–8.1 kg)
13–14 hh	—18–20 lbs (8.1–9 kg)
14–15 hh	—20–22 lbs (9–9.9 kg)
15–16 hh	—22–24 lbs (9.9–10.8 kg)
over 16 hh	—24–26 + lbs (10.8–11.7 kg)

(In fact, feeding by weight can be unsatisfactory if the horse is overweight when you start. Yearlings, if you are using the height chart, should be fed according to the estimated height at maturity.)

Feeding is particularly important for the yearling since this is the period in the animal's life in which the most rapid development occurs. It is probably advisable, so as to encourage growth and bone formation, to switch the nut portion of the ration to a specialist yearling product or to higher feed value lucerne nuts.

Headcollar and bit

As the youngster grows, the foal slip has to be replaced by an adjustable headcollar. As such this presents no problems but it is a convenient moment at which to introduce a browband to the headgear. This simple addition may provoke resistance out of proportion to its size and importance because it involves pulling the ears through the space between the headstrap and the browband. The easy way is to have a stud-fastening browband which can be fitted independently of the headcollar. Failing that, slide the headstrap through the off-side loop of the browband, bring the strap over the head and then pass it through the browband's near-side loop before fastening it up.

The horse will soon get used to the browband and it will not be long before he allows the complete headcollar to be fitted in the usual way. Do, however, make sure that the browband is too large rather than too small. If it is too tight it will pull the headstrap against the back of the ears.

Well-fed yearlings as they grow older and stronger may become too boisterous to handle, or to show, in just a headcollar and it will be necessary in the interests of control to introduce a bit. Certainly, if one is to show a well-grown two-year-old a bit may become an essential piece of equipment.

Usually, it is advocated that a mouthing bit should be employed, i.e. a straight mouthpiece with mouthing 'keys' set in the centre. The theory is that the horse will play with the loose keys, thus relaxing his jaw and increasing the flow of saliva. Both actions are entirely desirable. Nothing is worse than a dry mouth which is always set and unmoving. On the whole, however, I am not convinced that the key bit is all that advantageous. The 'mouthing' action it encourages can cause the horse to become unsteady in his head carriage and far from 'seeking' contact with the bit he withdraws his mouth, getting 'behind the bit' in order to avoid accepting it.

To employ a jointed bit in the first instance is to risk all sorts of evasions. Most commonly it will encourage the horse to pull back his tongue and put it over the mouthpiece, an action which renders him quite outside its control.

I use a plain rubber or vulcanite bit made in a mullen (or half-moon) shaped mouthpiece. The horse quickly has a 'wet' mouth and he relaxes in his jaw without making exaggerated movements of his head.

To fit the bit to the headcollar and in the mouth is simplicity itself, so long as the job is tackled intelligently.

Fasten the off-side ring of the bit to the off-side headcollar dee by means of a flat clip or a small strap. Now take the mouthpiece, together with some slices of carrot, in the left hand and pass them quietly into the mouth. The right hand can help by inserting the thumb and first finger into either side of the mouth with the hand held under the chin. One then has only to secure the near-side bit ring to the headcollar by the same means.

Give the horse a small feed whilst the bit is in place and he will quickly relax his jaw in order to be able to eat. The bit can be left in place for half an hour or so each day to accustom the horse to its presence. I am not in favour of leaving the bit in position for longer periods of time, nor of trussing the horse up in side-reins in order to force him into 'mouthing' the bit. He is far more likely to spend the time working out how he can evade the pressure and the discomfort he experiences.

Adjust the bit sufficiently high in the mouth to wrinkle the lips in a horsey smile, but make sure the bit chosen is neither too large nor too small. The butt ends of the bit should protrude about $\frac{1}{2}$ in. (12 mm) from each side of the mouth.

The education content during the yearling period may be slight but it is very important. Ideally, the horse needs to spend a short time in the stable each day, during which he is taught his stable manners and is fed. He

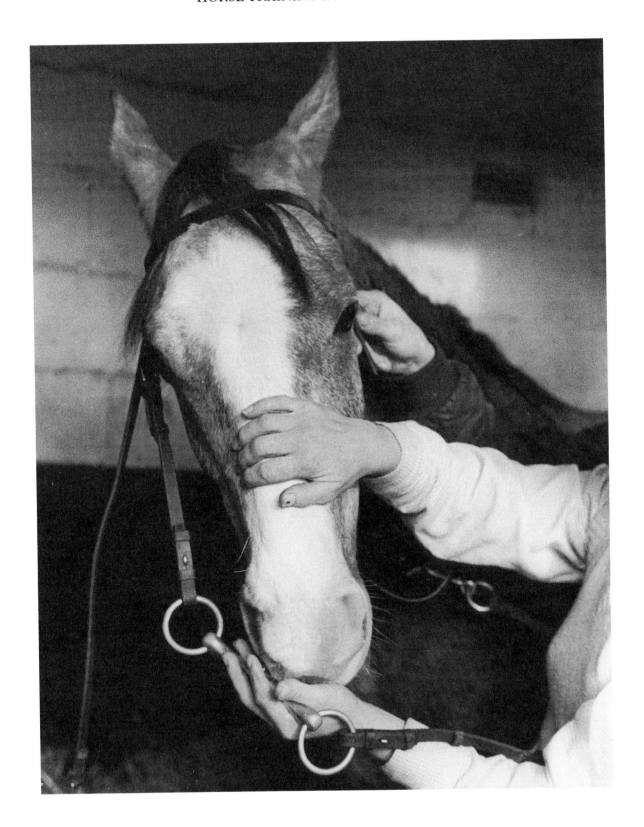

The easy way to insert the bit into the mouth of a young horse.

needs also to be schooled in-hand outside for very short periods.

The stable, in particular, provides an environment in which the vocabulary can be increased.

Tying up

The first lesson is that of submitting to be tied up. It is an essential accomplishment of the modern horse and makes life easier in a whole variety of ways.

All sorts of methods are advocated. You can acquire a stout headcollar (a *railway* headcollar used to be the one most frequently recommended) and a very strong rope with which the horse is attached to some virtually immoveable object like· a telegraph pole. However much the horse struggles to free himself it will be of no avail in those circumstances. Eventually, exhausted and resentful he accepts defeat but I doubt very much that these strong-arm methods do much to cement the trusting relationship of willing co-operation with the human.

It may, very occasionally, be necessary to assert one's authority with an unusually recalcitrant equine, in the same way that some high-spirited boy may have to be reminded of the limits of reasonable behaviour. I know two or three salutory methods of persuading horses to submit to the restrictions of the tie rope, all very much less violent than the telegraph pole/railway headcollar method, but I find it unnecessary to use them.

Horses can be taught to tie by fastening a length of rope to the headcollar, passing the end through a wall ring and then back to the hand. One can then begin to groom the horse, the rope being long enough for one to attend to his hind legs. If he moves backwards, one gives with the rope, then he is put back in his original position and once more a light tension is taken up on the rope. On each subsequent occasion that he moves one says 'No' firmly and repeats the process, making sure that he is rewarded by the voice and a pat when he does what is wanted.

I am quite prepared to continue doing this for an hour or more. Usually, in far less time, I am able to tie the horse up with a quick-release knot while I continue to work round him.

Horses are tied up to facilitate grooming or mucking out and there is rarely any necessity to leave a horse tied in the stable on his own for any period of time. For that reason I cannot support wholeheartedly the advocated safety measure which recommends that the horse be tied to a loop of string which will break easily in the event of his running back. There is no reason at all why the horse should want to run back whilst I am in the box with him, or for that matter whilst I am out of it but very close at hand for 30–60 seconds. If the horse should run back for some reason and finds that he can easily break the tie he may well continue to do so until it becomes an habitual practice.

Horses that were stabled in stalls used to be secured by a rope from the headcollar which was fastened, via a metal loop, or a hole made for the purpose in the manger, to a 'manger log', a round piece of *lignum vitae*. The length of the rope allowed the horse to feed and to lie down but the weight of the log always ensured that there was no slack in which a leg might be caught up.

No provision was made for the rope to break if the horse ran back, and I never heard of an accident being caused by one doing so.

'Move over'

Youngstock given adequate feeding are quite able to live out (with supervision) throughout the year but if we are concerned with their future schooling it is a good idea to bring them in once a day, as suggested, to be fed and checked over. The horse then becomes familiar with the stable, he can be groomed and handled and he can learn some simple lessons in obedience which will stand us in good stead when it comes to the more serious business of schooling.

The first of these lessons teaches the horse to move over on command when being groomed or when the box is being cleaned out.

It is taught by holding the horse's head inclined towards you and tapping his flank with a short stick or even with the hand. At the same time the command 'Move over' is given.

Inevitably he moves his quarters away from the tap. With constant repetition he soon learns to move over in both directions and it is then possible to rely on the tapping hand alone and in time to dispense with that also. When that is the case you can stand further down the flank, almost in a line with the dock, and using the voice alone get him to move over.

The secret lies in positioning the body so that the horse understands easily what is wanted. Stand, therefore, well to the left or right. It is no good standing directly behind the horse, where he cannot see you clearly, and asking him to move over. There is no way in that circumstance that he can understand to which side you want him to move.

Remember, also, to preface the actual request to move over with some preparatory introduction which will alert him to the command which follows. When he obeys reward him with a quiet, encouraging word – it works wonders.

'Lift'

As the youngster becomes increasingly attentive and obedient to the voice more words can be added to the vocabulary.

Every time the feet are picked up accompany the action with the word 'Lift', or even 'Lift, please', which is even better. Gradually the horse can be taught to raise the leg almost entirely on the word of command.

'Open wide'

Since it is important to examine regularly the mouth of young animals, for signs of new teeth erupting, gum inflammations, etc., we should also teach the youngster to open his mouth.

Horses that make a fuss about opening their mouths usually do so because somebody has frightened them by being rough.

The easy way is to stand just in front of the horse's shoulder, facing forwards. Place the left hand *very lightly* on the nose, without grasping it, and then, from behind, insert the thumb and forefinger very gently into each side of the mouth. Since there are no teeth there you won't be bitten and so long as you make no effort to force the jaws apart the horse will open his mouth.

If, in conjunction with the finger and thumb being put in the mouth, one makes the request 'Open wide', or something similar, the horse once more associates the words with the action.

To examine the mouth closely it is usually necessary to take the tongue and hold it out to the side so that the horse keeps his mouth open for the time required. But *be careful*. Hold the tongue gently, not in a vice-like grip which only causes the horse to become apprehensive, and *let go at once* if he should pull away. Quite appalling injuries have been caused by 14 stone men hanging on to a tongue in that mistaken spirit of mastery.

'Come here'

'Come here' is even more easily taught. I confess to using a titbit for this one but the results probably justify a slight bending of the rules.

Stand in front of the horse holding the end of the lead rein and apply a little tension to the rope whilst you say 'Come here'. The moment he takes a step forward relax the tension and then, when he comes up close, make much of him and give him his reward.

Step by step, this can be extended until you are using a full-length lunge line.

Have an assistant hold the horse facing you, tighten the lunge rein, give the word of command and initially let the assistant walk alongside the horse as he comes up to you. As before, release the tension on the line as the horse responds. It does not take long before you can do without an assistant but you do need to be adept in handling the rein. Ultimately, of course, you won't even need that.

If the horse will come to you, you will also need to teach him the opposite obedience, to stand still when requested, even if you are some yards away from him; this, however, is best left until the lunge lessons begin in the third year. There is no advantage at this or any other stage in the horse's education to do other than 'hasten slowly'.

'Out of the way'

There are two more stable lessons, one which should be taught at the outset and the other which can be introduced when the horse is in the latter part of his second year.

The first is to teach the horse to stand at one end of the stable whilst you are inside and when entering or leaving. Nothing is more awkward, irritating and potentially dangerous than the horse who rushes to the door, regardless of your presence, at every opportunity.

To persuade the horse to stand quietly and out of the way one has to continually put him in the place required. If he moves put him back, saying 'Stand', 'Stand still', or whatever phrase appeals to you. Go on doing this

until he gets the message. It takes time and patience but it is basic to good stable manners.

'Back'

The second movement which can be taught in the box is moving backwards, a proceeding which involves submission and obedience in equal measure and is an essential preliminary to the rein-back under saddle.

Put the horse against the stable wall. Take the lead rope loosely in the left hand and touch the horse lightly on the chest giving the command 'Back'. He can be kept straight by laying the whip, held in the right hand, along his flank.

Success depends upon getting the horse to drop his nose and then in the lightness of the touch. If you push strongly, resistance is provoked and any movement to the rear is ugly and unco-ordinated.

Two backward strides, made diagonally, i.e. left fore and right hind followed by right fore and left hind, or the other way about, are quite sufficient, after which ask the horse to come forward and, of course, reward him for his co-operation.

In-hand leading

The brief lessons outside the stable, which can be practised as the horse is being brought in, are concerned with teaching him to walk and trot in-hand. They, too, involve obedience to the spoken command. These simple exercises are the basis of the work on the lunge and are the first exercises which lead to the fulfilment of the second part of L'Hotte's trilogical commandment – unrestrained FORWARD MOVEMENT.

The trainer places himself at the shoulder facing the front. He holds the lead rein lightly in his right hand about 10–12 ins (25–30 cm) from the bit. The slack of the rein passes

The young horse learns to walk in hand. The trainer follows behind to encourage the forward movement.

across his body and is held in the left hand. Also in the left hand is held a schooling whip, long enough so that it can be used behind the trainer's back to tap the flank.

The command 'Walk-on' is given; the whip end reinforces the spoken word with a light tap on the horse's side; the trainer steps off smartly *and* an assistant can follow up behind to encourage the horse to march forward.

The horse is then moving in front of the trainer and his whip, just as in the later mounted training he will be 'in front of the legs'. As in the ridden work the hand must allow the movement; it must not restrict it in any way. The principle of leading in-hand, from the whip into the rein is, indeed, no way different to riding from the legs into the hand.

Halt

To halt the horse involves the use of the body, hand, whip and voice. The trainer moves in front of the shoulder by lengthening his stride. He alters the grasp on his whip so as to hold it about halfway down its length. The body is turned inwards towards the horse; the rein checks the movement; the butt end of the whip is raised in front of the horse's face and the command 'Whoah' is given.

The horse has then to be made to stand square, without trailing or resting a leg, before he is rewarded. This is important, since if the horse is made to stand square every time he is brought to halt it becomes an habitual action which will make the halt under saddle so much easier to obtain.

What we are asking is for the horse to halt in balance. From that state he can *march* into walk without sacrificing the straightness of the movement, i.e. his hind legs will follow the track of the forelegs without any initial deviation to one side or the other. Later, when we ask for the rein-back under saddle the square halt is a vital prerequisite to the movement.

Occasionally, the horse will have difficulty in coming to this square halt, usually because of a trailing hind leg. He can be helped by asking for the halt on a shallow curve so that he is compelled, in order to follow its line, to bring his inside leg further underneath the body. So if he trails the left hind leg ask for halt on a gentle curve to the left. If the right hind is at fault use a right-handed curve.

The horse will not, of course, be able to halt squarely unless his head, neck and shoulders are held straight to the front. If the handler brings the head towards him when asking for halt the balanced movement is made impossible because the quarters will swing outwards and away from the directional line of the movement.

Trot

The trot in-hand is taught in the same way as the walk and in the same command sequence, i.e. voice, whip tap, corresponding movement from the handler.

Should the horse lose the forward movement, which is bound to occur from time to time with young horses, the solution lies in falling back a pace, lengthening the rein and employing the whip to send the horse into contact with the hand.

Always, the horse must be taught to lead from *both sides* and since most of us are happier leading from the near-side, it is as well to begin every lesson from the opposite, right side just to make sure it is not neglected.

When leading the horse in trot keep the pace balanced, and slow rather than fast. There is a trend towards showing horses at speed, originating, I suspect, on the Continent where young horses are run out by white-trousered sprinters wearing 'trainers'. Those who exhibit Arab horses in-hand are, if anything, even more guilty of this inelegant, unnatural and damaging practice.

To trot a horse flat out is really inexcusable and the very antithesis of thinking horsemastership. In young horses, and in older ones too, it causes the action to become wide behind, the hind legs being compelled, lest they strike into the forelegs, to be carried *outside* the line taken by the latter in what has been described most graphically as 'the wet-knicker trot'.

An active, slower pace, with the hind legs engaged well under the body contributes to both the rhythm and the cadence of the trot, the joints being flexed to the full extent. (By definition *rhythm* is the regularity and properly ordered flow of the pace. *Cadence* is the expression, animation and extra quality given to the rhythm and to each succeeding foot fall by increased upward impulsion – a controlled power, if you like, which has nothing to do with that undisciplined tearaway run.)

Showing

Showing is a good experience for yearlings and two-year-olds with a number of peripheral educational benefits. Manes and tails have to be pulled and made tidy. Tails need to be bandaged prior to the show (but don't bandage so tightly as to break the hairs and interfere with the circulation, nor leave the bandage on for more than a couple of hours) and manes can be plaited.

To keep the coat clean and flat the horse wears a sheet or rug, which has to be kept in place by either a surcingle or a roller, in themselves precursors to the saddle.

Do not, however, overdo the showing. Continual circling of show rings restricts the natural stride, and a lot of travelling, making the horse balance himself by bracing his hind legs, is no good at all for young limbs. Where youngstock are shown from a bit it is better to use a three-way couple so that control is achieved by pressure applied to the poll rather than directly on the mouth. (A three-way couple has three adjustable straps connected to a central ring – two fasten to the bit rings and the third to the rear of the nose-band. The lead is fastened to the central ring.)

Lungeing

In other countries two-year-olds and year-lings are lunged and even jumped. I am not of that school which spends years analysing and perfecting the walk to the exclusion of every-thing else (by the time the horse is asked to canter he is probably too old and too arthritic to comply), but I set my face against the practice of systematic lungeing and jumping at this age.

Apart from the damage which can be caused to the limbs, the action can be affected seriously. It is early enough to begin work on the lunge during the third year. There is, of course, no harm in the horse occasionally being asked to circle the trainer on the end of a lunge line in order to combat any disinclination to go forward, but that is sufficient.

However, I have no objection, if it can be arranged, to encouraging youngstock to jump low obstacles like logs. A pole or a log, or two or three of them, set across the route leading from paddock to stable and feed are an ideal introduction to leaving the ground – so much so that jumping becomes virtually habitual and a pleasurable experience.

At the end of Stage 1 we should have a young horse well prepared both physically and mentally and very much ready for the primary schooling in the third year of his life.

8

Stage 2 – Training the Three-year-old

THE HORSE begins Stage 2, the primary schooling, in the April of his third year. It extends over a period of about four months up to August, when the horse can be turned away to grow naturally (with, of course, the help of some good supplementary feeding) until the following April when he begins Stage 3, the secondary education.

The *objectives* to be achieved in Stage 2 are these:

(1) To extend the horse's acceptance of discipline and handling. During this period, for instance, the horse will be shod and, if he is not already familiar with boxing he has to be schooled in his boxing drill.

(2) He has to be prepared physically to carry weight.

(3) He has to be taught to *accept* weight on his back.

(4) He learns how to *carry* the weight of the rider, which involves him in making adjustments to his natural balance.

(5) Finally, he will be taught the rudiments of the aid system – the language of the aids.

To attain these objectives involves much of L'Hotte's first principles: CALM, FORWARD, STRAIGHT.

A state of *calm*, even in potentially exciting circumstances, is a prerequisite for training. The horse makes no progress unless he is calm, and therefore receptive, in his mind; and until he is calm he cannot be taught to go *forward*.

Most of us understand going *forward* as the willing and immediate response to the action of the leg aids. It is, of course, that but in fact it goes further. It includes also a mental attitude producing a positive urge in the horse to go steadfastly to his front. You might indeed say that forward movement is the physical manifestation of a mental quality.

To be *straight* the hind feet must follow directly in the track of the forefeet, the acid test being that they should do so on the circle. If the hind legs deviate from the track to one side or another, like the hind legs of a lurcher dog, the efficiency of the movement and the propulsive power of the quarters is diminished. For maximum efficiency the thrust of the hind legs has to be delivered directly to the front, into the track of the forefeet, and not partially expended by being directed outside that track.

If the horse is straight it follows, by implication, that the rider will be capable of controlling the position of the quarters, and is able to ask for a movement away from the action of a single leg or, conversely, and very importantly, he will be in a position to counter and correct any unwanted shift to either side.

The practical advantages of the straight, forward-moving horse are obvious and, of course, extend to jumping. Horses that stop at fences do so for the very good reason that they cease to go *forward*. Horses that run out at fences do so because the rider has lost control of the quarters. In order to deviate from the line of approach to a fence the horse alters direction *not* by moving his head but by shifting his quarters. He can quite easily go to the left when his head is pointing in the opposite direction. The position of his head is not the source of the directional movement, that is the prerogative of the quarters and where they point there the horse must surely go – unless, of course, the rider is able to alter their position.

In fact in the stage of primary education we cannot expect to do more than make an approach to the ideal of straightness, although we shall hope to inculcate forward movement to the extent that it becomes virtually habitual.

How completely the objects of the primary education are attained depends very much on the competence of the trainer and is the governing factor in the success or otherwise of the subsequent secondary schooling.

First steps

The three-year-old's education begins when he is brought in and a routine established. In essence, this preliminary period is one of acclimatisation. If the horse has already as a two-year-old been schooled on the lines suggested it is of short duration, possibly no more than two weeks. If, on the other hand, the horse is brought in as a big, raw and almost unhandled three-year-old it will take commensurately more time.

Whatever the routine decided upon the horse should be turned out every day for a couple of hours so that he is able to relax and generally unwind.

The following is a suggested routine which obviously can be adapted to fit individual circumstances. I would stress, however, that a daily routine of some sort is very necessary. With young horses you have to keep at it and keep them occupied. It is really not advisable to attempt the schooling of a three-year-old if you can only spare two or three hours over weekends.

7 a.m.	First feed. Pick up droppings. Quartering (i.e. a quick brush over and cleaning out of the feet.)
8 a.m.	Clean out and then groom.
9.30–11 a.m.	Exercise period.
1 p.m.	Second feed.
2–4 p.m.	Put out in paddock.
4 p.m.	Give 4 lb (1.8 kg) hay net.
6 p.m.	Groom – stable training.
7 p.m.	Third feed.
9 p.m.	Last haynet (10 lb/4.5 kg).

Health inspections

As a preliminary a check has to be made on the worming programme, and dates when worming doses are due entered on a wall-chart. Teeth also need to be inspected before the horse is put into work and it is a sensible precaution to establish the animal's average temperature and pulse rate, since it may vary between one individual and another.

As the temperature is inclined to rise slightly during the day it is as well to take two or three readings at different times. The nomal temperature is between 100–101.5°F (37.7–38.6°C). Above this level there is reason to suspect some general infection. The temperature is taken by inserting a greased clinical thermometer, well shaken before use, into the rectum for about 3 minutes. Do, however, hold tight otherwise the instrument may be sucked in by contraction. (After use wash the thermometer in cold water; hot water is not advised since clinical thermometers burst at about 110°F/43°C.)

The normal pulse rate is between 35–40 beats per minute. An increase signifies a problem, usually connected with a feverish condition. A pulse rate between 40–50 beats is serious and indicates that the horse is in some pain. Such a pulse rate will, of course, be accompanied by other symptoms. The pulse is taken most conveniently on the inner surface of the lower jaw or just behind the elbow.

Strapping

Grooming during this stage becomes progressively more thorough and by the end of the schooling period it should be possible to *strap* the horse vigorously.

Ideally, once the horse is really in work, the routine needs to be altered so that grooming takes place *after* exercise when the horse is warm and the pores are open. Strapping, or wisping, is better left to the evening for the reason that it encourages circulation which will naturally slow down during the night hours.

Strapping a horse has two important purposes:
(1) It develops and hardens muscles and improves *tonus*.

(2) It stimulates the skin and the circulation.

As a bonus, the exercise produces a bloom on the coat caused by oil being released from the gland surrounding each hair follicle.

To strap a horse effectively you need a wisp or pad of hay, strong muscles, good lungs and a persevering nature. Given those requirements remarkable results can be achieved in both horse and human.

A wisp can be made from hay, or rather from a tightly woven rope of hay about 8 ft (2.5 m) in length. The way to do it is to open a hay bale, shake it out a little and then start twisting it into a rope whilst keeping your foot on the bulk of the hay. Make two loops at one end, pass the rope around each alternately, tuck the end in and you should finish with a fine, woven pad.

If you are insufficiently dextrous to aspire to a woven hay wisp make a small bag out of chamois leather and stuff it tightly with hay until it is very firm, then stitch it up.

To use the wisp it has to be dampened. Standing well back, so that one is able to put weight behind the stroke, the pad is thumped down rhythmically on to the horse following the lie of the coat. It can be used on the quarters, shoulders and neck but *not* on the loins, head, belly and legs.

If it is introduced gradually most horses enjoy being strapped, but it would be most unwise to start thumping a young horse without working slowly up to maximum effort. As a steady rhythm is achieved the muscles will visibly contract and relax as the pad is brought down; they are, therefore, exercised and circulation is encouraged.

Massage

A further technique which can be practised with advantage is to massage the horse's body with the dampened forearms and once or twice a week to extend the session by muscle rubbing and stretching.

It is very hard work and those who undertake it conscientiously may feel justified in moderating their physical exercise programme, and even relaxing their diet to include one or more of life's little pleasures. (A good friend of mine calculates that the expenditure of energy is equal to the intake of two large whiskys.)

The massage technique is not difficult but the muscle rubbing requires more practice.

Rub the body all over with the forearm and closed hand using a circular motion and considerable pressure. Increase the pressure in the area of the circle nearest to the heart and decrease it in the area furthest away from that organ.

In time one is able to detect tension in specific spots and concentrate on producing a relaxation. Further massage can be given along the neck and down to the withers, the fingers kneading the crest gently whilst rolling it from side to side. The thumbs and the heels of the hand can then be employed on either side of the spine from withers to croup, but be careful not to exacerbate tenderness in any area and do begin very gently.

Leg-rubbing using a spirit lotion is also useful and a certain way of detecting lumps, cuts or other irregularities. Begin by first squeezing and releasing the bulbs of the heels, then work up to the coronary band and pastern using stiffened fingers and a degree of pressure. Lock the hands round the leg and work *upwards*, towards the heart, the heels of the hands being used in a small circular motion. Work up the front and back of the legs to the knees on the forelimbs and the hocks behind.

Finally, and it need only be included in a once- or twice-weekly session, stretch each leg forward and backwards but no further than is comfortable for the horse.

Initially the extent to which the horse will allow the legs to be stretched out in this way will be surprisingly limited. In time, however, the extension will increase as the horse becomes more relaxed.

Shoeing

Within a week or so of being brought up it will be necessary to shoe the horse if he is to be able to work without becoming footsore. If he has been well-handled from foalhood, shoeing should present no problem. However, in addition to having his feet picked out twice a day it is no more than a wise precaution to tap the foot regularly, first with the hoofpick and then with a hammer, well before the farrier's visit.

Initially, if it can be arranged, it is better to shoe the young horse at home in his familiar surroundings. If possible let him watch an older horse being shod and stand the old horse close by whilst the farrier fits the shoes to the youngster. (The leg-stretching exercises mentioned previously are in themselves a good preparation for shoeing. Very often the reason a horse starts pulling his leg away is because of the discomfort caused when the farrier has a hind foot between his knees and the leg outstretched behind.)

When the first set of shoes has been fitted young horses may move awkwardly for a day or two until the shoes settle and they have got used to the weight on their feet.

Exercise and work

There is a difference between the two and one of which we should be aware. Exercise is the less strenuous and takes place over a longer period of time. Work is of shorter duration, is more energetic and is interspersed with frequent rests.

In the early stages the horse is *exercised* with *work* being introduced gradually.

At the outset the horse is exercised in-hand wearing his lunge cavesson, to which is attached a lunge rein. In fact, these first exercise periods are no more than walks, the horse being led round the place and being familiarised with the usual goings-on. The more he sees the better – tractors, farm machinery, animals and so on. Indeed, the presence of a dog is an advantage. Horses have to get used to dogs and accept them as being commonplace and no cause for anxiety, even though they represent one of the traditional predators, the wolf. Do not, however, allow dogs to chase or round up horses, much less encourage them to do so. Inevitably, the horse kicks at what he sees as an attacker and may thereafter behave unreliably when dogs or hounds are about.

If facilities permit the horse to be led through water, over small ditches and banks, or over a small log on the ground so much the better, for he will begin to accept these, too, as being commonplace occurrences.

Of course, the lessons at walk and trot can be repeated, *the horse being led equally from either side,* and any other obedience lessons recapitulated.

Boots

Right at the beginning fit the horse with protective boots all round. Young horses lack co-ordination and can as a result easily damage themselves. Once more, however, give the horse time to get used to wearing boots. Initially he will raise his legs high in a sort of equine goose-step.

Lungeing

Whilst walking and trotting in-hand and being led about is a good introduction to his working life it does little towards developing muscle and preparing the physique to carry weight. To accomplish those objects we need to have recourse to the lungeing exercises, which are, indeed, critical and basic to the primary stage of education and are essential to the lessons under saddle which follow.

Lungeing, if well done, is an art and is of enormous benefit in the development of the horse. If badly done it is in every way counter-productive and can lead to incorrect muscle formation affecting the outline of the horse, as well as a restriction of the natural paces. In extreme instances lungeing, carried out improperly, may put the limb components under such strain that disease and unsoundnesses may develop.

However, it is an art which can be learnt by the average intelligent horseman who is prepared to apply himself. There is no mystique about it but you do need some basic equipment both for lungeing and for the subsequent backing and early ridden work.

Lungeing equipment

(1) A well-fitting lightweight *cavesson*. It must fit snugly round the nose and there must be no possibility of it pulling across the face so that the headstrap comes up against the eye. To this end a jowl strap is essential. It should have three rings on the nose, each set on a swivel, one on either side and one in the centre. Never compromise on the fitting of a cavesson. It is either right or wrong – nearly right won't do.

(2) A *lunge rein* made of soft tubular web with the fastening (either a hook or a strap and buckle) set on a swivel, otherwise it can become twisted in use. Tubular web is preferable to any other material as it is less likely to burn if pulled violently through the hand. Rope and nylon are best avoided. The web need not be more than 1 in. (25 mm) wide, otherwise it becomes too heavy, and between 22–36 ft (6.5–11 m) in length. My own preference is for a 30 ft (9 m) rein. Short reins, 22 ft (6.5 m) and below, compel the horse to be worked on too tight a circle. An additional rein will be needed for long-reining or one can switch over to an altogether lighter pair which will not hang so heavily on the mouth. (Soft cotton plough reins which are tapered at the bit end are probably the best.)

(3) A *lunge whip* – the modern fibreglass or nylon whips are light and well-balanced. A heavy, clumsy whip, or one that is too short, is of no use at all. It is never necessary to hit the horse but you do need a whip and thong long enough to be effective.

(4) A pair of *gloves* – to prevent burning if the rein is pulled through the hand. Light hogskin gloves are the best.

(5) A *body roller* and *crupper* – a stout leather roller, adjustable at both sides, is needed so that it can be fitted precisely. It should be made with three large rings on each side, the lower one being about half-way down the flank. A breast-girth helps to keep the roller in place without it having to be too tightly adjusted. Also conducive to the comfortable fit of the roller is the crupper which, even if adjusted quite loosely, does 'bring the horse together' and assist the overall carriage. Additionally, of course, the crupper accustoms the horse to the use of pieces of equipment on various parts of his body, in this case under the tail. The dock piece in a properly constructed crupper is adjustable on both sides and the dock itself is stuffed with linseed. The heat of the body then combines with the linseed and the usual cleaning agent to make the leather soft and pliable.

The roller has a number of purposes. It acts as a very useful introduction to the saddle and gets the young horse used to pressure round his middle. Obviously, it provides a place for the fixing of the side-reins and at a later stage is necessary when the long-rein work begins.

Finally, it helps to develop the sternum curve in which the girth lies. Like small children young horses do not have a clearly defined waistline and wearing and working in a roller helps in that respect. (I have to admit that a decade ago I was somewhat against the use of cruppers, arguing that when employed with side-reins it was possible for the back to be hollowed in a sort of both-ends-against-the-middle effect. Indeed, that is possible, along with one or two other *imposed* resistances, if crupper and side-reins are adjusted improperly. Fitted intelligently and with great care I now advocate the use of the crupper. Used properly, along with the side-reins, it in no way forces a carriage on the horse. But it does, without causing restrictions, *suggest* a carriage and 'brings the horse together'.)

(6) *Side-reins* – in this respect, too, I was in the past guilty of misunderstanding the purpose of the reins and the effect of the types of reins I supported so strongly.

Quite wrongly I used and encouraged reins inset with elastic or rubber inserts. The idea of the soft give and take on the mouth was attractive but fallacious. In most instances the reins were an invitation for the horse to come 'behind the bit' rather than accept its action.

The elastic side-rein *did* give and take, but the 'take' part encouraged the horse to evade the tension by tucking in his nose and thus avoid contact with the mouthpiece.

I now use and recommend light, leather side-reins made with plenty of adjustment and fastening to the bit and the rings of the roller with neat clip hooks.

The purpose of the side-reins is once more 'suggestive' in terms of carriage. We use them so as to get the horse to 'seek out' the contact with the bit and they are integral to the little-understood art of 'making a mouth'. In skilled hands they are adjusted more loose than tight so that only a minimal pressure is put on the mouth. Ideally, it is the *weight* of the rein which gives the lightest of 'feels' on the mouth and induces the required relaxa-

tion in the lower jaw.

(7) A *lead rein* – a simple web lead rein, preferably with a hook fastening which can be attached and undone quickly, is necessary. It should be about 8 ft (2.5 m) in length.

(8) A *bit* – the types of bit available have already been discussed in the previous chapter.

(9) A *snaffle bridle* fitted with reins and a plain, thick-mouth snaffle or with a Fulmer-type snaffle which has cheek-pieces. If the latter is preferred you need a pair of small retainers to fasten the cheeks to the cheek straps of the bridle. Initially, an ordinary cavesson noseband which can be adjusted so as to effect a partial closure of the mouth will suffice but it is as well to have a drop noseband to hand as well.

(10) A *saddle*. One of the less intelligent conventions observed in the backing and early schooling of young horses is the employment of an old, well-used but out-dated saddle. Since it is just as necessary, if not even more so, for the rider to be in balance at the outset of the young horse's education as in the later stages, choose a modern saddle which by its construction contributes materially to the correct positioning of the rider's weight. The only proviso is that it should not be exaggeratedly dipped in the seat. You need to be able to get on easily and you may, also, require to get off quickly and without throwing the leg so high in the air as to startle the horse.

Use with the saddle a soft, lampwick girth for the sake of the horse's comfort and in regard for his soft skin use a numnah as well.

(11) *Boots* – choose a set of boots which give

the leg complete protection from the coronet up to the knee or hock joint, and use ones which are equipped with easy fastenings.

(12) A *long whip* is an essential piece of equipment for schooling on the ground or from the saddle. Sometimes called a dressage whip, it is long enough to be applied without the hand being taken from the rein. Choose, however, a firm whip rather than the very flexible kind which delivers a rat-tat-tat rather than a single tap.

Facilities

To school young horses a training area, well away from the stables, is a necessity. It can be a simple arena marked out in the corner of a field, taking advantage of enclosing hedges on two sides, or it can be a far more elaborate affair with an all-weather surface surrounded by a post and rail fence or even, if funds permit, lap-type wood garden fencing or hurdles so that the horse cannot see through the walling. The object is to reduce possible distractions to an absolute minimum. An area 120 ft × 60 ft (40 m × 20 m) would do very well but it is possible to manage with a smaller arena. The going, however, needs to be level and, indeed, rideable in most weathers otherwise the progression of lessons is interrupted and much time can be wasted. Failing the professionally laid all-weather surface a mixture of rough sand, bark, ash or peat can provide an acceptable surface.

In the primary stage jumping equipment is not a major consideration. Half a dozen stout poles 8–10 ft (2.5–3 m) long, either left natural or painted so that the horse gets used to coloured poles right from the beginning of his schooling, will be sufficient, with the possible addition of a set of five cavalletti, made to give heights of 10 ins (25 cm), 15 ins (38 cm) and 19 ins (48 cm).

Recently, the official horse organisations in Britain have discouraged ('we do not recommend') the use of cavalletti on safety grounds.

There is, of course, some danger in piling cavalletti to make a fence and it is right that people should be reminded of the risk, but that is only one aspect of these versatile pieces of equipment which otherwise constitute a perfectly sound and safe training system. Don't build silly fences from cavalletti, straw bales, barrels or any other material but don't, on the other hand, ignore a valuable item of equipment which has played an important role in the most logical of the world's training progressions for something over three-quarters of a century.

The greater the range of facilities the easier, in theory, is the trainer's job but it is still possible with very simple arrangements and the exercise of imagination and ingenuity to produce some very nicely schooled horses. In the end it may be that the horse is only as good (or bad) as his trainer.

There is one last and very important facility: the possession of an older, schoolmaster horse who will teach the young one by example. It is possible to manage without in a number of respects, but in others the experienced horse who gives confidence to his companion is an invaluable asset.

Objects and benefits of lungeing

The simple definition of lungeing is that which states: 'The horse describing a circle around the trainer – the two being connected by a line from the horse's head to the trainer's hand.'

If that was the sum total there would be no point to the exercise. In reality it goes, or should go, so much further.

The mature horse is lunged when for some reason he cannot be given ridden exercise: or he is put on the lunge when he is very fresh and needs to have the itch taken out of his heels before the rider gets into the saddle. This is a sensible precaution. It is far better to allow the horse to get rid of his high spirits in a situation where he does no harm to anyone rather than risk a battle and a possible fall and injury.

For the young horse, however, lungeing is the basic gymnastic exercise which prepares him to carry weight and develops his powers of concentration.

There are two aspects to the lunge exercise, the physical objectives and those which are concerned with the mental development. Both are of equal importance and neither have anything to do with the idea of lungeing as some form of equine treadmill, much less with that inane theory which demands that the horse should make a perfect circle round a trainer who pivots on a fixed heel rammed firmly in the ground. That is nonsense and impossible to boot so far as the young horse is concerned, and if persisted in leads to the ruin of potentially good horses.

The *physical objectives* are these:

(1) The promotion of muscular development *without it being formed in opposition to the rider's weight*. Additionally, the *equal* development of muscles, whether working in pairs or in opposition, on either side of the body.

(2) The suppling of the horse laterally by the equal stretching and contraction of the dorsal, neck and abdominal muscles on each side.

(3) The induction of a degree of tension in the spinal complex (which does not mean or imply stiffness) by encouraging an extension and lowering of the head and neck and the engagement of the hind legs. On the circle the inside hind leg is bound to be more actively engaged beneath the body.

(4) The increase in the flexion of the joints, which occurs as the result of greater and more supple muscular development.

(5) To correct any natural curvature in the body which causes the hind legs to be carried away from the track of the fore-legs. A natural curvature is present as the foal lies in the womb and it can be increased still further by the practice of always leading and handling the horse from the near-side.

(6) The improvement of the balance as a result of the need to engage the hocks and the refinement of the paces in terms of rhythm, cadence and tempo (the rate of the stride or footfall).

By working the horse on the lunge all these benefits are obtained without the inhibiting weight of the rider.

These are the *mental benefits*:

(1) The inculcation of *calm*.

(2) The acceptance and development of habitual discipline and, in particular, obedience to the *voice*.

(3) The development of *forward movement*, which is both a mental and physical quality.

Method of lungeing

Work on the lunge is a natural extension of the work in-hand and is taught from that base.

The first lessons (duration no more than 15 minutes) require the horse to be wearing his cavesson, with the lunge rein fixed to the central ring on the nose, and a set of protective boots on all four legs – no other equipment is necessary at this stage.

As a start, the horse is walked and trotted in-hand and put through the transitions from halt to trot and then downwards to halt again. The trainer can then back away from the horse and ask him to move round him in a number of small circles. Holding the lunge rein in the 'leading' hand, i.e. left on the circle left and vice-versa, the slack of the rein is taken across the body and held in loops in the opposite hand. The lead hand should hold the rein in the same manner as it is held when riding. On no account should the rein be wrapped round the wrist. Good hands – or more correctly, 'educated' hands – are just as much a requirement when lungeing as when riding.

The lunge whip is carried in the whip hand, i.e. the right on the circle left and conversely. Held in this way it can be used behind the horse to encourage him to go forward and into the hand holding the rein.

The whip is held, point down on the ground, behind the trainer, from which position it can be employed in a low sweeping movement with the thong trailing.

At this point an assistant will be helpful to lead the horse round the trainer on *both* reins. She should lead from the *outside* so that nothing comes between the trainer and his pupil. The former has to concentrate on the horse, watching the movement and trying hard to assess the horse's attitude. He is, in fact, seeking to establish a *rapport* and that is made more difficult by interposing the physical presence of a third party between the two principals.

The assistant can remain in position, holding the lead rein very lightly, until the horse walks, trots and comes to halt on the trainer's spoken command and when working in both directions. If necessary she can reinforce the command by encouraging the horse to walk and trot and by using the rein when he is asked to halt or to slow the pace when it is becoming hurried. In this last instance the trainer will use the words 'Steady, boy, steady,' or something similar. Indeed, as the training progresses the importance of this command increases. It is used, in conjunction, with the hand and whip to obtain the sub-divisions within the paces of walk and

trot, i.e. medium, working, collected and extended in trot. Although much later in the training, when the horse is approaching an advanced level, it is possible to obtain collection on the lunge, the collected paces are outside the primary and secondary stages of training.

It should, however, be possible to obtain variations in the paces towards the end of the primary stage, between a medium walk and a more extended one; and in trot, the definitive pace of the lunge, between working and medium. (Medium walk is a free, swinging movement of moderate extension. The steps in this four-beat pace are even and clearly defined, the hind feet touching the ground just in front of the prints made by the fore-feet. In collection the steps are shorter and more elevated as a result of increased flexion in the joints. Extended walk, where the horse stretches out the head and neck, sees the hind feet touching the ground clearly in front of the prints of the forefeet. The fourth sub-division is the free walk, a pace of rest when the horse under saddle is allowed complete freedom of head and neck.

In the two-beat trot pace, working trot is the pace between medium and collected. The hind feet touch the ground just behind the prints of the forefeet. In medium trot the action is rounder with the hindfeet touching down in the prints of the forefeet.)

In a surprisingly short space of time, no more than two or three lessons, it will be possible to dispense with the assistant, who can then drop behind the horse and follow him tactfully to maintain his forward movement.

However, before the assistant leaves the horse's head it is very important to establish the halt.

When the command is given, accompanied by a little rippling movement on the lunge rein which will run from the hand to the nosepiece of the cavesson, the horse must be taught to halt *on the circle* and must not be allowed to turn inwards. The trainer then *goes out to the horse,* stands him up in a balanced halt and rewards him. The horse remains in that position whilst the trainer moves back, preparatory to asking the horse to walk on.

To allow the horse to come into the centre is a grave error. He never learns to halt squarely and once he has been allowed to turn in without correction, particularly if he has been rewarded for doing so, he becomes confirmed in this most annoying and non-productive habit. Indeed, the habit can make a nonsense of the whole exercise and prevent any sort of constructive progress, the horse losing his concentration on the work in hand.

To turn the horse so as to work on the opposite rein, he is led round a half circle and placed on the track facing the other direction. The trainer then takes his time about changing over the rein and the whip before stepping back to take up his control position.

The success of the exercise depends on the ability to position oneself correctly in relation to the horse.

The trainer needs to place himself in line with the horse's hip, from which position he is able to send the horse forward from his whip (the extension of the hand that was used to urge forward a foal) into the rein-hand.

If the horse ceases to go forward or attempts to spin round and go on the other rein, the trainer has to move swiftly to re-establish his control position behind the animal so as to frustrate the attempted disobedience.

Attempting to spin round is a common fault in horses who have not been taught to go in both directions and have not been handled from both sides. Usually, it occurs when the horse is asked to go to the right rein, which he finds more difficult.

From the outset, therefore, the lessons should begin, and probably end as well, on the right rein.

In the early lessons no attempt should be made by the trainer to fix his position, instead he should operate on a small circle moving concentrically in respect of the larger circle being taken by the horse. To do this successfully, without falling over the rein or the whip, requires a certain knack. The secret is in moving the leading leg (i.e. the left on the circle left) and then bringing the right leg up to it before repeating the movement. In dancing terms (ballroom dancing terms, anyway) it is the simple *chassis*. Crossing the legs over has a purpose in another context but it is not to be recommended in this one.

Less likely, but by no means impossible, is the resistance exemplified by the horse seeking to escape the restraint of the rein by taking off. It cannot be allowed to succeed but we have to be careful about the ways in which this rebellion is countered.

Since it is quite impossible to stop half a ton of horse moving at speed we must disregard those manuals which advise us to dig our heels in and pull. (One wonders if the authors have ever tried it.) Of course, we have to stop the horse but we want to do so without the risk of damaging him. The cavesson is a powerful piece of equipment and I know of no more certain way of straining and spraining immature ligaments, tendons and joints than by pulling the horse sharply round on his forehand. Even then it is unlikely that we shall have stopped his wild career.

Should the horse go off we must, initially, yield to him, following for a few strides before acting strongly on the rein and then giving and taking again. On occasions a horse that is over-fresh and, therefore, not in a receptive frame of mind, may ignore the commands to halt. In most instances repeated verbal requests, accompanied by a noticeable relaxation in the trainer's posture, will result, in the end, in compliance. If the horse persists, however, he has to be driven directly into the wall (hedge or whatever) of the arena, the action being accompanied by the vocal command.

Sometimes with a fresh horse he will break into a faster pace, often anticipating a command. To check him is to frustrate the very forward movement which is to all intents the Holy Grail of the schooling exercises. Therefore, immediately the trainer perceives the horse's intention he should give the command to trot or whatever, so that the horse instead of succeeding in his disobedience, is made to think that he has done what the trainer was wanting. With the dominant horse this is the approach to make and is exemplary of the way in which we work with him.

Lungeing – Weeks 1–3

During this period the emphasis, certainly, is upon the horse moving freely and correctly at walk, but also at the more demanding trot. The trot represents work, whilst the walk is the introductory pace in which, and from which, one consolidates obedience to the commands and begins the variations in the pace.

However, it serves another vital purpose also, which is all too frequently ignored, even at advanced levels. In fact, a really good walk is rarely seen, even in the rarified atmosphere of the Grand Prix test, probably because riders use it only as a rest after more strenuous paces.

That apart, each lungeing session, and each ridden session, should commence and terminate in walk periods.

At walk the body is using a great many muscles without any being under extreme exertion. They remain, therefore, more or less flat and with a gentle pulsating action slide easily and smoothly over each other. Prior to the more stressful work at trot the walk pace prepares the muscles, removing stiffnesses and causing increased circulation. Were the horse to be worked directly in trot, without this preparatory loosening and suppling phase, the muscle fibres can become bunched and the movement stiffened and

The young horse working quietly on the lunge and in excellent balance. Note the light contact of the side-reins.

restricted commensurately.

After a period of work, and trotting continuously on a 25 ft (7·5 m) diameter circle is *hard* work, the gentler action of the walk and particularly the pumping movement which occurs in the muscles helps the latter to get rid of waste products which will have accumulated in them during the period of work in which they were under stress. At the same time the movement in walk smooths out the muscle fibres which may have become taut and even tangled.

Waste products which are not released and bunching muscle fibres cause stiffness and even cramp. But that does not mean that the walk should be allowed to become sloppy, a common fault with riders who are, indeed, confusing relaxation with a less than co-ordinated looseness. The walk is of no use, and can indeed be harmful, if it is other than active, rhythmical and controlled.

In trot one should aim for the working pace with the horse being encouraged to stretch the head and neck downwards so that the hind legs are engaged and the top-line is nicely rounded. The latter will, therefore, be long whilst the bottom line will be short. The converse is to be avoided, for the horse will then be on the forehand and out of balance – an upside-down horse, in fact.

A horse in the correct outline is building up muscle on the top of the neck whilst that awkwardly strong and unhelpful muscle on the neck's underside will be used so little that it will be reduced.

The horse will be helped to stretch down if he is pushed up actively into a nice contact with the rein and then asked to stretch by the hand tightening and relaxing the contact.

Towards the end of this three-week period we can ask for a few lengthened steps in trot and we can spend a few moments each day varying the size of the circle, decreasing the radius for a few circuits and then enlarging it. (Lengthening can be achieved by pushing the horse forward from the whip, thus increasing the engagement of the hocks and quarters, into a hand which resists momentarily to prevent the pace quickening). In time this valuable exercise improves the balance so that the horse is able without difficulty to work on a small circle with hind legs engaged and begins to raise his head and lighten the forehand, but that takes quite a long time and we shall not see a significant move in that direction until the end of the primary stage and perhaps not until we are a little way into the secondary, four-year-old training.

Smaller circles, however, are more difficult for the horse so they should not be overdone. If the horse starts leaning away from the rein and/or the quarters swing out so that the hind feet cease to follow the track of the forelegs, the circle is too small and one must go back to working on a larger one.

The tracking up of the hind feet has to be watched continually and there are other physical indications of good movement and relaxation which tell the observant trainer how well or otherwise the work is going.

The mouth is closed (when the horse wears a bit the lips will have a covering of white foam); the ears are relaxed and the tail is carried freely, swinging loosely away from the quarters. If it is clamped down and tucked in, the back will be stiff and hard. Watch, in particular, that the ears are not carried one up and one down. If they are the head is being twisted at the poll in resistance. This, in fact, will occur more frequently when side-reins are used and is a sure indication that they are too short.

The state of the stomach muscles is particularly revealing. They should be relaxed and not tensed. If they are held up tightly it is noticeable and, of course, it affects the freedom of the pace.

This relaxation, producing the more fluid movement, develops as the lesson proceeds and may not be complete for upwards of 10 minutes and sometimes twice as long as that with highly strung animals.

Until, of course, this physical relaxation occurs the horse is similarly tense in his mind and that, too, becomes more easily discernible as the work progresses and horse and trainer develop increased sympathy with each other.

By the third week the horse should be working with a bit in his mouth, fitted comfortably under the cavesson on a simple headpiece, but still without side-reins. He can also wear his roller and crupper. These can be introduced to him in the box, the roller being tightened gradually over a period of days. He can then be walked about in the tackle so that he gets used to it before his lesson on the lunge.

The actual working time of the lessons should by the third week have been extended to 30 minutes or upwards of that, so long as the horse is quite capable of working for this length of time without experiencing discomfort.

Pole grids

To encourage still further the rounding of the top-line, the engagement of the hocks, the muscular development of the quarters and second thighs and the overall agility of the horse, an additional exercise can be introduced during this period involving the use of stout poles laid on the ground which may later be replaced by cavalletti. Furthermore, since the horse needs to raise all four legs to cross the poles he has to increase the 'give' in the lumbar muscles of the back – a most important consideration.

It is easier to treat the poles as a separate exercise carried out towards the end of the lesson. The horse can then be taken back to the stable and his feed on its completion. If an arena is available it is best to put the poles down the long side and straighten the horse to make an approach off the circle.

To start with only one stout pole is necessary and it need not be more than 6–8 ins (15–20 cm) high. When the horse will walk and trot quietly over this pole another can be placed about 4 ft (1·2 m) away and the horse walked over the two. To trot over the poles the distance needs to be increased by some 10 ins (25 cm). After a couple of lessons it should be possible to make a full trotting grid by adding two more poles, but only if the horse is working rhythmically with a rounded outline.

The aim is to achieve an unaltered length of stride in the approach, the crossing of the grid and when coming away from it.

The distance is critical and there can be no hard-and-fast rules on this score. For most horses 4 ft 10 ins-5 ft (1·45–1·5 m) will be convenient but there will be horses with both shorter and longer strides and the grid has to be adapted to their requirement.

If the approach, the pace and the distances are correct the horse should not trip over the poles. If he does then something is wrong in one or other of those departments or in all of them. The answer is to go back to the beginning. First establish the rhythm and outline over the single pole again and then continue over two poles until you and the horse have got it right.

The pole grid and later the cavalletti grid, which causes the legs to be raised higher with a corresponding increase in the flexion of the joints, are an invaluable training aid throughout the schooling period and after, since they can be used in the re-schooling or correction of older horses and also in teaching the horse to jump.

Properly used the grid can also act to regulate the length of stride, the latter being made to extend or shorten according to the distance between the poles. One is, therefore, developing the horse's ability to adjust his stride, a very necessary accomplishment in the competition horse. Moreover, this lesson can be taught on the lunge and the necessary muscular development brought about before the horse is asked to perform the exercise under saddle.

Side-reins

The value of the pole grid extends even to the work in side-reins which can be commenced at the end of this initial period. To begin with adjust the side-reins to the bit rings at nearly their full length so that there is a definite loop and let the horse become accustomed to the slight pressure imposed on his mouth by the weight of the reins. This is followed by continuing the work over the grid when the horse will take up the slack of the rein on his own accord as he lowers the head and neck and stretches forward over the poles. *The horse is then making contact with the bit of his own accord*; in no way is it being forced on the mouth, and that represents a very significant peak in the training programme.

Thereafter for the trot work on the circle we can tighten the side-reins to a point where the rein just dips at its centre. They must not be so tight that the horse retracts the nose to come behind the bit and evade contact with it. Even with the reins fitted lightly horses will occasionally come behind the bit in this way. They do so when they are tired and/or when the hind legs are insufficiently active. The solution is obvious.

There is a school of thought which advo-cates that the inside rein should be adjusted shorter than its partner. It sounds logical until one examines the implications. By enforcing a bend there is every possibility that the horse will either hang on the inside of the bit or retract his nose to avoid the contact. His weight is thrown on to the inside shoulder and his quarters must, willy-nilly, be pushed outwards and off the track. I prefer the reins to be of equal length. They should, however, be adjusted according to the pace. The correct tension for trot (really the only pace suitable for side-reins because in trot the horse moves the limbs whilst keeping the head still) is not applicable to either walk or canter when the head swings with the altered movement.

It is not a matter of too much importance in the walk and does not prevent practising the transitions up and down to trot and halt, but a longer rein is needed when the horse does any cantering on the lunge.

Long-reins – Backing (Weeks 3–6)

For many years I made little or no use of long

Introduction to the long reins–the safe way.

Working in the long reins. The carriage and overall impression is excellent.

reins, believing that I could obtain the same results from the saddle. I omitted long-reining for the best of reasons – I was not very adept in their use!

In time, as I became less inept, I learnt to appreciate the value of long-reining as a means of furthering the 'mouthing' of the horse, teaching obedience to the indications of the rein and improving the balance, carriage and quality of the paces. From the human viewpoint long-reining is equally rewarding. It gives a new concept to the use of the hands; provides a wonderful opportunity to observe and influence the horse in movement; represents the almost ultimate exercise in body positioning and allows for a closer and very fascinating relationship with the horse.

There are four methods of long-reining, all of which have their particular advantages and objectives. There is the Danish system, derived from the Neapolitan style of the Renaissance, perfected by Colonel Egede Lunde and exemplified in Britain by Mr Einar Schmit Jensen and his pupil Miss Sylvia Stanier. In this the horse wears a driving pad with the reins passing from the mouth to the hands via the terrets. The French method employs a collar from which the rein is passed downwards through a ring set low on a body roller and thence to the hand.

In Vienna, long-reining is used to show off a horse already highly schooled under saddle and is not, therefore, relevant in our context.

The so-called 'English' method is the least sophisticated of the four and in its popular application probably the least effective. It differs from the others in that it is the only one in which the outside rein is passed round the quarters.

However, if the principle is employed with a roller, instead of the reins being passed through stirrup irons, it can, in the right hands, produce good results. Additionally, it has the advantage of being within the capacity of the trainer of average ability.

Method of long-reining

The lunge rein, to which the horse is well accustomed, is moved onto the inside ring of the three on the nosepiece of the cavesson. A second rein is then attached to the opposite side ring and passed, via the top ring on the roller, round the quarters. This can be done without help but as always a good assistant simplifies the matter and reduces the risk of the horse becoming out of hand.

If single-handed the horse is lunged in the usual way with the rein coming directly from the cavesson to the hand. The second outside rein comes to the hand round the quarters. Should the horse object strongly, the outside rein can, in an emergency, be dropped whilst the trainer continues to maintain control through the inside lunge rein.

With an assistant the process can be short-circuited. She can lead the horse while the trainer operates the reins, both of which can be passed through the roller rings.

At this stage the trainer has to continually reassure the horse with the voice. It is all right so long as the horse is able to see the trainer clearly, as when he or she is positioned threequarters-on to his rear, but when the trainer steps directly behind he is almost out of vision and the horse is likely to lose confidence and to be hesitant about going forward.

Before operating single-handed, therefore, one has to be sure that the horse accepts the situation and has also learnt, with the help of the assistant, how to change direction on a simple S bend. Even then he will need to be encouraged by voice and by small movements of the whip. To commence, the horse is worked at walk on large circles, the trainer making the horse pass in front of him when he wishes to change rein.

Once forward movement is established the horse can be driven from the bit and worked from trot as well as walk. An important part of the work in long-reins takes place outside the arena, the horse being driven quietly round the yard, through fields and so on and, if they are to hand, over small banks and ditches.

Changes of direction and changes of pace – 'slow-downs and speed-ups' within the trot and walk pace – can be practised for short periods.

It is, however, important to recognise that tight circles, as on the lunge, can be damaging to the horse's still immature frame.

Sympathetic, light use of the reins is an obvious essential. The hands must take up a slackness in the reins but they must *never* pull. The guiding principles are that the inside rein produces flexion and the outer one contributes to a degree of balance. Ideally, one needs to work the reins in rhythm with the hind legs but it is easier, I think, to look at the forelegs, taking up the rein to maintain contact in rhythm with the movement as the appropriate foreleg is raised, i.e. left rein in time with the raising of the left leg and vice-versa.

In changes of direction we comply with the classical principle of giving with the *outside* rein instead of pulling with the inside one – a principle which will be maintained throughout the subsequent ridden work.

Long-reining has also to include work on straight lines when the horse is driven forward from directly behind his quarters. The horse can be put into increased contact with his bit by being driven forward and the carriage and self-carriage can be much improved. One does, however, need a wall, hedge or rail to work along and then the horse can be kept straight by the use of the outside rein.

Towards the end of Stage 2 it should be possible to teach the rein-back in the long reins, but first the transitions from halt to walk to trot and back again must be entirely consolidated, the rein-back being practised within those transition exercises so that there is no possibility of the horse anticipating the command or becoming confused by it. In any case it requires *finesse* and until you are confident of your hand is better not attempted.

The rein-back is obtained from halt by asking the horse to go *forward*. Just as he begins to obey, the hands, instead of allowing the movement by giving to the mouth, close on the rein in time with the movement of the legs, i.e. the right hand closes as the right leg begins to rise and then the left hand repeats the action. This will result (or it should do so) in the horse moving backwards in balance and in two-time without the reins having pulled him back.

With the Danish method, particularly, it is possible to obtain movements like *renvers*, *travers* and *shoulder-in* without too much difficulty, but the encircling rein of the English system hardly permits such movements with any degree of fluency, if at all, and certainly not with the use of a correct directional rein.

Backing

For all too many horses, and people, backing (i.e. mounting the horse) represents the apogee of training. The horse is then 'broken to saddle'. What rubbish. Up to the rider getting into the saddle the schooling is concerned with a physical and mental preparation for that moment and with the teaching of exercises in-hand which will later be practised under saddle. Only after that does the horse's ridden education begin.

Because the backing of the horse represents a divide in his training it is all too frequently endowed with some sort of mystical property.

In fact, if the preparation has been logical and thorough, backing the horse is no more difficult than teaching him to walk and trot in-hand or any other of the early lessons.

Preparation is, nonetheless, essential. Before the rider can think of getting on the back, the horse has to become used to wearing a saddle and working in it on the lunge.

Anything which might be potentially exciting or upsetting is best introduced after work when the horse has settled. Putting on a saddle is no exception to this rule. For a week or so the saddle is put in place in the box and girthed loosely. The rider can press down on it and even lean over it and the horse can be led out for a short while to get used to the creak of leather. Within a few days it should be possible to stand on a straw bale placed alongside the horse and lean over the back with the toe in the near-side stirrup. Then the process can be repeated from the opposite side on the principle of all things being done equally from both sides of the horse.

In preparation for the rider's legs the leathers and irons are moved backwards and forwards along the flanks and even banged on them.

The next step is to lunge the horse in the unmounted saddle (i.e. without irons) and then to do so with the irons in place, having first taken the precaution of tying the irons together with a piece of twine under the belly to prevent their swinging about excessively.

The actual backing takes place after the horse has been worked rather more comprehensively than usual.

One handler, preferably the trainer, holds the horse's head whilst the rider, either from a straw bale or not, is given a quiet leg-up until she is lying over the horse. Keeping the body low she slips a leg over. Meantime, the horse can be distracted by much petting and a bowl of oats. With the horse standing still the rider makes slow, deliberate movements, leaning forward and swinging the legs back and forth. This last is important and the horse should be accustomed to legs swinging right from the start, otherwise he might explode as the rider is compelled to swing the leg to get on and off. At this stage the rider 'creeps' on and off without making exaggerated movements which might startle the horse and, of course, stirrups are not necessary.

On the next day, after work, of course, the horse can be led forward with the rider in place. Within a week with the rider up and employing stirrups it should be possible for the horse to be led round the arena at walk and trot, the rider remaining quite passive since the object is no more than to get the horse to accept the weight on his back.

Teaching the aids – Riding on (Weeks 6–9)

Then it is time to lunge the horse with the rider in the saddle, first having a pair of reins attached to the cavesson and then to the bit itself. Following on from that some simple aids can be taught.

Since the horse is already schooled to the voice on the lunge he will soon associate an action upon the part of the rider with the spoken command.

From halt, for instance, the command 'Walk-on' is given accompanied by the movement of the whip. Fractionally before the voice the rider applies the legs – voice and lunge whip, in effect reinforcing that aid.

The same applies to the trot and to the downward transitions back to halt, but at the outset the rider's aids have to be applied in the manner in which they will for ever after be employed. This is the time to attempt refinement of the aids, not years later when the horse has learnt a set of signals which are clumsy, unbalancing and woefully incomplete.

It follows, therefore, that the rider needs to have more qualifications than the mere ability to stay on board. At this time the horse, attempting to adjust to the unaccustomed weight on his back, is more easily unbalanced than at any other time later in his education.

Under saddle, calm and attentive. The rider/ trainer is the late Mrs Alison McInerney and the horse a three-year-old Arabian bred by Major and Mrs T W I Hedley.

The rider's seat has, therefore, to be exemplary.

From halt to walk the aids first *prepare* by a momentary closing of fingers and legs; they *act* by the legs being put lightly on (just behind) the girth in a gentle forward squeezing movement; the fingers open to allow the horse to obey and as the horse responds the legs, too, *yield*, being held lightly in contact with the sides.

To halt, or in any downward transition, the same principle applies. The horse is *prepared* (forerunner of the half-halt which serves to re-balance within the pace) by the brief squeeze of hands and legs. The aids then *act*, the legs preceding the action of the hands by half a second or so. In effect the legs push the horse, with engaged hind legs, into an intermittently closing hand.

From the circle, the horse can work round the whole arena, still on the lunge but increasingly under the rider's control. The trainer's voice and whip just reinforce her aids as necessary. It should now be possible to achieve variations in the pace – the 'slow-downs' and 'speed-ups' if not the precisely clear divisions between working and medium etc.

Finally, there are the directional changes. To alter direction on the arc of a circle as at the corners of the arena, there is once more no sense in employing aids other than those which will be used in the subsequent schooling. They may, however, be a little more exaggerated so that the horse is left in no doubt as to their meaning. Approaching the corner, the rider increases the activity of the pace so as to maintain impulsion on the turn; the inside hand is opened outwards – not pulled back to restrict the forward movement and compel the quarters to be shifted outside the track – whilst the outside shoulder, elbow, hand and hip is advanced to correspond with the balance and posture of the horse's body.

One absolute essential in this early ridden work and in all that follows, too, is that the rider should on changing the rein at trot change the diagonal also.

It is usual for the rider to sit on the inside diagonal, that is as the left foreleg and right hind leg touch down on the circle left, the opposite being the case for the circle to the right. The seat rises from the saddle on the outside diagonal as the right shoulder moves forward on the circle left. From the rider's viewpoint it is held, quite rightly, that it is easier to apply the inside leg, the operative one on circles and turns since it activates the horse's inside hind leg, when sitting in the saddle than when the seat is raised.

So far as the horse and his movement is concerned the rider's changing of the diagonal is of even more importance. Were the rider always to sit on the same diagonal (which many do) the horse would develop his back muscles to cope with the situation, developing the back on one side at the expense of the other, and becoming one-sided as a result – which, of course, all our careful training is designed to prevent. (The diagonal can be changed by the rider sitting for one stride, or bump, before rising on the opposite diagonal. If one 'bump' is insufficient allow for three or even five).

Once the horse is no longer reliant on the pressure of the lunge he can work daily in the arena under saddle as well as continuing with his lunge and long-rein lessons.

Riding out

Having accomplished these early lessons, then – and the sooner the better, for the arena is bound to have an inhibiting influence – he is ready to be ridden out, but in company with a steady, older horse. He can, of course, continue with his daily lessons in the arena learning to jump small obstacles on the lunge and so on, but the emphasis has to be shifted towards the daily hacking period during which he is learning in a natural way how to carry weight, adjusting his balance in accordance with the ground he traverses and to the weight of the rider on his back.

It is also an opportunity for him, under the wing of his more experienced companion, to come into closer contact with traffic conditions.

The periods of work and exercise can now be up to, say, 30–40 minutes in the arena, interspersed with frequent rest periods and with the addition of a 1–2 hour period, either in the morning or afternoon, devoted to straightforward hacking, the length depending on the individual's development.

It is advisable, even though the older horse can act as a shield for the young one on lanes and roadways where traffic is likely to be encountered, to take the precaution of riding out in fluorescent tabards inscribed with a suitable slogan, e.g. 'SLOW – YOUNG HORSE' – or, perhaps, 'DANGER – EXPLOSIVES'. Obviously, one chooses routes carefully and gives the young horse plenty of opportunity to watch traffic from safe vantage points before actually riding through it.

The more the youngster is ridden on straight lines at walk and trot the better the paces will develop, so long as the rider remembers to change diagonal frequently.

Keep a light, even contact with the mouth but otherwise allow him to carry his head as he will, whilst riding him firmly from the legs and *in front* of them. He must be allowed freedom to adjust his balance and to do that he uses the head and neck as a balancing agent. We must not, therefore, interfere with the process, but neither must he be allowed to slop along.

Uneven ground compels frequent balance adjustments and it does the world of good to ride him up and down even quite steep slopes. Hills are grand for trotting up so as to build muscle but to trot downhill puts too much strain on the horse. Later on, in the four-year-old training, trotting down gentle inclines is necessary as a way to improve and confirm the horse's balance.

The more variety that can be brought into

the hacking sessions the more valuable they become. It should not be impossible to find some water to cross and on country rides there is usually a log or two about or perhaps a low bank over which the youngster can follow the schoolmaster horse.

So far no specific attempt has been made to teach the canter, although it is probable that during schooling sessions in the arena the horse will have broken into the pace for a few strides. The sustained canter on a lunge circle and certainly in the early ridden lessons is beyond the balance and ability of a young horse.

However, by the end of Stage 2 the canter has to be introduced and the horse taught to lead with the correct inside foreleg.

This is most easily taught on the lunge and is described subsequently in the suggested lunge work for this and the ensuing periods in the three-year-old's education.

Nonetheless, it will do no harm and a great deal of good if the horse is encouraged to canter during his hacking sessions.

For the first attempts it is probably wiser to choose an uphill slope for cantering is an exciting, forceful pace for the horse. Indeed, young ones may even express that excitement, as well as their pleasure and well-being, in an exuberant buck or two. Going uphill, a buck, if it comes, is not too uncomfortable, for it is difficult for the horse to get his head down low enough to perform one of the full-blooded variety.

A buck or two on a fresh morning is, indeed, to be expected from any normal young horse who is feeling on top of the world. Whilst not wishing to spoil a little innocent fun it should not, of course, be allowed to become habitual. When bucking goes beyond an acceptable level it has to be countered by the head being raised, *before* the buck has time to develop, and by driving vigorously forward with the legs.

The first essays at canter will be far from polished performances, but that does not matter. The purpose is to let the horse experience the swing of the pace whilst teaching him how to carry his rider and himself at this new gait.

If the older horse sets off in canter at a suitable piece of ground the young one will usually follow suit, particularly if he is encouraged by a vigorous, if less than scientific, driving with the legs.

In fact, in order to preserve his balance, he may fall into canter and initially he may want to use our hands as a sort of fifth leg. This, too, is of no concern. The rider has only to sit quietly, following the movement with an even, light contact on both reins and interfering as little as possible. Do not, however, make the mistake of always cantering at the same point. If you canter at A on one day, make sure that you walk that stretch on the next, otherwise the horse learns to anticipate the rider's requests and will always expect to canter there. If he is prevented from doing so he is then confused and in danger of becoming resentful of the imposed restraint.

Steady trotting on the level and up hills is a recognised body-building exercise but it must be carried out carefully, particularly in respect of the change of diagonals. On relatively straight lanes trot for 5 minutes on one diagonal before changing to the other for 5 minutes. Intersperse the trotting with rest periods at walk, letting the horse stretch out his head and neck whilst keeping a light contact with the lengthened rein. Once he has been out for half an hour or so the horse is unlikely to take advantage of the situation and explode uncomfortably and the thought that he might should not deter us from letting him relax in this way. (In fact, he is less liable to do anything untoward in this relaxed, swinging walk than otherwise.)

The relaxation is important in itself but it also represents an expression of trust by the rider in the horse. Just occasionally a pheasant getting up unexpectedly may cause that trust to be betrayed momentarily, but there is always a mane or a neckstrap – the latter being a sensible piece of equipment to in-clude in the wardrobe of the young horse.

Further work on the lunge

The lunge and long-reining work is continued in parallel with the horse being ridden out and it is now advisable to teach the canter. As well as establishing the correct leads at the pace, the three-time rhythm of the canter compels muscles in the back and quarters to work that much harder and thus benefits their development.

Cantering a circle is difficult and initially demanding, it has therefore to be made as large as possible if we are to avoid the risk of strain. Also, the side-reins must be lengthened to allow for the altered posture.

The canter is obtained by shortening the trot, the horse being pushed up to a hand that resists in little tweaks on the rein. The trick then is to get an increased bend, as though the circle was to become smaller, whilst raising the head, and then to ask for canter, with the voice and whip whilst simultaneously yielding with the rein to allow the inside shoulder to stretch out in the final sequence of footfalls constituting the canter pace. If the rein is held fractionally too long, the shoulder is closed and the horse will be unable to extend the inside foreleg. (The sequence of footfalls at canter left, for instance, are (1) right (off) hind leg; (2) right diagonal (off-fore and near-hind); and (3) left (near) fore). Be content to let the horse circle at canter just once or twice before asking him to return to trot and then walk.

It helps very much if in these early departures into canter the trainer himself moves in the rhythm of the canter in much the same way as we did when we rode a hobby horse in childhood.

If difficulty is still experienced a ground pole or a cavalletto at lowest height can be placed in the corner of the arena and the horse lunged over from trot. Almost inevitably he will land in canter and on the correct lead.

Cavalletti

To encourage greater activity the ground pole grid can be replaced with the slightly higher cavalletti, starting at the lowest height and progressing to the intermediate position.

There will be no harm also in asking the horse to jump small obstacles on the lunge.

It is sufficient probably to do no more in this stage than to jump fences of up to 2 ft (60 cm) high and low spreads of, say, 3–4 ft (90–120 cm).

Place a ground pole just after the corner of the arena and 9 ft (2.7 m) away on the long side put down a cavalletto at the top height. Trot the horse into this small fence and practise jumping from both left and right, altering the disposition of the ground pole and fence accordingly.

To make a spread add a second cavalletto alongside the first.

When both are jumped quietly a small fence of crossed poles, no more than 2 ft (60 cm) high, and with a ground-line (i.e. a pole on the ground close up to the fence), can be built between two uprights. Balance a pole on the inside upright with the top end projecting some 18 ins (45 cm) so that the lunge line may pass smoothly over it. The pole also acts as a wing for the fence and a discouragement, therefore, to any ideas of evasion.

Trailer and boxing drill

If the two-year-old has been educated in the manner suggested, trailer drill is no more

A confident entry into a carefully positioned trailer by a horse well-schooled in his trailer drill.

than a recapitulation of lessons already learnt. If, however, the pupil is a new and unknown three-year-old we should start at the beginning, leaving nothing to chance, and trailer drill should form part of the training programme, time being devoted to it on a daily basis initially.

What follows relates to trailers, which are more frequently the cause of loading problems than horse-boxes. Nonetheless, the principles which apply to loading horses in trailers are just as relevant to putting horses in and out of boxes.

There should be no trouble at all. A horse should walk up and down a ramp as easily as he enters or leaves his box, particularly if he has been schooled to walk in-hand, but we should take every possible precaution to ensure that we make boxing easy for the horse and do not introduce unnecessary difficulties.

Method

Place the trailer against a wall, so that at least one 'wing' is provided. That way fifty per cent of the danger of running out is at once eliminated. Put the stabilisers down so that the ramp is firm. Nothing upsets horses more than an unsteady footing. Park the trailer with the front opened up and the ramp facing towards the sun, otherwise the inside resembles a dark cavern which will be discouraging for most horses. Move the central partition over to make the entrance wider and more inviting.

After the horse has been worked, take a feed bowl in one hand and circle in front of the box at an active walk. Circle to the left if the left side of the box is against the wall and the opposite way in converse circumstances. This enables the approach to be made from a slightly oblique angle and this in itself reduces the likelihood of a run-out. I use the last word advisedly because loading is very similar to jumping so far as the approach is concerned, and the secret of successful jumping is fifty per cent in the approach and fifty

per cent about rider determination. For 'rider' substitute 'handler'.

When the horse is walking forward actively make the approach off the circle so as to strike the ramp at a slight angle. Have an assistant walk up briskly behind and let the horse see the feed bowl as he puts a foot on the ramp and begins to walk into the box. Halt the horse, in the box, give him his reward, make much of him and walk him straight out. If there is no front unload facility he has to come out backwards, but insist that he does so one step at a time. Move him back a step, halt him, make much of him, and repeat the movement. Do, however, have the assistant standing by the ramp to guide the quarters with a directing hand.

Repeat the exercise for a few days, reducing the reward to no more than a carrot or a sugar lump. Then begin to put the breeching strap in place and the ramp up, whilst the handler remains with the horse. The chest bar will then, of course, be in position. When the horse is quite happy to enter the trailer in this way move the container to different positions until the horse loads easily in the middle of the yard.

It is always advisable to have a lunge rein handy and attached to a point on the trailer so that in the event of the horse becoming hesitant the assistant can pass the rein behind the quarters as an additional incentive to move forward.

One does not always have an assistant, however, and on occasions we may well have to manage single-handed. Against that time it is wise to get the horse used to 'Professor' Sydney Galvayne's lead harness, a most useful loading aid.

In its simplest form it comprises a loop of soft, strong rope passing round the quarters and then upwards to the withers, where it is kept in place by a breast rope, the ends being continued through either the bit or the headcollar. It represents something of a puzzle for the horse and thus has a psychological effect as well as a physical one. Its effect is much intensified if the loop round the quarters is modified to make a crupper round the dock. A rope round the dock was one of the basic training devices of the old-time horse tamers of whom Galvayne (real name Osborne) was particularly notable.

When the horse loads as a matter of course, he and a companion should be taken for short rides, the greatest care being taken to ensure that the vehicle is driven smoothly and steadily – one bad ride can put a horse off travelling for a long time.

Purpose can be given to these journeys by driving to some particular spot, unboxing and taking the horses off for a ride before loading up and returning home. Make sure, however, that all the loading aids are taken with you.

Completing Stage 2

Before turning the horse away in August he should be checked over thoroughly for any small injuries he may have sustained. His teeth should be looked at, as well as his worming and inoculation records. His shoes should be removed and replaced with 'tips', which will prevent the foot breaking up.

9

Stage 3 – Work on the Flat

IN HIS fourth year the horse begins his secondary education. The overall objective of the training within this period is not dissimilar to the aims of the rider intent upon improving the physical capability by means of an exercising programme (as in Chapter 6), and the schooling is, of course, just as applicable to older, educationally deprived horses.

The purpose of the human exercises was threefold. They were designed to increase SUPPLENESS, STRENGTH and STAMINA, all qualities which we need to encourage in the competition horse at whatever level. The combination of the three provides the necessary foundation for the teaching of competitive skills in this secondary stage; and even if competition is not a principal concern they are skills which contribute entirely to an obedient horse, comfortable and a pleasure to ride in all his paces and in a variety of circumstances.

The secondary schooling can be divided into a number of interrelated activities carried out as part of an overall curriculum.

Exercise is provided by daily hacking sessions, whilst the *work* divisions comprise the exercises and movements on the *flat,* the subject of this chapter and the basis for much of the jumping training, as well as the actual *jumping* lessons in the arena and over cross-country fences.

In some respects, particularly in the jumping exercises, the lunge work is continued and extended to prepare the horse to jump under a rider. For the sake of clarity and convenience the various aspects of the secondary education are described in two chapters, this one and the one which follows.

However, since the quality of the work on the flat, and indeed over fences, is entirely dependent upon the competence of the rider and his/her understanding of basic equestrian theory it will be as well to remind ourselves of the principles involved.

The system of signals

We communicate with the horse through the medium of the mind, the voice, the seat, weight and limbs.

The influence of the mind is enormously important, but it is an acquired art, for the accomplishment of which no specific instruction can be given. It is a matter of awareness, of sensitivity, concentration, projection and receptivity. Once we become aware of the ability to communicate on the mental plane then it becomes a matter of application and practice.

Certainly, we can communicate with the voice, but only to a degree. It is an insufficiently sophisticated and subtle instrument with which to obtain other than a basic response.

The physical aids, however, provide a system of communication which can reach a very high level of sensitivity, their application, if sufficiently skilful, embracing the most delicate gradations of expression.

How well, or otherwise, the system works in respect of the clarity of the message and the horse's ability to respond appropriately depends upon the acquisition of a seat 'independent of the reins for its security and in which the limbs and bodyweight are in a state of physical freedom' – which is what the rider exercises on the lunge attempt to achieve.

For a definition of a man's seat on a horse we have to go back over 2000 years to the first Master, the Greek general, Xenophon (c.430–356 BC).

He wrote that the seat of a man on a horse was not 'as though he were sitting on a chair ... but rather as though he were standing upright with his legs apart'. The only addition that has to be made is 'and with the knees bent'. Thereafter, the rider has to be sufficiently relaxed to be able to follow the horse's movements from a supple, muscular back.

Shoulder, hip and heel form one straight line; elbow, hand and horse's mouth form another. The late Colonel Hans Handler, Director of the Spanish School at Vienna, wrote this: 'The torso is in a natural position but erect, the hips pressed slightly forward. This position of the spine ensures that the pelvis is tipped so that the weight of the body rests on the seat bones where there is almost no covering of muscle. The seat is broad, the buttocks open. The broader the base the better the balance.' Such a seat permits the back to be held in its natural curve. Used in conjunction with hand and leg, the seat/back then has a most powerful and effective influence upon the horse.

(Nonetheless, if the rider is to be in balance with his horse, i.e. with the bodyweight carried lightly over the centre of the horse's balance, where it causes the least possible interference to the movement, the choice of a saddle to assist in the maintenance of that position has to be given a lot of consideration.)

Additionally, the rider uses his weight on one seat bone or the other to cause a shift in his centre of gravity and that of the horse, reinforcing the rein and leg aids in turns, leg-yielding and so on.

Legs

Paramount in the interdependent combination of aids and regarded as the principal forward driving aid is the *leg*. It is, however, used in a variety of ways to communicate to the horse what is being asked of him. Used carefully, almost as a precision instrument, it speaks with the utmost clarity. Used carelessly, its potential to confuse is immeasurable.

It should be held still and in light contact with the horse's side so that the rider 'feels' the horse and, of course, the horse the rider. It is an essential contact between the two and perhaps the instruction that it should be *still*

is a trifle misleading. It should be still in the sense that it must not swing about irrelevantly, for that would cause confusion. In fact, although it has the appearance of being still, the effective leg is always moving, even when passive, in response to the movement of the horse's flank, for it, like the rest of the rider's body, has also to be supple. (I have a pair of excellent hunting boots made by a notable maker. As hunting boots they are well suited to their purpose, being made of very stout leather, able to withstand the onslaught of thorns and bramble and to protect the legs against blows from a swinging gate or even, on one occasion, a kick from an unruly horse. But I cannot school a horse in them because they are so heavy that I cannot feel him through the thick leather and therefore cannot communicate with him.)

Just as we develop the horse's vocabulary in respect of the spoken word so it is necessary to teach the language (or at least the alphabet) of the legs. Indeed, by not doing so we make a rod for our own backs and our efforts to teach even the elementary movements are made more difficult.

A horse will certainly learn to go forward from that *backward* kick of the legs which represents for far too many riders the whole sum of their leg vocabulary. He will even get the idea that he should increase his speed if the legs go on kicking, but anything more than that, the canter departs, the suppling work on two tracks and so on, become impossible – the vocabulary is exhausted.

To fulfil the function of the aids in the sequence of PREPARE, ACT, YIELD, the legs, in conjunction with the other aids, of course, prepare the horse by closing *inwards* as nearly 'on the girth' as possible. In fact the leg will either be at the rear edge of the girth or just behind that point. This is no more than a *smooth* momentary *inward* squeeze warning the horse that another signal is about to be made.

To go forward, or to go forward more energetically, the leg goes on in the same smooth inward squeeze at what we can call Point A, but is then moved forward very slightly against the lie of the coat. This inwards and forward rolling motion of the leg is quite easily acquired with a little application. It is more effective because it acts on the most sensitive part of the horse; it does not disturb the seat and it is more logical – why push backwards to go forwards?

The emphasis on the smoothness of the action is equally logical. An abrupt action of the leg produces a response of a corresponding quality, whereas a smooth aid results in a smooth movement.

What may happen if pressure is applied all the way down the leg is that the toe may turn slightly outwards, although by no means to a point where the back of the calf is brought into contact. The inside of the heel will then be in touch with the horse and if a spur is worn it too may come into contact, but it will only slide forward, disturbing the lie of the hair. It will not dig into the horse as is usually the case when spurred legs are applied in the backward kick.

Used in this way the spur (a blunt one) is absolutely humane. Obviously, one does not use spurs on a young horse in the very first stages of training, but thereafter they are a legitimate aid in obtaining a more refined response to the legs and far better than those bruising kicks.

Quite distinct from the inward forward push of the leg is its application when it is used to move the quarters or when it is held passively to resist an unwanted shift to one side or another. (Resistance to an unwanted movement is the fourth function of the aids.)

The leg is then taken back to a point (call it Point B) *behind* the girth and behind Point A, where it is applied in an inward squeeze. This is the only time, excepting when the leg goes even further to the rear in the flying changes at canter, in *piaffe* and *passage,* that the leg is taken backwards, so there is no likelihood of the horse being confused so long as we limit the leg's application to these two points.

There is a fourth point of contact in front of the girth which advanced riders may use to obtain more extension, but like the third point to the rear of the point controlling the quarters used in the advanced elevated paces, it is of no concern in the secondary training.

Hands

Modern riding and, alas, modern teaching lays great emphasis on contact with the mouth but precious little on good hands or even 'educated' ones. (There is a difference: good hands give as the horse takes and vice-versa; educated hands, on the educated horse, do just the opposite, but with some subtlety.)

Good, educated hands are quiet and their possession is only possible when the seat is to all intents independent of the reins. The connection between legs and horse is a delicate one, but that between the hands and the mouth, the most sensitive part of the horse, is even more so.

The hands receive the impulsion created by the legs. They act as regulators for the created energy, containing or releasing it to the required degree, or it is possible for the hands to re-channel that energy as when a rein is applied to block the surge of forward movement and redirect it to one side or the other. In very basic terms they combine, in conjunction with the legs, the functions of a brake and steering wheel.

Distil that definition still further and, whilst it remains essentially correct, we can say that the hands maintain in balance the forward movement of the horse – they are in the last analysis regulators of the balance.

The ultimate aim, the very Nirvana of the equestrian art and the aim of the French Masters, is when the reins, whilst regulating the balance, control entirely the direction of the movement, including the lateral work, whilst the legs supply the impulsion. That, too, is worlds beyond what we can expect to achieve with anything other than the very advanced horse, but it is a thought worth bearing in mind.

Of course, even in these advanced functions, the reins act as restraining aids in conjunction with the seat and legs which impel the horse forward. Like the legs they prepare, by a momentary closure of the fingers following the inward squeeze of the legs. They act, by the fingers opening to allow the horse to obey the request of the legs or, following once more the legs, they close to reduce the speed or to make downward transitions in the pace.

They control the direction of the horse by being applied in one or more of the FIVE REIN EFFECTS all of which contribute materially to the armoury of the serious rider and should be understood by those who undertake the training of young horses or seek to improve older ones.

The rider can be prepared physically by the exercises on the ground and on the lunge. But these physical skills are of no help in influencing the horse unless there is background of knowledge and an understanding of the theory involved.

Rein effects

There is an infinite variety of possible rein aids but five are generally recognised. They are these:

(1) The direct or opening rein.
(2) The indirect rein.
(3) The direct rein of opposition.
(4) The indirect rein of opposition *in front* of the withers.
(5) The indirect rein of opposition *behind* the withers.

The last one is frequently termed the *intermediary* or *intermediate* rein because it comes between the third and fourth effects by virtue of its acting on *both* shoulder and quarter. The third rein effect, on the other hand, shifts only the quarters, whilst the fourth

The five rein effects (from left): direct or opening rein; indirect rein; direct rein of opposition; indirect rein of opposition in front of the withers; indirect rein of opposition behind the withers.

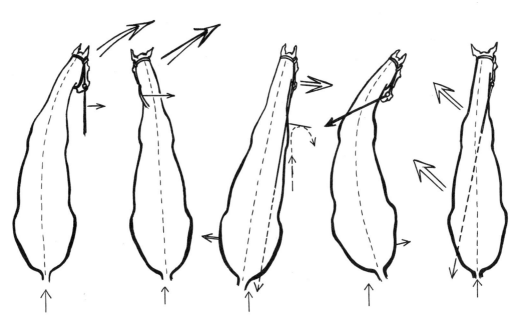

moves the shoulder.

The difference between *direct* and *indirect* reins is that the former act on the same side of the horse as the rein is applied; the latter influence the opposite side of the horse.

Reins of opposition, as the name implies, oppose the forward movement causing it to be redirected. The movement, as the diagram shows, may be re-channeled through the shoulder or the quarters or, in the fifth rein effect, through both.

The direct or opening rein is applied by the hand being carried slightly outwards in the direction of the movement required so that the rein is taken off the neck. It is used on turns and circles where the horse is bent to the inside i.e. when the horse's head and neck is aligned to the direction of the movement.

The indirect rein is really a neck rein. If, for instance, the left rein is applied in the indirect rein effect, the right shoulder is moved forward and to the right. It·is used in turns and elements of circles which require the bend to be to the outside as it is when teaching the turn on the forehand.

Direct rein of opposition. It opposes the forward movement on the side on which it is applied. If, for instance, the right rein is used in this effect the thrust from the quarters is blocked on the right side of the mouth. As a result the quarters are shifted to the left. It is used in the turn on the forehand and (with both reins) for the rein-back. The rein is frequently used, and perhaps unconsciously so far as its effect is concerned, in riding turns and circles. To use this rein for that purpose will inevitably cause the quarters to be moved outwards and out of the track made by the forefeet. To a degree this outward move of the quarters can be countered by the application of the rider's outside leg behind the girth, but this is really a contradiction of applied forces, the aids being used in opposition to each other.

The indirect rein of opposition in front of the withers moves the shoulders to the left when the right rein is applied and vice-versa. There is also a secondary movement of the quarters in the opposite direction. It can be used to turn the horse on the centre with outside bend.

The indirect rein of opposition behind the withers. In addition to being called the intermediate or intermediary rein this one is also referred to by the eulogistic title, the Queen of Reins. It moves the whole horse sideways and forwards by acting on the shoulders and quarters. It is used in leg-yielding and shoulder-in.

These reins can only be effective, of course, whilst there is ample and sustained impulsion. Without active forward movement there can be no result: the horse is, as it were, becalmed.

It is a great mistake and similarly non-productive to think that any one rein can be used in isolation. It has to be complemented and supported by the action of its partner so as to moderate or increase the action and must always be subordinate to the impulsion created by the legs.

Perhaps the greatest benefit the rider obtains by understanding the five rein effects is to be able to recognise when the reins are being used incorrectly or even in contradiction to the movement required. How many times do we see the rein crossed over the wither and effectively preventing the required movement as a result?

A lot of problems concerned with the hands are caused because of their being held incorrectly. For the hand to be soft the rein runs between the little and third finger and is passed over the index finger, being secured by the thumb. The thumb always remains on the top of the hand pointing towards the base of the horse's ear on the opposite side. The back of the hand should be in line with the forearm and never, ever should the fist be clenched. It there is tension in the hand there will be tension in the forearm, elbow, upper arm and the shoulder and all the way up to the head. From the horse's viewpoint there will be a corresponding tension in the mouth.

Hands may move upwards, downwards and sideways but never backwards. When the hand pulls, moving to the rear, the pace is immediately interrupted, the balance is affected and the stride shortened on the side on which the rein is applied.

The most common faults are for the hands to be held with 'broken' wrists, i.e. wrists turning outwards or inwards from the forearm, or held knuckles upwards as though riding a bicycle. In each case the forearm becomes stiff and tense. Hold your right forearm with the left hand and see how the muscles stiffen if the hand is held in any of those three positions.

A good way to check the hand position and to encourage it to be maintained is to ride with a cane held under the thumbs and across the body. The ends of the stick moving forward as the horse circles or changes direction are useful reminders of the way in which the hands are being used.

The school figures

The figures performed within the arena are the equivalent of the rider's physical exercises, increasing the strength and suppleness of the horse certainly, but also contributing materially to the overall balance and straightness.

They are based on the horse working on circles and elements of circles and they include exercises calling for transitions and the variations within a single pace which will improve the longitudinal suppleness of the horse. By that is meant the ability to lengthen and to shorten the outline and the base in response to driving aids creating impulsion which is either contained by the hand, to produce shortening, or released to produce lengthening.

The work on the circle leads ultimately to the *straight* horse and additional work towards that desirable end is described in more detail later in this chapter.

The lunge work on either rein acted as a preparation for riding the school figures. Lateral suppling was achieved by the stretching of the muscles on the outside of the body whilst those on the inside of the turn were contracted. The weight of the rider, however, presents an additional problem for the horse and although the trot is the most rewarding and suitable pace for the riding of these figures it should be preceded by some work at walk to accustom the horse to the pattern of these new exercises. (The trot compels full and even utilisation of the body, more so than either walk or canter. It is also easier for the horse to bend at this pace and then to straighten.)

The first of the school figures to be ridden is a full circuit of the manège. This will involve the execution of four quarter *voltes,* one at each corner of the arena. A *volte* is a small circle of determined size, a *circle* proper being of any size larger than that.

Academically, the radius of the volte is equal to the length of the horse. Taking that to be on average around 3 m, then the radius of the volte is the same and the diameter will be 6 m. To ride so small a circle in level balance (i.e. without the horse leaning over towards the centre) is *very* difficult and is by no means within the capability of horses in the secondary stage of schooling.

The quarter voltes are clearly less difficult, but they still require the horse to move on a 6 m bend and that too is well beyond a horse at this stage of training who will almost certainly be compelled to swing his quarters outwards.

It is easier for the horse if the corners are made rounder, so that the bend is the equivalent of a much larger circle of, say, 15 m. He should then be able to follow the track of the forefeet with the hind legs.

Corners should be thought of and ridden as elements of a circle, which is what they are, and not as distinct left or right *turns*.

Following the full circuits of the arena, we can ask for the simple changes of rein, the circles to either hand, the figure-of-eight using 20 m circles, and after those the changes through the circle and simple serpentines.

The longitudinal suppling exercises also begin on the full circuit of the manège and though they are simple enough they too have to be approached with care, since they involve shortened strides at sitting trot. If they are introduced too early in the training programme when the horse is insufficiently muscled up there is a danger of his being driven into resistance, stiffening his back to avoid the discomfort he experiences. These exercises are, therefore, best left until the young horse has been in work for three or four weeks.

The easiest exercise is to shorten the stride at the ends of the arena. The reverse exercise, shortening down the long side, is more difficult and it is only when the horse is absolutely comfortable in both these figures that one should attempt the 20 m circles and the change of hand which forms a figure-of-eight. (In an arena measuring 20 m × 40 m, two 20 m circles can be accommodated. In fact, of course, the horse describes something nearer to a 19 m circle since he has to work about half a metre from the wall.) Circles smaller than 20 m should not be attempted in trot until the horse has reached a more advanced stage of training and is in level balance.

To start riding 10 m circles too early puts so much strain on the horse that he is likely to resist the bend by 'falling' either in or out, that is he evades by carrying his quarters inside the track of the forefeet in the first instance and outside in the second. Either of these two failings are a sure indication that the horse is not ready for the exercise and is insufficiently supple to perform it. The answer lies not in persisting but in going back to the general strengthening process which will be realised by intelligently planned hacking sessions and by working on the lunge without the weight of the rider to inhibit either movement or balance.

(It is important to ensure that the arena markers are placed at the correct distances so that the rider is helped in riding accurately from one point to another. It is also helpful if circles can be marked with sawdust or something similar so as to familiarise riders with the sizes – 20 m circles can all too easily take on an undesirable ovoid character.)

Paces and school movements

Within this secondary schooling the aims include a refinement of the paces, brought about through an improvement in response, rhythm, impulsion and balance, and the teaching of the school movements which are fundamental to the horse's education.

Before beginning to work seriously on the circles it is necessary to have the young horse moving *forward* willingly and with sufficient energy to make it necessary to exert just a modicum of restraint. Additionally, we have to demand, increasingly, an improvement in the *rhythm,* and that will not come about until the horse accepts a steady, equal and very light contact with the hands.

This will remain a prime consideration throughout the horse's training but until we see signs of it being realised there is no point in working on more advanced figures and movements which may well make it more difficult to establish the basic requirements.

Young horses and even older ones will sometimes give the feeling of holding back rather than making an immediate response to the legs. It may be an attempt to assert themselves. It can arise as a result of irritation or resentment, or out of plain old-fashioned laziness. If the horse is stiff from overwork or because of some physical weakness he will certainly be reluctant to comply with the requests being made of him. That situation should not arise if we are observant and careful in our management of the horse. If it does the horse has to be rested and put on a lighter work programme, with all the loss of time and continuity that entails.

Otherwise, we have to take action to correct the failing. We dare not allow the horse to get into the habit of disregarding the aids and as the schooling progresses we have to be ever more demanding in this respect.

If there is no answer to the leg aid, or if the response is delayed, don't repeat the aid but use the whip in a couple of firm taps behind the leg. If that fails then the spur must be brought into play, but only sufficiently to make him aware of its presence. By employing the aids in this sequence, each being a degree more imperative, but hardly more severe, than the preceding one, we can in time obtain a more instant response to an ever lighter leg aid.

With the lazy horse there is a greater degree of difficulty. The temptation is to wake him up with a sharp cut of the whip or by a stronger application of the spurs. It may work in some instances, but we run the risk of the horse becoming resentful, particularly in respect of the spurs. Resentment of the latter can just as easily become habitual as disobedience and that could place a serious limitation on the horse's future performance.

There is, of course, no cut-and-dried answer. It all comes down to the individual horse and how developed is the 'feel' of the rider.

A skilful, positive trainer may get over the problem from the ground by working both horse and rider through the medium of his voice and, if it is not too pie-in-the-sky, the projection of his personality supported, ever so tactfully, by the material presence of a lunge whip.

Without doubt, there has to be a more demanding use of the aids. Many lazy horses respond to a slap down the shoulder with the long whip combined with a sharp click of the tongue. In other cases, an increase in the energy content of the food ration will be helpful. Again there can be no more than a rule-of-thumb guide, but if the heating element is increased until the horse is a little too bright for comfort – a condition best and more safely ascertained by his behaviour on the lunge – it can then be reduced to produce an acceptable level of energy. Far more 'lazy' horses than one would imagine could, indeed, be made more forward-going as a result of an increase in their ration of energising foods than by the more positive application of legs, whip and spur.

Another practical, if less than purist solution, to the lazy horse, so long as you are well attuned to the character of your pupil, is to take the reins in one hand allowing them to loop a little; the legs are then applied and almost simultaneously one delivers a sharp reminder with the whip with the free hand and behind the leg. The horse will most probably bound forward, hence the need for that looping rein, but he may well have learnt his lesson.

The object is to produce forward movement *with enthusiasm*; it is not sufficient for the horse to go forward in a quiet, lack-lustre style. The ideal is for the horse to go forward energetically enough for the rider to need to apply a little restraint.

Thereafter, the aim is to establish a steady, regular rhythm in the paces. In plain words we shall seek to maintain the correct order of the footfalls in each pace – four distinct, equally spaced beats at walk, two at trot, three at canter.

The flow from one step to the next is smooth and the regularity of the beat even. Both rider and horse will benefit if the schooling sessions can be accompanied by some judiciously chosen music. Modern recorders are so small that they can easily be carried by the rider if outside assistance is not

A pleasing walk by Julie Hughes and the four-year-old Welsh cob cross, Friar Tuck.

available.

The essence of rhythmical movement is in going no faster – in fact just a shade slower – than the speed at which the horse can maintain his balance. If the horse is pushed into going above the speed at which he is comfortable the quality of the pace deteriorates and the strides become shorter and more hurried.

Inherent to rhythmical movement is the contact between bit and hands.

The principle involved is concerned with the legs pushing the horse forward whilst the hands gradually take up a level contact. The horse has then to work within the frame dictated by legs at one end and hands at the other. The frame, however, cannot and must not be rigid for that would imply constriction and restriction. At all times the hands follow the movement of the head, maintaining the contact even, and particularly, when the horse seeks to evade it by shortening his neck, retracting the nose, opening the mouth and so

on. The horse then begins to learn and to accept that contact is constant, unescapable and even comforting.

Whatever happens, contact must not be maintained by the hands moving back to pull. If the horse reduces, by one means or another, the degree of contact he has to be made to retake it by the rider's legs pushing him forward more energetically, whilst not allowing any increase in the speed of the pace.

The circles

The introduction to the circle is the quarter *volte* which has to be performed in describing the full circuit of the arena.

When riding on a straight line it is comparatively easy to keep the horse in level balance.

The trot showing an excellent bend with the horse relaxing well in the lower jaw.

Changes of direction, however, be they ever so gradual, upset the balance. This imbalance, in turn, results in a loss of impulsion, and an interruption to the rhythm of the pace.

The secret in riding the quarter *volte* and therefore when entering the whole circle is to create more impulsion – that is, the energy created in the hind legs and controlled and directed by the hands. It involves an increased use of the legs combined with a slightly firmer contact but no increase in speed. As the curve is entered emphasis is given to the inside leg, the inside rein is opened slightly by the hand moving outwards and the outside rein is lengthened by the advance of the outside hand, elbow and shoulder *and* the outside hip.

The philosophy is that of riding from the *inside* leg to the *outside* hand and is one which necessitates the rejection of some pretty sacred cows.

Deeply entrenched by continual repetition, both in the written word and in actual instruction, is the time-honoured formula relating to the changes of direction.

The instruction given is for the rider to *act* with the inside rein, supporting it with the outside hand. Action entails the use of the *direct rein of opposition*, the third rein effect. *Support* should mean that the outside rein cedes, or is 'given', to allow the inside bend. I suspect, however, that in reality 'support' means just that: the acting hand operating against a base provided by the outside, supporting hand and thus restricting the movement quite hopelessly.

The manuals, having, it is true, urged the use of the inside leg to provide impulsion, ask for the outside (*supporting*) leg to act behind

Wonderfully active extension in trot with the horse in the correct balance.

the girth so as to prevent the quarters swinging out and off the track of the forefeet.

The truth is that it is the opposing action of the direct rein which causes the quarters to swing outwards. Hand and leg are therefore at cross-purposes, the action of the former being opposed by the latter. The hand has created an unwanted movement which the leg seeks to rectify. It is hardly logical and is surely an unnecessary difficulty for both horse and rider.

To a degree it is probable that even with the employment of the opening rein the quarters will tend to shift a little to the outside and that movement will need to be countered by the outside leg, but there is no need to exaggerate the problem by an incorrect and restrictive use of the rein.

Half-halt

The use of the aids to *prepare* the horse for a subsequent request is in effect a half-halt, but it can be carried further with much advantage.

Essentially, the half-halt acts to re-impose the balance within any pace. It causes the horse to make use of his quarters and to lighten his forehand. He is then in a posture from which he is well able to make a subsequent movement.

To make the half-halt the rider increases the influence of the back, seat and legs, the inside leg predominating, to drive the horse forward, even to the extent of bringing the shoulders slightly to the rear of the hips. Almost, but not quite simultaneously, the hands are raised and the fingers closed to prevent any increase in speed. As a result, the hind legs are compelled to engage further under the body and, since the forehand has been subjected to the restraining lift of the hands, it will be raised and lightened.

The danger lies in the hands being brought to the rear in a backward pull. To avoid this the rider has to think of them moving on an arc pivoting on the mouth, the action being upwards and forwards rather than otherwise and then descending smoothly on the same arc.

The half-halt is only as effective, however, as the response made to the legs. Unless the horse goes forward immediately from the leg the second part of the operation, the raising of the closing hands, achieves nothing since it depends upon the movement from the leg.

If there is a failing in impulsion the action of the hands does nothing more than shorten the neck and force the back to hollow. There can be no question of rebalancing the body mass.

For the horse to benefit from the half-halt it needs to be practised continually during the schooling session, up to half a dozen times, indeed, for every circuit made of the arena –

Good position at halt. The horse is balanced, attentive and looks happy.

and that is hard work for the horse but far more demanding of the rider.

Halt

The half-halt will, of course, prepare the horse for the full halt, which is a defined movement and, indeed, it may be preceded by a couple of discreet half-halts.

The halt itself is then no more than an extension of the latter, the restraining aids being applied a little more strongly until the horse stops. It is, however, important to keep the legs on the horse when the rein is relaxed (not 'given') so that the halt is made correctly. They may thereafter be *relaxed* but not to the point where all pressure is removed.

The usual failing in the halt is for the horse to trail a hind leg, which can be felt from the saddle as that side will be lowered. To correct this, the rider squeezes forward from a little

behind the girth with the leg on the side of the errant hind leg to bring it forward as a result of the contraction of the stomach muscles. A foreleg too far under the body can be corrected by easing the rein on that side and giving a little push with the corresponding leg.

If the horse halts badly it is never any good trying to correct him at that juncture; instead ride forward and try again.

If the horse has been accustomed to halting squarely in-hand and on the lunge and then confirmed in the half-halt, the halt itself should not be a difficulty.

Turn on the forehand

This is a movement to which the horse has already been accustomed by those early lessons in the stable when he was taught to 'move over' and there should be no difficulty

The aid applied. (a) Aids for half-pass; (b) for the turn on the quarters; (c) for the turn on the forehand; (d) for the leg-yield.

in teaching him to move his quarters round the pivot of his forehand from the saddle.

This turn on the forehand is not natural to the horse. Very occasionally a startled horse at liberty may perform something approaching a turn on the quarters, when the forehand turns round the pivot provided by the latter, but never will he turn on his forehand. The natural way for the horse to turn is on his centre when he moves his four legs round the vertical axis at the girth.

Nonetheless, in the schooling of the horse this unnatural turn is of enormous importance. Indeed, the turns on the forehand and quarters mark the watershed between the partially schooled horse and the trained one.

The reasons for teaching this turn are these:

(1) When the horse moves his quarters either to left or right in response to the action of a single leg he is compelled to lift and cross the hind legs. It is, therefore, possible to supple and strengthen each hind leg individually, improving the joint flexion and also increasing the power of the all-important loin on which all movement

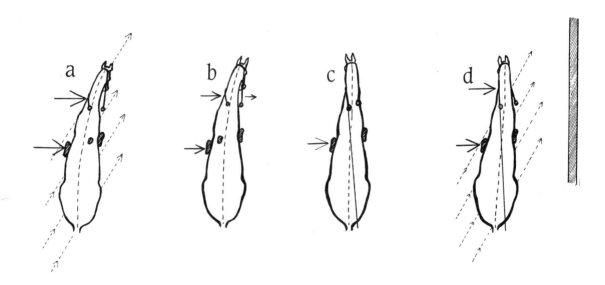

must be based.

(2) Once the rider has the ability to move the quarters at will it follows that he is also able to prevent any *unwanted* shift. He is, therefore, by being in control of the quarter, equipped to *straighten* his horse.

(3) The turn which gives us mobility of the quarters also gives us mobility of the jaw, and thus the ability to obtain flexions on either side of his mouth. (There is therefore a beneficial influence extending through the horse from the mouth to the loins and the hind legs.)

(4) It represents the essential introduction to lateral work.

(5) It is quite impossible to open a gate with any degree of competence unless the horse is capable of performing a turn on the forehand.

As a start the horse can be taught to shift his quarters from a tapping whip applied behind the girth whilst the trainer stands at his head. Within two days one should be able to walk the horse forward (for the turn is just as much concerned with forward movement as anything else), the trainer necessarily walking backwards and leading him from his bridle. One then checks the horse and moves the quarters over with a touch of the whip. It is, of course, essential to practise the movement in both directions.

When the horse is ready to attempt the turn under saddle the rider needs to be very clear in his mind about the aids he is going to apply. An incorrect combination of rein and leg will confuse the horse, whilst any contradictory requests made through the aids will very effectively prohibit the execution of the movement.

The turn is approached from walk, the horse being checked (half-halt) before being brought to halt. If the quarters are to be moved to the right the left leg is placed flat well behind the girth and is pushed inwards. (Avoid at all costs the digging heel and turned

out toe which might disturb the horse's composure.) The right leg is held ready in case it is necessary to limit any excessive movement.

In concert with the left leg we use the left rein in the fifth effect, i.e. the indirect rein of opposition (to the haunches) behind the wither, placing the rein (without pulling backwards) carefully towards the right hip, whilst easing the right rein to permit the head to turn slightly to the left. Both hand and leg act simultaneously and intermittently. The intermittent use of the aids is far more persuasive than an unbroken pressure and less likely to disturb the horse.

To increase the mobility and to carry the horse a stage further the turn (through 180°) can be practised from the *reversed half volte*, a ponderous title for a very simple movement. It involves riding off the track and returning to it and, therefore, turning about, by means of a 6 m circle. As the circle is entered the same aids are applied, following a slight half-halt, and the horse takes his quarters round his forehand to return to the track.

Leg-yielding

This is the first of the lateral suppling exercises and the obvious follow-on from the forehand turn. It imposes no strain on the horse and is very easy for him to perform, since we are not asking that he should bend his body.

The horse is now well used to the lateral aids which have been applied in the forehand turn. The same aids are now applied to move the whole body to the side away from the pressure of the rider's leg.

The exercise begins in walk and we should take advantage of the inside track, that is a track some 2 m inside the perimeter of the

(a) Half-turn on the quarters; (b) half-turn on the forehand; (c) position of horse in shallow shoulder-in.

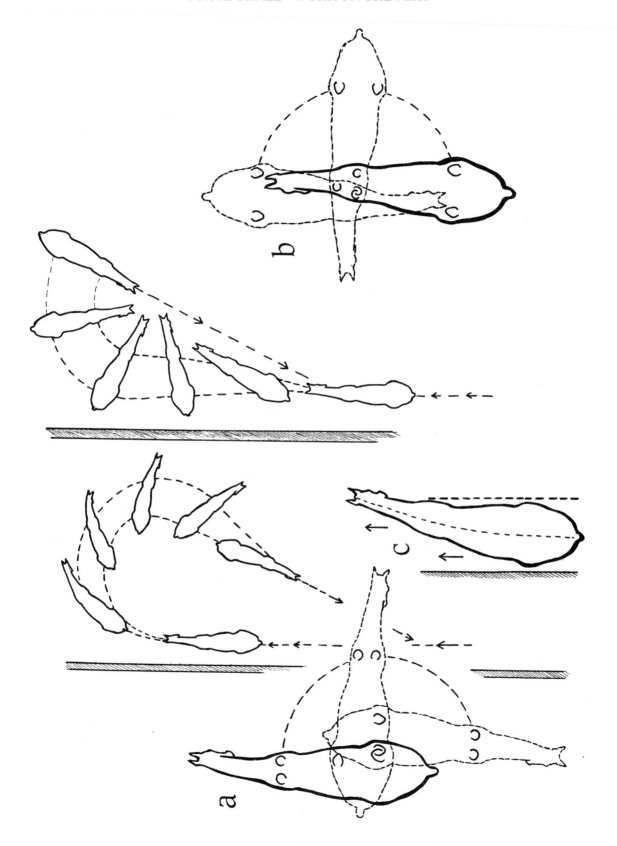

arena and parallel to it. Put on this new circuit, the horse, being a creature of habit and always happy to return to the familiar, will be willing and even anxious to move outward in order to take up the original track.

With the horse moving in an active walk the lateral aids are applied on the long sides to move the horse sideways onto the track. If we are moving to the left (right leg, right indirect rein of opposition) the supporting hand (the left one) is carried slightly outwards to emphasise the direction in which we want the horse to move. Additionally it supports the right rein by preventing the bit from being pulled through the mouth and it checks any tendency for the neck to be bent more than a shade to the right. Only a slight flexion to the right is needed. We use the left leg to maintain the impulsion and, if necessary, to control any excess movement.

Leg-yielding can not only be practised in the schooling arena, but also on the lanes when out hacking, the horse being moved into and away from the side of the roadway.

Within a week or so the horse should be able to yield in either direction from trot and to do so without interrupting the rhythm.

The only real difficulties that may occur in the leg-yielding exercise are those which may arise because of the rider exaggerating the movement and producing a sort of false shoulder-in with far too much bend in the neck. For this reason do not attempt the leg-yielding exercise on the outside track when it is only possible to produce a travesty of the shoulder-in.

Shoulder-in

This exercise, first practised by the eighteenth-century French Master de la Guérinière, has been described as the ultimate suppling exercise. It is certainly that, but also, once perfected it gives the rider a very

Leg-yield to the left.

high degree of control over his horse and it leads to both straightness and collection. It is valueless if done incorrectly so the rider must understand what the shoulder-in seeks to accomplish and then be absolutely clear about the execution of the exercise.

The ideal is for the horse to be 'bent' round the inside leg of the rider, the quarters square in relation to the wall and moving parallel to it. The hips, therefore, are virtually at right angles to the wall. The head and neck is to be inclined slightly away from the movement, which is led by the outside shoulder. 'The inside foreleg passes and crosses in front of the outside leg and the inside hind leg is placed in front of the outside leg.' That is the official definition of the FEI and can hardly be bettered.

The shoulder-in becomes a path leading to collection because of the increased engagement of the inside hind leg under the body. This is facilitated by the increased freedom of the diagonal partner, the outside foreleg, as a result of the shoulder being 'opened' by the inward inclination of neck and head. Furthermore, if the position is correct, the inside hip has to be lowered and that in itself contributes to a greater engagement of the leg and, of course an increase in the flexion of the leg's three joints.

The classical shoulder-in is, in the opinion of some authorities, a movement on three tracks. However it can be on four tracks and still be correct. It all depends on the degree of the bend.

Shoulder-in is ridden off a circle, so if we approach the exercise from a 20 m circle with the horse correctly bent to correspond with a circle of that diameter, the curve will be too shallow to produce a three-track movement. If the quarters are held square, as they should be, the movement will be on four overlapping tracks. A little more bend on a 10 m circle will result in a three-track movement but we cannot expect that from a young horse who will be insufficiently supple at this stage of training.

The advanced horse who can be ridden through the corners in a true quarter volte, i.e. on a 6 m bend, will produce a four-track movement as a result, if the 6 m bend is held as it should be.

In both instances it is only the forelegs which are actually crossed.

Unhappily this is not always understood and one frequently sees riders deliberately attempting to produce a movement in which both legs cross and in which the quarters are not as a result held square. That is not shoulder-in. If it is anything it is a kind of exaggerated leg-yield and is of no gymnastic value.

The pace for shoulder-in is the trot, in which greater impulsion can be obtained, but initially the movement is best attempted from walk, which is easier for both horse and rider and is less likely to be confusing.

To begin, ride a 20 m circle. It will, in fact, be about 19 m and if it can be reduced comfortably to 18 m that will be even better. However, it must be a very good circle and the rider has to ride positively from active inside leg to the outside hand. When it is established we can begin shoulder-in between the quarter and half markers. The optimum moment is when the quarters are in line with the quarter marker and the horse is bent to continue on the circle.

In fact, it can be said to begin a stride or so before that when the head is in line with the marker. At that point we demand the horse's attention by a light half-halt and then, in simple terms, we ask the horse to move down the long side whilst the bend is maintained.

When the horse can execute the movement easily at walk *and to both left and right* the shoulder-in can be ridden from trot to the point where it can be approached from a 15 m or, better still, a 10 m circle, although the

A good effort by a young horse in the shoulder-in exercise. No more than this is necessary at this stage in the training.

latter cannot be expected until the closing stages of the four-year-old's training and, indeed, probably not until the following year.

Aids for shoulder-in

The inside leg acts actively on the girth in the prescribed rear-to-front motion to push the outside shoulder along the track. The outside leg is held behind the girth to stop any twisting or falling-out of the quarters. However, should there be any failing in impulsion it must be used to reinforce its partner.

The rider's weight is concentrated more on the inside seat bone than otherwise, by the leg being stretched and the foot pressing into the stirrup. This shift of the balance to the inside accords with the horse's position and encourages the sideways movement.

The inside rein acts behind the withers in the fifth rein effect, whilst the outside rein opens slightly to indicate the required direction in the initial steps. Thereafter it acts to support its partner in holding the bend in the neck. Both hands have to be carried to the outside without the inner hand crossing the wither.

The temptation is to lead the movement with the outside hip and allow the inside leg to be held behind rather than on the girth. That will only result in the quarters moving out of their square position and becoming twisted.

The rider has, instead, to keep his hips aligned to those of the horse *but* his shoulders must turn to the *inside* to follow the movement and remain in parallel to those of the horse.

This is a paramount consideration and it emphasises the need to have a full understanding of the movement, the rein aids and the positioning of the body in relation to that of the horse. The rider has to conform to the movement of the horse in relation, particularly, to hips and shoulders. Secondly, he must ride with his mind as well as his body.

If the horse should display hesitancy in his

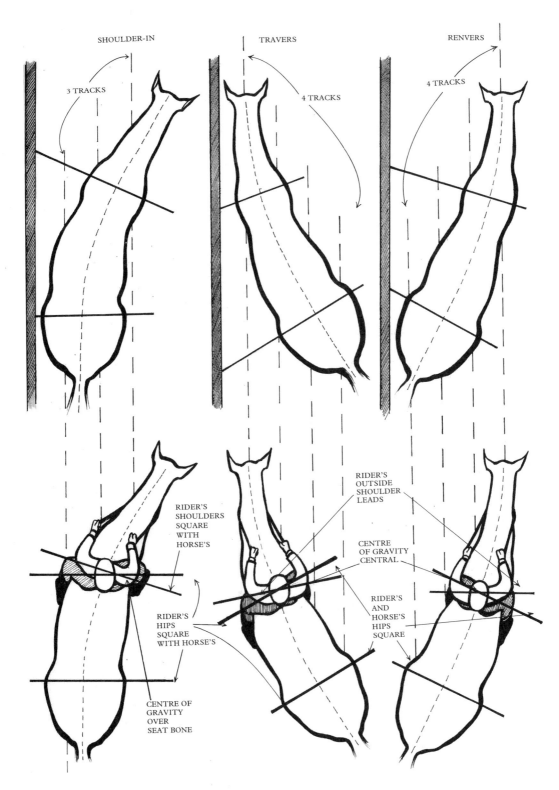

From left to right: shoulder-in, travers and renvers.

progress down the long side in the shoulder-in position he can be helped by the inside rein being laid on his neck and used in a raising, slightly pushing, movement in time with the lifting and sideways movement of the inside foreleg.

The shoulder-in position is maintained for the strides between the point of departure from the circle and the corresponding point between the half and quarter markers at the further end of the long side, when the horse, in the same bend, resumes the circle at the opposite end of the arena.

Travers – renvers – half-pass

It is possible to teach the half-pass, an uncompromising four-track movement, from the shoulder-in, but it is far more easily approached from the exercise known as *travers*, which is also called *head to the wall* or *quarters-in*, and is another four-track movement.

Once more it is approached from the circle but now the bend is towards the movement. It begins at the moment the neck and shoulders become virtually parallel to the wall, the exact opposite of the shoulder-in movement. The forehand then proceeds directly on the track, the quarters are bent inwards and the hind legs cross.

The rider holds this bend and maintains the forward movement by the inside leg acting on the girth as in the shoulder-in. The outside leg is held *flat* on the horse and behind the girth. The hands are carried to the inside without the outside one crossing the withers. The outside hand predominates and acts in conjunction with the inside leg. The rider's outside shoulder is well forward but the seat is otherwise held centrally.

Renvers, *tail-to-the-wall* or *quarters-out* is the reverse movement and in this the horse becomes independent of the guiding wall.

In *half-pass* the horse moves obliquely forward, slightly bent round the rider's inside leg and with the head inclined towards the direction of the movement. It is approached from the circle and the object is to move forwards and sideways with the horse's body as nearly parallel to the long side of the manège as possible. The outside legs pass and cross over the inside ones.

The rider's weight is on the inside seat bone; the inside hand is opened a little, the thumb pointing in the direction of the movement. The outside rein supports by being on the neck. The outside leg is laid flat on the horse behind the girth to push the horse both forwards and sideways, whilst the inside one is acting on the girth.

All these movements are best commenced in walk before being attempted in trot.

Ramener

This is a French term describing the carriage of the head, and involves the horse being on the bit, the jaw and poll being flexed and relaxed, the head close to the vertical with the poll at the apex. This high carriage is brought about, or it should be brought about, by the *advance of the body towards the head*, the horse being pushed up to gently resisting hands in accordance with the classic precept of riding from the back to the front.

In theory it is not a matter of difficulty, in practice it can be just the reverse, with the horse avoiding the assumption of this position in all sorts of ways. He can, for instance, drop the bit or swing his quarters off the line so that we cannot obtain the necessary engagement of the quarters and the impulsion which we need.

Nonetheless, it has to come about and the longer it is delayed the more difficult it will be to accomplish, for the muscles of the neck and gullet will have stiffened and become inflexible. At first the rider has to be satisfied if the horse works within this shortened frame for a few strides and then, in time, for a few minutes. When the horse moves in the

frame without resistance he has to be rewarded with a pat and a short period of
relaxation before he is asked to shorten again.

Properly done the top-line is tautened and
the horse is shortened both at the base and
top by the increased engagement of the
quarters. But that can only come about as a
result of a back which is free and that in turn
depends upon the poll and jaw being flexed
and supple.

The danger lies in riders seeking to impose
a carriage either by retreating hands or the
employment of some forceful gadget. All that
is then obtained is a semblance of *ramener*
which lacks the essential requirements of
engaged quarters and a free back.

Half turn on the quarters – demi-pirouette

This difficult movement should not be
attempted until the horse has acquired an
acceptable carriage and is capable, as a result,
of lightening his forehand and carrying the
weight over the quarters.
The purpose of the turn is:

(1) To eradicate still further the resistance to
be found in the quarters by increasing
our control over them. In this instance
they have to be held in place to prevent
the horse turning on his centre.

(2) To supple the shoulders in the same way
that the forehand turn suppled the
quarters.

(3) To rebalance the horse by lightening the
forehand. The forehand turn lightened
the quarters in similar fashion and both
therefore contribute to the overall
balance.

From an established walk the turn is preceded by a half-halt. If we wish to make the
turn from left to right the right rein is opened
to lead the horse round; the left rein supports
and is laid against the neck preventing too

much movement forward and limiting the
bend of the neck. Both hands are carried to
the right.

The left leg, held back, prevents the
quarters slipping away to that side whilst the
right leg controls the turn and, with a little
help from its neighbour, maintains the impulsion. By far the most powerful incentive,
however, is for the rider to place the weight
on the outside seat bone so as to push the
horse over in the required direction.

Ideally, the forefeet and the outside hind
foot will move on the pivot of the inside hind
leg.

A useful way of obtaining the turn is from a
half-volte (just as the forehand turn can be
obtained from the reverse half-volte). The
half-volte is progressively decreased in size
until it becomes a turn on the quarters and
does so without endangering the forward
impulse.

Canter

Whilst out hacking in this secondary stage
the horse will have been encouraged to canter
quietly but with no particular regard for a
strike-off being made on a particular lead.
During the school work he has now to learn
about striking off on one leg or the other
dependent upon the direction in which he is
circling the school.

He will, indeed, have been prepared pretty
well by the lunge work and those lunge
lessons in the canter strike-offs should be
repeated before the canter is attempted under
saddle. The trainer can then support the
rider's aids with the vocal command, and
there's the rub. What aids are to be used?

Once more, as in so much of equitational
theory and practice, there is no overall uniformity of opinion.

It would, of course, be perfectly possible to
teach the horse to strike off by pulling his
mane, pinching his wither or whatever, but
that would hardly be fair for any subsequent

owner of the horse and in the show ring might cause difficulties for judges.

The sequence of footfalls at canter begins with one or other of the hind legs. In canter left it would be the right or off-side hind leg, followed by the right diagonal (i.e. right fore and left hind) and then after a moment of suspension the third beat is made by the leading leg, the left fore.

There can, of course, be no disagreement about that, but there is sufficient variety in the aids recommended by those who have committed themselves to the written word to cause understandable confusion in the less than highly expert. It all hinges on the horse being straight when making the strike-off, and the lack of uniformity, I believe, is because a tendency towards being unstraight can be countered in several ways.

The basic instruction given at riding schools all over the world is to sit at trot when in the approach to the corner of the school and then, at the optimum point of the bend, to act with the inside rein and the outside leg, the two being supported by their opposite numbers.

This works, but there are one or two in-built disadvantages, not least the action of the outside leg which, if applied too strongly, pushes the horse into unstraightness, although it does, of course, activate the out-side hind leg, which is first in the sequence of footfalls.

After many years, in which I have been as confused as most, I have at last settled on an aid sequence which satisfies me in respect of the logic behind it. It is not difficult to accomplish by a rider of reasonable proficiency and, most importantly, horses at this stage of training find it easy to understand and respond without difficulty.

In my book, therefore, we trot into the corner, straightening the horse if need be, by using an active outside leg and an inside leg which presses inwards. The trot strides are shortened; the rider stretches the inside leg to

put more weight on the inside seat bone and immediately prior to the optimum point of the bend gives a warning upward tweak on the inside rein whilst the outside leg is slid to the rear and held flat and lightly on the horse's side. This, too, is a warning and, of course, a way of keeping the quarters in place.

The executive command comes from a distinct forward push on the girth from the inside leg made at the optimum point of the bend and a fraction of a second after the warning aids. In time this aid sequence can be refined to a point where legs and hands are used almost imperceptibly.

Initially, the horse should be allowed to canter for just a few strides and then brought back to trot. It will take time to canter the full circuit of the arena and even more time before 20 m circles can be ridden in anything like a state of balance. The strike-off should be established on one lead before the horse is asked to operate on the other. To alternate the leads in the early lessons only produces confusion.

Of course, the horse will be helped enormously by the rider who sits in balance and is able to adjust his seat to conform with the movement. In the canter pace, for instance, the horse will carry his inside shoulder and hip somewhat in advance of the outside ones – with the off-fore leading the right shoulder and hip will be in front of the left. To remain in balance with the horse the rider conforms to this arrangement by slightly advancing the corresponding seat bone, the right one on the canter right and vice-versa. Much later in the training this positioning of the hip bones becomes an aid in itself as in the change of leading leg.

Towards the end of this secondary period it should be possible to make a simple change of rein at canter, the horse coming back to trot for a few paces in the centre of the arena before being asked to strike off on the opposite leg. It will, of course, be much facilitated if the rider's aids have followed a consistent form on the lines indicated.

Straightening

The early precautions taken to prevent the horse becoming one-sided, the method of lungeing, etc., all contribute significantly to improving the performance in this respect.

Nonetheless, horses will continue throughout their training (and sometimes throughout their lives) to have a stiff side which, after all, is the reason for their being more or less unstraight. Human beings are not that different, being either right- or left-handed. It is very rare to find someone who is completely ambidextrous.

A prime consideration in the training of the horse is concerned with this matter of straightness and we seek to achieve it through exercises like shoulder-in. But before we reach that point, and after, we need to be constantly concerned with straightening the horse in every stage of the school exercises. For that reason we need to have a general appreciation of what constitutes crookedness and of the techniques employed to eliminate it.

In almost every instance the problem is with the off-hind. Most horses have difficulty in engaging and flexing that leg in comparison with its partner and they may often put the foot down outside and thus to the right of the track made by the corresponding forefoot.

The resulting stiff side causes the horse to lean on the opposite rein and against the rider's leg on that side.

There is no point in trying to force the horse into bending the stiff side. He will only respond with an increased resistance because of the discomfort. Nor is it any use trying to correct the situation at halt or walk. One has to work at a good active trot, giving and taking with the rein on the stiff side, the hand acting as though it were squeezing a rubber ball. The opposite rein is held in support, whilst the right leg is active in asking for engagement of the off-hind.

Work on turns and circles, opening the stiff rein and directing it towards the hip, and then ride circles with the hands in even contact so that the horse describes the circle in the *wrong* bend. This is uncomfortable for the horse and should not therefore be overdone, but because it is uncomfortable he will, after only a few circles, slowly begin to give on the stiff side and accept the outside rein.

In the school figures the horse can be straightened after passing through the corners if his shoulder is kept away from the wall or the outside of the arena. It is done by moving the inside hand a little to the side and laying the outside rein lightly on the neck.

Rein-back

This much misunderstood movement should be left alone until the horse is more advanced in his training at the end of the secondary stage. Nothing is less edifying than seeing a horse, or a pony ridden by a largely untutored child, hauled backwards by brute force.

The horse can be prepared for the movement in the stable and in-hand but before attempting it under saddle the square halt has to be established and the suppleness and flexibility of the joints increased.

The easy way is to bring the horse to halt square and on the bit with poll and lower jaw flexed and relaxed – that is a prerequisite of the movement. The legs are put on in the aid asking the horse to step forward in walk and as the horse begins his response the hands close on the reins (in the third effect, the direct rein of opposition). To ensure that the hands do not move *back* to *pull*, the elbows should be closed into the sides. The voice, which the horse understands, can also be used and it is helpful if the seat is lightened. When the horse obeys the aids by going back we can release the pressure of the legs whilst keeping them in place.

After two or three steps at the most, the legs are applied again and the hands open to permit the horse to move off in walk. It is an exercise which horses find difficult and there is never any need to ask for more than five or six steps even when the horse is adept at moving back in a straight line.

If the rein-back is overdone or forced the horse stiffens in the back, even hollowing it, and moves his quarters sideways.

Should the horse not at first understand that he is to move backwards, ride forward and then start again. If necessary, have an assistant tap his front lightly, to emphasise still further what is wanted of him.

(It is possible, and is often advocated, to apply the reins alternately, but whilst effective it can be a little more difficult for the rider. If it is not done with some sensitivity the horse, too, may become a little alarmed and resist the aids.)

The rein-back, with the horse moving correctly in two-time. The rider has lightened her seat to facilitate the movement.

10

Stage 4 –Jumping and Cross-country Riding

THE OBJECTIVE at the end of the third stage, so far as the jumping schooling is concerned, is to produce a free-going horse who is well able to jump a variety of small fences, up to 4 ft (1.2 m) in height and/or width, confidently and with a notable gymnastic quality.

The work on the flat, carried on in this stage in parallel with the jumping training, provides the foundation for the jumping exercises. Properly executed, the school movements prepare the horse in the best possible way. The work develops, supples and balances the horse; it ensures a willing obedience and submission and it increases the rider's control.

All these factors contribute materially to the horse's gymnastic ability and, therefore, to his subsequent performance over fences.

So long as they are not overjumped or overfaced, the majority of horses enjoy jumping and seem to regard it as relaxation after the frequently demanding school work. There are the occasional horses who are not entirely enthusiastic about jumping but ones that steadfastly refuse to leave the ground are rare.

Almost every horse can be taught by progressive exercises to jump fences up to the standard we set in the secondary stage.

The first two weeks or so of Stage 3 are devoted to recapitulating the pole grid and lunge jumping exercises which were done in the previous stage and then extending those early lessons. It should be possible after a fortnight to jump the horse on the lunge over a 3 ft (90 cm) upright fence and over a parallel with a 4 ft (1.2 m) spread. It is not, however, necessary to make the latter a true parallel; it is easier for the horse if the second element is placed 6 ins (15 cm) higher than the first to give something of a staircase effect. In both cases provide a ground-line and a distance pole, or cavalletto at lowest height, placed 10 ft (3 m) in front of the fence. The latter prevents rushing and assists the horse to judge the approach and take-off more accur-

ately.

The fences should be jumped out of trot and from both directions. On landing the horse may make a few strides at canter, which is of no consequence, but he must then be asked to return to trot and then to walk before he jumps another fence.

Jumping on the lunge has every possible advantage but it can produce a problem unless the trainer is adept in the use of the rein and appreciates how easily inexpert or unthinking use of the lunge in these circumstances can encourage a most undesirable habit – that of jumping to the left or right.

The horse must jump the fence from a straight approach and continue for a few strides after landing on the same line. He must not be jumped on the arc of a circle with his head and body inclined towards the trainer's hand by the rein, otherwise he is being taught to jump to one side or the other.

To avoid that happening the trainer has to move parallel to the horse, not asking him to return to the circle until a few strides after landing.

Lunge and/or mounted jumping lessons can be practised daily for a period of about 30 minutes.

A particular benefit to be derived from lungeing over fences is the opportunity it affords the rider to study the attitude of the horse in the phases of the jump. These are regarded as being TAKE-OFF, FLIGHT and LANDING, with the possible addition at either end of the spectrum of the APPROACH and GETAWAY strides.

The ideal which should be imprinted on the rider's mind is that *if a position is maintained in which the rider sits in balance with the horse and, therefore, without interference to the movement, the outline in each of the phases should not differ from that assumed when the horse is jumping free.*

An analysis of the phases shows the horse raising the head in the *approach*, in order to focus on the fence and to judge the take-off, and bringing the hind legs under the body preparatory to entering the next phase.

At the point of *take-off* the hind legs are brought further under the body whilst the forelegs lift upward the forepart of the body, an action necessarily accompanied by the raising of the head and neck. Finally, the engaged quarters thrust powerfully upwards, propelling the horse into the *flight* phase, when head and neck are extended and the forelegs tucked up. Almost simultaneously the horse forms an arc over the fence with the back rounded and head and neck at full stretch.

On *landing*, the forelegs are outstretched and the feet meet the ground one after another. For a split second, therefore, the horse's weight is carried on one foot.

In order to adjust the balance, re-distributing the weight carried over the forehand, the head and neck, acting as the balancing agents for the body mass, are raised. When the hind legs touch down the head and neck are lowered and the horse goes into the *getaway*

stride.

Should the rider hinder or unbalance the horse, either by the disposition of the body-weight or the limiting action of the hand, at any point during the leap the outline will be altered, the jump made less effective and the horse will be subjected to additional and unnecessary strain.

Mounted jumping

The first ridden exercises follow the pattern and sequence of the lunge exercises that have gone before, returning therefore to the pole grid, which has to be ridden from both directions.

With a shortened stirrup the horse is ridden in a few circles to either hand in rising trot. When the horse is moving actively with

An introduction to jumping, Friar Tuck jumps a small fence on the lunge with confidence and in good style.

An active trot over the pole grid with particularly good engagement of the hocks. An excellent balancing, suppling and strengthening exercise.

a regular rhythm, dropping the nose and relaxing the jaw on either side of his mouth, a wide turn is ridden from which a straight approach can be made to the grid.

Still in rising trot, the legs act in time with the stride to make the horse cross the grid without alteration to the speed and rhythm but, of course, with increased flexion of the joints.

Contact has to be maintained with the mouth by relaxed elbows and hands moving forward to follow and allow the stretching movement of the head and neck. It is just as important to ride accurately and correctly in the jumping exercises as in those on the flat.

Once the rider becomes careless in respect of either rhythm, contact or balance the quality of the work deteriorates and will be reflected in the horse's performance.

The usual failings in this simple grid exercise, other than losing the rhythm, are (a) for the rider to lose contact by letting the rein slip through the fingers, and (b) for the trunk to be inclined too far forward, i.e. in advance of the movement and thus out of balance with the horse.

The next stage is to raise the ground poles by about 8–10 ins (20–25 cm), placing them on bricks or resting the poles on short logs which have had a vee-shape cut in the top. Alternatively, use cavalletti at the lowest height (15 ins/37 cm).

The effect of the increased height is to make the horse use himself more actively and increase the flexion in the joints of the hind leg.

Trotting over a slightly higher cavalletti grid this pony shows exemplary hock engagement.

First jump

The first jump can be made by moving the last pole or cavalletto 10 ft (3 m) (double the trotting distance) from the penultimate one and raising it to make a small fence between 18–20 ins (45–50 cm) high. The rider need hardly alter the position over this fence, it is, after all, only a very small obstacle, but hands and shoulders will need to be advanced a little in order to follow the extension of the neck. The legs remain active in time with the stride through the grid, being applied more firmly in the final squeeze as the horse passes the penultimate pole.

The obstacle can be jumped up to half a dozen times during the lesson, but that is

Jumping exercise employing a cavalletti grid followed by a small fence.

sufficient. Thereafter, make much of the horse, do a little more work and finish the lesson.

Simple combinations

When 'jump-perfect' over this small fence the exercise is made more demanding by the addition of a second fence at the same height built 18 ft (5.4 m) from the first. This distance allows the horse one *non-jumping canter* stride between the two fences, that is between landing over the first and the take-off point for the second. (The average canter stride for a horse is between 11–12 ft (3.3–3.6 m) and becomes longer as the speed increases. In general, the optimum take-off point for a 4 ft

Balanced approach to a small upright fence by Friar Tuck. The rider's contact with the rein and her quiet position could hardly be bettered.

(1.2 m) fence is one and a third times the height. At this height and when the approach is from trot 18 ft (5.4 m) is an easily manageable distance for anything except a very big, long-striding horse.)

To ride this simple combination the rider crosses the grid in trot as before. As the horse *lands* over the first element of the combination the legs are put on firmly; almost inevitably the horse will take one canter stride and the leg action is then repeated even more decisively to ask for the take-off over the second element. Let the horse go on for a few strides in canter before bringing him back to circle quietly at trot and then at walk before asking for another jump. (Always in schooling, bring the horse back to a slower pace after a jump but equally make sure that he is allowed to canter on after landing for a few strides so that there is no encouragement for him to 'dwell' in the getaway stride.)

The words 'firm' and 'decisive' in relation to the leg action are deliberate. They mean just that, and the leg aid must never be allowed to deteriorate into a vulgar kick which disturbs the rider's balance and in consequence that of the horse. It is just as important to observe the measure of the aids when jumping or riding cross-country as when schooling on the flat. They will, of necessity, be stronger, but it is pointless to teach the horse obedience to the lightest of aids on the flat and then to employ extra strong and disturbing leg actions when jumping. It is also unnecessary. Indeed, by using over-strong aids in the schooling over fences we are reducing the range of pressures at our disposal and are coming close to *punishing* the horse into the fence instead of *riding* him. If you kick to jump a 2 ft (60 cm) fence what is

The final bar of this parallel is a little higher than the front one, an arrangement that makes the fence easier to jump than a true parallel.

there left to do when the horse is asked to make a special effort over a big and difficult obstacle?

The next step is to raise the fences to 2 ft (60 cm) using whatever materials are available to make the jump look solid.

The increase in height is insignificant but it involves the rider in closing the angle between upper body and thigh still more whilst concentrating on getting the weight down through the knee to the ankle. The closing of the body/thigh angle causes the seat to be raised a little from the saddle at take-off. The shoulders have then to be taken further forward with the elbow and hand advancing to follow the mouth. The seat needs to return lightly to the saddle on landing – an important point this for it contributes to the rider's security in the event of the horse pecking.

Finally, make the last element of the double a parallel 2 ft (60 cm) high and 4 ft (1.2 m) in width. This will cause both rider and horse

to be more active in the approach and take-off. Initially, so as to improve the horse's judgement of this new obstacle, fix the second element of the parallel some 3 ins (7.5 cm) higher than the first.

These exercises, involving the jumping of small fences from a grid approach, are valuable because they encourage balanced jumping in a state of calm. Additionally, they increase the suppleness and gymnastic ability and give the horse confidence in himself. They ensure, of course, that the horse will arrive automatically at the right point of take-off and that in itself improves his judgement of the fence.

The last exercise can be extended by following a three-pole trotting grid with a 2 ft (60 cm) fence 10 ft (3 m) away. Then allow

A combination with one non-jumping stride between the fences. The horse and rider partnership oozes confidence.

Friar Tuck jumps his first 'bounce' fence. It encourages the horse's confidence, initiative and gymnastic ability.

18 ft (5.4 m) (one non-jumping stride) before putting up a parallel 33 ft (10 m) away (two non-jumping strides) measuring 2 ft 6 ins (75 cm) in height and 4 ft (1.2 m) in width.

This calls for concentration by both partners in the enterprise and the rider needs to be quite clear about when the legs are to be put on. The one-stride distance called for the legs to be applied twice – once on landing over the first element and once more to ask for the take-off over the second. Two strides between the fences require the legs to act with increasing definition *three* times, the last decisive squeeze, not kick, asking for take-off.

For the rider to concentrate on the maintenance of good style in jumping is not a pious declaration of intent. Good style, on the contrary, is highly practical since any deviation from the ideal disturbs the balance

of the horse and probably his confidence too.

The principal faults, which occur even in experienced riders, are:

(1) *Rounding the shoulders and dropping the head.* It loosens and unbalances the seat. The back should be flat and be carried as nearly as possible in line with the horse's spine in the take-off and flight phases of the jump.

(2) *Lowering the toe and raising the heel upwards.* It obviates the effective use of the lower leg. It pitches the rider forward to the detriment of balance and security. It displaces knee and thigh, causing the weight to be carried in advance of the movement, and makes it very easy for the rider to exit over the shoulder should the horse peck on landing.

(3) *Kicking with the heels*—a failing already discussed.

The jumping seat

The seat is no more than a modification of the balanced position adopted for flat work and is based on a shortened leather. The seat is then pushed further to the back of the saddle and when the rider stands in the irons the seat will be raised a little above it.

The effect of the shorter leather is to make the angle at the knee, between thigh and lower leg, more acute and to close correspondingly the angle between the upper body and thigh when the shoulders are inclined forward in front of the hips.

The seat allows the rider to assume a more forward position to correspond with the horse's advanced centre of balance when jumping and it places the weight, via the bent knee, more upon the ball of the foot and less upon the seat bones.

The salient features of the seat are these:

(1) Trunk inclined forward from the hips.

(2) Head held up, rider looking directly to the front.

(3) Back held flat with shoulder open.

(4) Elbows lightly into the side. Using a necessarily shorter rein the hands are held either side of the wither and a little below it, but not so low as to break the straight line from elbow to bit.

(5) Seat in light contact with saddle or minimally raised from it.

(6) Knee pointed and well down the saddle so that the thigh is in contact.

(7) Lower leg held slightly to rear of the girth and in contact, toe raised and weight sinking into the heel.

Distance poles

So far the horse has been helped by the correct siting of the grid and the combination of small fences to arrive correctly at his point of take-off. Now it is time to remove that dependence and encourage the horse to work out the problems for himself – with, of course, help from the rider and some carefully planned fences.

However, it is still advisable to retain a distance pole in front to prevent rushing and to provide some assistance in the judging of the take-off. (So far as the rider is concerned the distance pole is a useful aid in 'seeing the stride'.)

Two fences can be built, one on each side of the schooling area. The height by degrees can be raised to 3 ft (90 cm) but both must be solid in appearance and both should be supplied with a ground-line. One can be a straightforward upright and the other a parallel. Build the latter with a 4 ft (1.2 m) spread and have the second element a hole higher than the first. In front of each place the distance pole 18 ft (5.4 m) away, and approach from trot. To encourage the horse provide wings to the fences. In the absence of properly constructed wings a pole resting on the standard at one end and on a bale or something similar at the other will serve the purpose. Once the horse is within the enclosing wings, which at the standard end will be considerably higher than the obstacle, it is easier for him to jump the fence than to attempt to run out to one side or the other. We should not, however, place too much reliance on the wings, nor allow the horse to do so. By gradual stages as the horse becomes increasingly confident we should aim to dispose of them altogether.

The distance poles can then be varied so as to give one or two non-jumping strides, and finally the fences can be approached from canter with the distance pole placed 45 ft (13.5 m) away to give three non-jumping strides between landing over the pole and take-off over the fence.

Changes of direction

Jumping single fences is relatively undemanding. Jumping which calls for precisely executed changes of direction is considerably more complex and puts a premium upon the approach and the maintenance of impulsion and balance.

Depending upon the horse's progress it should be possible to introduce the figure-of-eight exercise about half-way through Stage 3.

The exercise involves four fences sited on a figure-of-eight which can be made as large as the schooling area allows.

The fences can be varied but should initially be kept very low, certainly no bigger than 2 ft 6 ins–3 ft (75–90 cm) and should be preceded by a one-stride distance pole set at 18 ft (5.4 m) from the fence, which will be approached from trot. In effect this involves trotting round the 'short' sides at the top and bottom of the figure-of-eight.

Follow this by placing the poles to give two non-jumping strides, or three if space is available. After which dispense with the distance poles in front of the second and fourth fence, siting those fences so as to vary the number of non-jumping strides between one and two and three and four.

The exercise is amongst other things a lead-in to the change of direction and leg at canter which, ultimately, may have to be made in mid-air over a fence.

(Before attempting the figure-of-eight exercise over fences put out some strategically placed markers and ride the figure very accurately at trot, keeping to the track exactly without cutting corners and whilst maintaining the impulsion and the rhythm.)

complete accuracy, then go on to jumping from canter returning to trot round the short ends and then striking off on the opposite canter lead as the approach is made off the opposite diagonal.

Therafter build a small upright fence 2 ft 6 ins (75 cm) to replace the cavalletto. The fence, though not large adds a complication to the exercise. Sited as it is and approached from an angle it invites the unsteady horse to run out and down the line of the fence. Approaching from the left the horse can run out to the right and along the obstacle and vice-versa. It demands, therefore, concentration on the part of the rider and obedience and some initiative from the horse.

The extension to the exercise and the introduction to the change in mid-air is accomplished by placing a fence of crossed poles in the centre of the arena but parallel to the long sides. The crossed poles encourage the horse (and the rider) to jump accurately over the centre, and to do that the circles have to be ridden with equal accuracy if the approach is to allow them to do so.

A single circle ridden at trot commences the exercise. As the horse jumps the fence, the rider has to incline the horse's head and the upper part of her own body in the direction of the movement whilst applying the canter leg aids. In almost every instance the horse will land in canter and on the correct lead. The exercise has to be practised on both reins and when the strike-offs are established the circle can be ridden in both directions at canter. Thereafter the full figure-of-eight can be ridden.

The angled fence

To get closer to the ideal of changing direction over the fence begin by placing a cavalletto at the centre of the figure-of-eight. Trot the figure, jumping the cavalletto at an angle until the horse can perform the exercise with

Bounce fence and jumping grid

Bounce fences (those allowing no stride between the two elements) increase the gymnastic ability and suppleness of the horse and can also, along with the jumping grid, be looked upon as a strengthening exercise.

As an introduction put up two small fences 12 ft (3.6 m) apart with a distance pole 18 ft (5.4 m) from the combination. Trot into the fence strongly. Apply the legs on landing, and since there is no room for the horse to take a stride he will 'bounce' out over the second element. A more advanced exercise is to include a bounce fence as part of a combination of related fences. For instance, one might commence with an upright, followed 33 ft (10 m) away (two non-jumping strides) by the bounce combination and then by an obstacle placed so as to give either one- or two non-jumping strides. The distances can, of course, be varied to produce progressively more difficult exercises.

A useful, easily constructed training aid, usually much enjoyed by horses and their riders, is the jumping grid. It is a line of up to six fixed fences, 18 ins (45 cm) high and placed 12 ft (3.6 m) apart, which is ridden at canter. If the side can be enclosed by a rail so much the better.

Fence variety

Essentially all fences fall into one of four categories, although, of course, the appearance can be varied by the addition of filling materials etc. and the substitution of walls, gates, planks, etc. for the basic pole.

There are **upright, staircase, parallel** and **pyramid** fences, all of which should be included in the horse's training since they present different problems in respect of take-off and angles of descent.

At an *upright* the take-off zone, in general terms, is between a distance equal to the height of the fence and up to one and one-third times its height – the latter being closer to the optimum take-off point than otherwise.

For the fence to be jumped successfully the point of take-off and landing should be equidistant from the bottom of the fence.

The horse reaches the highest point of the arc made when jumping the fence when he is directly over the top of the obstacle.

The upright fence is the most difficult to jump since if the horse takes off too close he hits the fence on the way up, whereas if he stands off too far he is likely to hit the fence with his hind legs in the descent.

A ground pole, judiciously placed, reduces the difficulty and can be used to teach the horse how to judge his take-off. Placed in front of the fence at the appropriate distance in relation to its height it can be used to produce a correct take-off since the horse judges the latter for the most part by looking at the bottom of the fence.

A further pole placed on the ground at a similar distance on the landing side will control the angle of descent if it should become too steep, as the horse will reach out to clear it.

A *staircase* is a much easier and more encouraging obstacle. It is a fence built with two or three bars set at ascending heights, as in the case of a triple bar obstacle, and its shape corresponds to the parabola of the leap. The highest point of the leap will be in line with the highest element in the fence and it occurs in the middle of the flight phase. The landing is well out from the fence and the angle of descent less steep than over an upright. In consequence the getaway stride after landing is relatively long in comparison with the shorter stride following an upright.

These are factors which have to be taken into account when estimating distances between combination fences.

Parallel fences comprise two elements which in a 'true' parallel are of the same height. Lowering the first element introduces a staircase quality and makes the fence easier to jump.

It might seem that the horse has to take off well away from a fence of this nature and he may, indeed, do so, but it involves his making a very big jump with increased effort and a probable decrease in accuracy.

The most successful way to jump a parallel is to take off closer to the fence than would be advisable in the case of an upright. The reason is because the horse has to reach the highest point of the leap when he is closer to the rear bar than to the one in front of the fence. In consequence the landing is well out from the fence and as a result of the less abrupt angle of descent the getaway stride is longer.

A *pyramid* fence comprises three elements, the first and last of equal height and the central one higher.

It can be jumped from both directions but it must not be built too big or with too great a spread as the horse cannot see the final element.

It comes, however, within the category encompassing spread fences and the getaway stride is longer than with an upright.

Distances

With combinations of fences 4 ft (1.2 m) in height and with spreads of the same measurement, the following distances take into account differences in the angle of descent and their effect on the length of the get-away stride. They are based on an average canter stride of 11–12 ft (3.3–3.6 m).

Upright to upright: 24 ft (7.2 m) – one non-jumping stride; 33–35 ft (10–10.5 m) – two non-jumping strides.

Upright to spread: 23 ft (6.9 m) – one non-jumping stride; 32–34 ft (9.6–10.2 m) – two non-jumping strides.

Spread to upright: 25 ft (7.5 m) – one non-jumping stride; 35–37 ft (10.5–11.1 m) – two non-jumping strides.

Spread to spread: 24 ft (7.2 m) – one non-jumping stride; 33–35 ft (10–10.5 m) – two non-jumping strides.

(The same formula is applied for three non-jumping strides (45 ft/13.5 m); four (56 ft/16.8 m) and five (67 ft/20.1 m), the addition or subtraction of a foot between different types of fences being the same. Fences are *related* between 39 ft 4 ins and 80 ft (11.9–24 m) apart. Below 39 ft (11.7 m) they become combinations.

Cross-country riding

There is a more rumbustious, freer character involved with riding across country over obstacles and natural hazards, and both horse and rider have to adapt their technique accordingly. Indeed, it is not untrue to say that much of the school work and the jumping exercises carried out within the training areas are no more than a preparation for riding outside the constrictions imposed by 'walls' and 'long' and 'short' sides.

Throughout the horse's training a lot of emphasis must be given to the 'exercise' periods exemplified by riding in the countryside.

Within this stage, up to September in the horse's fourth year, the objectives are these:

(1) To accustom the horse to cope with natural terrain, including going up and down hills in balance and maintaining an easy rhythm.

(2) To jump a variety of low, fixed obstacles and natural hazards, including water, out of his stride and both up and down hill.

Fences, since they are fixed, should be small and inviting and one has also to seek natural obstacles like ditches and streams.

Across country the rider adopts the jumping position, placing the weight over the centre of balance and keeping the legs in contact.

The faults to be avoided are straightening the leg so that the contact and the flexion of knee and ankle is lost and the seat is taken too far out of the saddle. Just as common a failing is for the rider to disturb the balance by getting in front of the movement.

The pace to adopt in cross-country riding is a good swinging canter and once the horse has settled into the rhythm (and all horses develop their own comfortable cruising speed) the rider's concern is to remain in balance whilst keeping steady contact with hands and legs.

However, there is a notable difference between horses ridden in the schooling area and being ridden in the great outdoors. Horses that in the school take up a nice light contact and may need active legs to maintain impulsion can be quite different in the open. The natural impulsion is increased and the formerly light-mouthed character may take a stronger hold of his bridle.

This is natural and to be encouraged, but clearly it has to be kept within reasonable bounds, but without the rider fighting the horse to keep control. Fighting against a strong pulling horse does no good at all. The horse's excitement increases; he pulls even harder against the discomfort caused by the bit and he becomes less and less receptive to his rider. For the rider, too it is an unnecessarily exhausting business.

There is a knack in restraining a pulling horse which is acquired with experience and it has nothing to do with brute force.

The first rule is to keep calm, thereafter restraint can be imposed by straightening the upper body so that the weight, in fact, is somewhat behind the centre of gravity and the seat a little out of the saddle to allow the powerful back muscles to be used with full advantage.

The lower leg, too, may advance just a little. The hands act by one of them holding a steady contact whilst the other closes and

Tackling a downhill fence in good style. Friar Tuck wears a gag bridle to give his rider more control over cross-country courses.

The opposite. A fence being jumped from an uphill approach. The point of take-off is exactly right.

opens in firm squeezes. One should not, however, always check with the same hand. The horse gets used to it and he stiffens that side of his mouth in resistance because we have more or less provided him with a base against which to pull, even though the check is followed by a release of pressure. Constant pressure from one or both hands is even worse and is, indeed, an encouragement to the horse to pull even more strongly.

The effective way to use the hands in conjunction with the restraining aids of the body is to make the checks with alternate hands so that the base against which the horse can resist is continually switched from one side of the mouth to the other.

When the horse responds and comes back to his 'natural' canter speed the rider can resume his position poised over the centre of balance and revert to the policy of minimal intervention.

Up and down

Riding across country must inevitably involve traversing slopes and hills. Riding uphill the horse has to be able to employ the full propulsive power of his quarters and so the rider needs to fold the upper body forward from the hips so as to give the quarters complete freedom. The hands must allow any extension of the neck that is made whilst keeping a light contact with the mouth.

Going downhill is not so easy and the young horse needs to be introduced gradually to slopes of increasing severity. Downhill slopes should beridden first at walk with the rider's legs insisting that the horse moves

A powerful, onward-bound jump over an awkward tree trunk. The rider's jumping position over the fences is good.

forward steadily and *straight*. If the quarters are allowed to swing out so that the horse is across the slope there is a real danger of his legs slipping from under him. If the horse attempts to hurry he can be restrained by the fingers closing on the rein. The contact with the hand is, however, necessary to the horse since it allows him to relate his balance to what is a still point.

Whilst the upper body should most certainly not be allowed to overweight the forehand by being inclined too far to the front, it should just as certainly not be inclined to the rear with the legs poked out in front.

The horse does need to have his hind legs well underneath him and for that reason sitting well back over the quarters is to be discouraged. Conversely, if the trunk is inclined too far forward the transference of weight to the front end may force the horse into going faster and faster in order to keep a semblance of balance. As in all things moderation is to be encouraged.

Position

In fact, moderation combined with reasonable prudence is the secret of cross-country riding, together with an ability to adapt to the circumstance.

In general, it is advisable for the rider to adopt a less than absolute forward position over cross-country fences. It would, for instance, be unwise to get in front of the centre of gravity at a drop fence. It is far better and much more secure to hold the body in the vertical plane and 'slip' the reins.

The more experience that the young horse can obtain over a variety of small cross-country obstacles, including drops, banks and small step type obstacles, the better will be his balance. Furthermore, he will gain confidence in himself and his rider.

A very good training exercise, if the facilities are available, is to build a number of small obstacles, even if they are no more than stout logs or low piles of brush on tracks through a small piece of woodland and to ride over them at a steady canter letting the horse jump out of his stride.

Hunting

Without any doubt at all the best cross-country experience for both horse and rider is gained in the hunting field. Hunting, indeed, is one of the most valuable training aids at our disposal, developing initiative and confidence and teaching the horse to look after himself in all sorts of situations.

Towards the end of September the young horse can be taken cub-hunting. This is the ideal introduction to hunting proper since it is unlikely, at least in the early part of the season, that any run of note will ensue.

From the hunting viewpoint there is, of course, far more to cub-hunting than the provision of a training exercise for young horses. The purpose is to introduce the young hounds to their quarry, the fox, and to provide the same opportunity for the fox cubs. In consequence much of the time is spent in covert and one expects no more than a modicum of galloping and practically no jumping, which is ideal for young horses.

On the first occasion the presence of an older companion, versed in the ways of hunting, will be reassuring to the young horse who will naturally be excited by the sights and sounds of this new circumstance. To settle the youngster down and get the itch out of his heels it is better to hack to the meet, if this is possible. Otherwise, unbox three or four miles away and hack from there. It does, of course, mean geting up early, for cub-hunting meets in the early part of the season are usually not later than 7 a.m.

At the meet keep the horse moving on the fringes of the gathering. When hounds move off, instead of following them, ride off in the opposite direction and take a route which will bring you back within a field or two of what is going on. Stay out for a couple of hours then take the horse home quietly and let him think about his experience over his breakfast.

Having been to two or three meets the horse should have settled sufficiently to allow his being ridden with the field, but with discretion. Keep him moving all the time. If you get a gallop, join in, but keep out of the way and avoid, if at all possible, groups of excited horses waiting their turn to jump a fence. Where it is possible to jump do so, just as you would in the schooling area at home – don't, of course, jump unnecessarily. That is called 'larking' and earns the severe displeasure of Field Masters.

When the season opens early in November there is no harm in taking the horse out regularly for a half-day whilst continuing his schooling programme.

Always hack quietly back to your box after hunting so that the horse arrives there dry and calm. If he is wet, trot the last half-mile, put the rug on inside out and he will be pretty well dried off by the time he gets home.

Refusals

Before concluding this chapter we should consider the matter of the horse refusing at a fence. In a carefully planned and executed training programme refusals should either not occur or occur only rarely. It is, nonetheless, appropriate to remind outselves of why and how horses decline to jump.

Horses refuse for one or other of the following reasons:
(1) They are over-faced, either by the fence being too high or because they lack the experience to tackle it successfully.
(2) They may be sore from having jarred their legs or from a strained back.
(3) They stop if they believe the act of jumping will cause them pain. Ill-fitting saddles which pinch as the back is arched over a fence are a sure way to cause refusals. So, of course, is a rider whose incompetence causes him to jab the horse in the mouth at take-off. Horses that have been compelled to jump when their mus-

cles ached or their shins were sore may refuse long after the trouble has cleared up. A bad experience at a fence resulting in loss of confidence may cause problems at similar fences and it will take time and patience to get the horse going happily again.

(4) Rider error, or just plain incompetence, is one of the most common sources leading to refusals. Young horses cannot be taught to jump by inexperienced riders at novice level.

A principal failing in the less than expert is the obsession with not being left behind. In many ways it is commendable but it can be carried too far and with disastrous results.

If the rider lifts the seat out of the saddle in the approach, inclining the trunk well forward, it is very likely that contact with the mouth will be lost. The weight of the rider throws the horse on his forehand and despite those flailing legs and increased speed the position worsens as the horse gets into the take-off zone. The easiest and probably the most sensible thing for the horse to do in those circumstances is to stop – and he usually does. Speed, incidentally, only causes a horse to flatten the trajectory of the leap. The ideal jump is made from impulsion out of a state of balance.

(5) Horses will refuse when they find themselves wrong at a fence. By doing so they display their good sense and should not be punished for that.

Horses refuse by stopping or by running out. In other words, they cease to obey the legs and they cease to go forwards.

All our training has been directed towards obtaining obedience and instant response to the driving aids of the legs but even so, for one reason or another, most of them connected with a faulty or too casual an approach, there will be an occasional stop.

If it is a run-out, circle quietly but swiftly in the opposite direction, turn him off the circle and present him at the fence at a slight angle from the side to which he ran out. That is, if he went out to the left bring him in from the left, which makes it nearly impossible for him to run out to the same side again. Be careful, however, not to make the angle too shallow otherwise you are inviting him to run out across the front of the fence.

In training, whether the horse stops dead or runs out, have the fence *lowered* and jump it for two or three days at the lower height before putting it up again – always, of course, assuming that it wasn't impossibly high to start with.

Earlier in this chapter it was mentioned that it was possible to cause a horse jumping on the lunge to jump to one side or another by the lunge line not allowing him sufficient freedom to go straight forwards after landing. This is the source of much crooked jumping but it can also develop later in the training. Obviously, the habit creates problems over a course, particularly in the negotiations of short combination fences.

It can be countered and cured by using a 'straightening' pole placed from the top of the upright to the landing side on that side of the fence which the horse favours. First place the pole at right angles to the fence, moving it inwards as the horse becomes accustomed to its presence and jumps the fence freely with the pole in position. When the horse jumps straight with the pole at an angle of, say, 30° to the fence one can consider the habit to have been corrected.

In cross-country jumping the horse has to be allowed to use his own initiative more so than over show fences.

Very often the rider will need to encourage the horse at a difficult obstacle but there will be many occasions when we can do nothing but leave it to the horse, sitting as still as we can and 'throwing' the reins at him. If the relationship between horse and rider is right the good horse will then return the compliment and get his rider out of trouble.

II

Saddle and Bridle

IN THE majority of rider programmes little emphasis is placed on the importance of selecting and fitting items of saddlery. This is a pity, because the equipment we use is very much a part of the business of riding and can contribute materially to the performance of both horse and rider, or conversely detract from it in the same measure.

The conditions of unnecessary stress and the consequent lowering of safety thresholds which can occur as a result of unsuitable or ill-fitting saddlery were mentioned in Chapter 5. To avoid causing difficulties of that nature and to ensure that the performance is not inhibited by failings in equipment, riders need to have far more than a superficial understanding of the action and purpose of the various items involved.

The saddle

The saddle is the largest single item of the rider's equipment and the most expensive. It can be put into perspective if it is examined under three headings:

(1) The fitting in relation to the movement and the structure of the back.

(2) The comfort and security of the rider.

(3) Its design in relation to purpose and the positioning of the rider in balance with the movement. (The importance of this last consideration is easily appreciated when we realise that a 14 stone (88 kg) man on a horse weighing 9 cwt (450 kg) is in fact one-fifth of the horse's weight, the equivalent of the same man carrying a very heavy suitcase on a cross-county run. Carried over the centre of the horse's gravity the weight is the least possible encumbrance to the horse's movement. Carried out of balance or in a state of constantly shifting imbalance it is restric-

tive of movement and enormously fatiguing to boot.)

Fitting

The construction of the saddle must be such that with the rider in position there will be no restriction of the natural movement.

In the first instance that requirement, which may be regarded as the first and great commandment, will be met by the tree fitting the horse's back. If the tree does not fit then neither will the completed saddle.

Subsequently, the fitting depends on the regulation of the panel, i.e. the regulation of the wool with which the panel is most usually filled and the shape and cut of the panel and the overlaying flap.

It is possible, if expensive, to have a tree made specially for a particularly difficult back but in general they come in three sizes: narrow, medium and broad.

If the tree is too broad or too narrow for the back the matter will not be remedied by adjusting the panel stuffing. Too narrow a tree will continue to pinch at the points, the extensions of the front arch; too broad a tree will, under the effect of the additional stuffing, become broader. Both will put the saddle out of balance.

If the tree is too long it will clearly put restrictive and possibly damaging pressure on the loins: if too short it concentrates the weight over too small an area of the back.

Placed on the back the saddle should sit quite level, the pommel and cantle being in line horizontally, and the seat so shaped that the rider is compelled to sit at its centre and in its lowest point.

Above all, the saddle with the rider in position has to allow *clearance of the spinal complex* along its length and across the breadth of it. This last cannot be accomplished if the channel dividing the two parts of the panel is too narrow or has become closed. From the rear it should be possible to see through the saddle from cantle to pommel. In practice it is desirable for three fingers to be inserted between the front arch (pommel) and the wither when the rider is in position. The effect of discomfort caused to the spinal complex has already been explained in Chapter 5.

A horse that is markedly more developed on one side, or a panel that is stuffed unequally, will cause the weight to be carried unevenly and thus out of balance and may also result in soreness.

The same can occur, however, if the tree has become twisted.

Twisted trees are caused in three ways. Either the basic construction is at fault or they have become twisted during the making up process, or in the case of a spring tree, the fault has occurred because of misuse by the rider.

A spring tree is one which is given resilience by being fitted with two strips of tempered steel from front to rear. Obviously, it is made from lighter wood. The spring is easily discernible if one places the pommel against the chest and pulls the cantle (gently, please) with both hands.

The opposite to the spring tree is the rigid tree, made from heavier materials and, as the name implies, with no provision being made for resilience.

The advantage of the spring tree is that it gives greater comfort to the rider and, arguably, to the horse's back, since it gives in accordance with the movement of the latter. It also permits the influence of the seat bones to be more directly transmitted.

Nonetheless, it has disadvantages, too. A strong horseman using the seat powerfully may cause soreness of the back through the concentration of pressure.

Furthermore, it is something of a precision instrument and must be treated with care if it is not to be damaged. It can, for instance, be easily twisted should the rider mount by holding the cantle rather than placing his right hand over the waist of the saddle.

Finally, the action will be restricted if the panel and its flap is cut so far forward that it lies on the shoulder instead of behind it. This is a common fault in present-day saddles, particularly in those described as jumping saddles, but in fairness the fault does not always lie with the saddle. The panel will lie on the shoulder if the conformation of the horse is at fault and the shoulder is insufficient and overly straight. (Arab horses and their derivatives often suffer in this respect, not because the Arab shoulder is always or necessarily straight but because it is set somewhat differently in relation to a distinctive wither formation.)

Comfort, security, position

Modern saddles contribute to the comfort and, therefore, the security of the rider in a number of ways and also, of course, in varying degrees. The spring tree is in itself an aid to comfort. Usually, it is made with a narrow 'twist' (or waist) and the panel has therefore to follow that line. The advantage of the narrow twist is that it does not force the upper thighs to be opened uncomfortably, a factor much appreciated by riders with short legs. However, it can be overdone and will then prevent the rider from assuming the desirable 'open' seat. From the viewpoint of the horse there is also a disadvantage if the panel is narrowed too much at the waist of the saddle. Then, the bearing surface is much reduced and the rider's weight is concentrated over a small area rather than carried evenly over the whole bearing surface.

Virtually every modern saddle is equipped with recessed bars, that is, stirrup bars which are attached to the underside of the tree, and which as a result do not form an uncomfortable lump under the rider's thigh, allowing the latter to lie flat down the saddle. Without doubt the recessed bar is beneficial not only to the rider's comfort but also to the assumption of a correct practical seat. It can, nonetheless, cause difficulties when it comes to putting the leathers on the bars and, of course, if they are difficult to put on they will not slide off very easily in the event of a fall. A heavy iron and a proper riding boot should, however, take care of that unhappy occurrence and prevent the rider from being dragged.

The bars, together with the slimmed down panel allow the rider to get close to his horse and this is further encouraged by the use of relatively light leather for the flap and the sweat flap lying underneath.

Finally, the saddle adds to the rider's security by the seat being dipped, encouraging the rider to sit deep, and the provision of a forward knee roll on the panel. Knee roll is, in fact, a misnomer and is also misleading. The forward roll gives support to the lower part of the thigh above the knee. Any attempt to use the roll to support the latter will result in the seat being seriously disturbed.

The shape of the seat is critical to the positioning of the rider over the centre of balance, but by no means all of them fulfil this essential requirement. The principal failing is for the dip to be too exaggerated so that the rider is tipped forward on the fork, off the seatbones and thus overweights the forehand. Less frequent is the opposite fault when the dip causes the rider to sit behind the movement. It is, nonetheless, not unknown in many of the German patterns.

Types

There are all kinds of saddles, all bearing different titles. Essentially, there are three basic types: jumping, all- or general-purpose, and dressage.

The ultimate example of the jumping saddle is the Toptani model built on the spring tree designed by Ilias Toptani. The old, pre-Second World War hunting saddle which persisted well into the 1960s, was built on a relatively wide-waisted rigid tree with a straight head. That is, the front arch was vertical in relation to the rest of the tree. As a result the bars, over which the rider's weight rests, compelled the rider to sit more to the rear than otherwise, if only by a little. Toptani, wishing his riders to adopt shorter leathers and to be positioned further forward and over the centre of balance in the approach to the fence and when making the leap, realised the impossibility of their doing so in the old-type saddles with the conventional vertical head. He therefore *sloped* the head by bringing the points *forward* and with them the bars.

To correspond with the inclination of the sloped head the panel and flap had then to be swept forward also, so as to allow for the shortened leg position. The tree was a little longer than usual, dipped, of course, and narrow in the waist.

As a jumping saddle it has yet to be surpassed, but it is a *jumping* saddle and not ideal for other pursuits, such as a long day's hunting, when for much of the time the rider sits in the saddle. If you sit in a Toptani with shortened leathers, a 'rock' develops in time causing it to shift forward.

In the middle of the spectrum is the all- or general-purpose saddle. The slope of the head is less pronounced, the bars and, therefore, the point over which is carried the rider's weight is just a bit further back, the flap and panel cut not so much to the front. In fact, it is a modified version of the jumping saddle in which one can do just about everything up to a certain level. Today, many saddles of this type are labelled 'event' saddles, a word which is thought to have more sales appeal.

And so to the dressage saddle. Since the rider has no need to follow an advancing centre of balance the head of the tree is vertical, as in the old hunting saddles and, indeed, in some dressage saddles the bars are longer than usual and set just a little more to the rear. These 'extended' bars place the rider's weight a *shade* further back to accord with the horse's raised forehand and the displacement of the horse's weight on to the quarters.

The flap and panel once more follow the line of the head and are, therefore, almost vertical. Now that, in conjunction with a slightly dipped seat, is all very well for the top-level dressage rider who has acquired a long, vertical line through the seat but it is a disastrous design for the less accomplished who, in their attempts to emulate the Klimkes and Boldts, come off their seat bones and are perched on their forks. Anyone below the level of the Masters is far better off, and far more effective, using a saddle in which flap and panel are rounded forward. Ideally, the dressage saddle for the expert does not come off the peg, it has to be made to measure.

The principal faults in both jumping and general-purpose saddles are for the panel to be cut too far to the front and for the seat to be too exaggerated in its dip. In the dressage saddle the failings are concerned with panels and flaps cut too close to the vertical or even, Heaven forfend, behind that line and for the seat to be too short, almost to the point of encasing the rider and prohibiting any movement to either front or rear. Encouragingly, there is now a movement towards a less-pronounced dip in the seats of all three basic types of saddle.

The German influence in saddle manufacture is all-pervasive and, in my view, has proved retrogressive in some respects. Saddles of German manufacture are generally well constructed and cosmetically attractive, and a few are well designed in relation to both horse and rider. The imitations are far less satisfactory and, again in my opinion, are much inferior to the saddles which were available twenty years ago.

Central to saddle design was the principle relating to the angle of slope of the head and the consequent placement of the bars relative to the saddle's function.

The German saddle-makers have disregarded this basic design concept, substituting the illogical (but more expensive) 'cut-back' head.

Structurally, the cut-back head detracts from the tree's strength. It places the bars further to the rear and also, therefore, the rider's weight (as in the hunting saddle of half a century or more ago). It can create a pronounced bulge behind the head which, once more, may persuade the rider, particularly the male, to shift backwards in order to avoid uncomfortable contact.

The purpose of the cut-back head, it is claimed, is to allow for a greater range of fitting over the wither – it is said to accommodate the wither that is higher than usual. But the sloped head permits just such a range of fittings, if not more, and without the disadvantages inherent in the cut-back tree.

I am loath to admit any significant advantages in the German-inspired saddle but I concede that the less-waisted tree employed and the resultant broader bearing-surface of the panel is easier and more comfortable for the horse, and it is his well-being that has to be our first consideration.

Bitting

The principles which apply to bitting revolve round the action of the five main groups of bits upon one or more of seven parts of the horse's head.

It follows therefore that to understand the mechanics of bitting it will be necessary to have some knowledge of the five bitting groups and of the construction of the bits belonging to them. Secondly, we have to know something about the parts of the head involved in bitting and quite a lot more about the conformation of the mouth.

We can go a stage further and apply to the subject a sort of Parkinson's law. It reads something like this:

The action and pressures applied through the agency of the bit to the head and mouth varies in intensity and character according to three factors:

(1) The construction of the bit used.

(2) The conformation of the horse's mouth.

(3) The angle at which the mouth is held in relation to the hand.

As a corollary it can be added that the action of the bit is made more or less effective by the rider's ability to use the supporting aids.

The seven parts of the head and mouth involved with the bit actions are: the *corners of the lips*; the *bars* of the mouth, i.e. the fleshy gum between the molar and incisor teeth; the *tongue*; the *curb groove*; the *poll*; the *nose*, in some circumstances, where use is made of a drop noseband, for instance; and rarely, and not in my view legitimately, the *roof* of the mouth.

Principal bit groups

The five groups are these: the *snaffle*; the *Weymouth* or double bridle; the *pelham;* the *gag;* and the *hackamore* or bitless bridle. Hackamore, in fact, is an incorrect term for a bitless-type bridle usually fitted with metal cheekpieces. The true hackamore is part of a progressive system of mouthing the horse by applying a succession of diminishing restraints to the nose, after which the horse is ridden in what is potentially a very severe bit but is controlled at speed and in complex movements by the weight of a light looping rein. It rightly belongs to a far older school of horsemanship than ours, reaching its apotheosis in the Iberian Peninsular during its long occupation by the Moors which had begun early in the eighth century and was to continue for nearly 700 years. It went with the sixteenth-century Conquistadores to the Americas where it survives in something close to its pure form in the horsemanship of the Californian cowboy. In its bastard form it

is used, mainly by show jumpers, in Europe and elsewhere and appears to be successful in some notable instances.

Of the five groups the *snaffle* is the most elementary form of control available. These bits come in a bewildering variety but for general usage three subdivisions predominate: the mullen mouth snaffle (i.e. the half-moon mouthpiece) made of metal, vulcanite, nylon or rubber; the single joint snaffle; and finally, snaffles like the French bradoon which employ a central link or spatula.

The snaffle is varied further by the diameter of the mouthpiece and by the fitting of different cheeks or rings. The simplest of the latter is the wire ring running through holes in the butt ends of the mouthpiece. The ring may vary in size in the same way as the diameter of the mouthpiece.

Thin mouthpieces will be sharper in their action but have the disadvantage of concentrating pressure over so small an area that the latter may easily become numb and insensitive. A thick mouthpiece covering a wider area and a larger number of sensory nerves avoids this difficulty and is, of course, milder.

Large rings reduce the possibility of their being pulled through the mouth and to a degree act laterally on the side of the face. The advantage of the wire ring is that it allows movement of the mouthpiece in the mouth and thus encourages salivation and the relaxation of the lower jaw. Should the hole, through which the ring passes, become worn there is a possibility that the lips may be chafed or pinched. The eggbutt snaffle obviates that danger but it also alters the complexion of the bit in one respect, for the mouthpiece will no longer be able to move so freely in the mouth. In the intermediate and more advanced stages of training this should not be of much consequence and, indeed, the action may be improved by being more direct. In fact, it can be taken a step further in this respect if a slot is made at the top of the eggbutt through which the cheekpiece of the bridle is passed. This will have the effect of 'fixing' the bit in the mouth, reducing the movement still further but making the action all the more precise.

On the other hand it would be very unwise to employ such a bit with a young horse who is not relaxing the lower jaw and whose mouth is inclined to be dry.

Cheeks on a snaffle bit like those employed with the Fulmer snaffle, intensify the lateral action against the face and, of course, cannot be pulled through the mouth. Movement of the mouthpiece is made possible by the loose ring attachments. However, it is advisable to secure the top of the cheek to the bridle cheekpiece by means of a small retaining strap. The bit is then kept nicely in place and there is no danger of it causing injury by the cheek becoming caught up in a nostril – something that has happened more than once in fraught circumstances.

Of the snaffles, the mullen mouth pattern, particularly when it is made in rubber, is the mildest in its action but its shape makes it insufficiently precise for slightly more advanced schooling. Additionally, many horses seem encouraged to hang on the soft mouthpiece. The jointed snaffle is obviously stronger in its action and it is often thought that those employing a central spatula are a degree more severe again. This is not so, the two joints actually reducing the severity of the single-joint bit's so-called 'nutcracker' action.

Snaffle action

The action of the snaffle group is not, however, constant. It differs in relation to the position of the head.

When the head is held low and somewhat outstretched, as in the early schooling stages, the action is upward against the *corners of the mouth.*

In the intermediate stages, when the horse has acquired a higher 'working' carriage, with the face being carried in a line up to 45° in advance of the vertical, the action of the bit is *less* on the corners of the mouth and more across the *tongue* and the *bars* of the lower jaw.

In the advanced horse, carrying his head in the vertical plane, the bit bears increasingly across the lower jaw and tongue, although there will remain a modicum of action against the corners of the mouth which can be emphasised, as necessary, by the slight upward movement of the hand.

The double bridle

The *double* bridle represents the most sophisticated bitting arrangement. Used skilfully it can be used to influence the advanced head position more easily and with greater finesse.

The bradoon, a light snaffle with smaller rings, needs to be adjusted fairly high in the mouth and it acts, primarily, against the corners of the lips in a raising effect.

The curb bit, fitted below the bradoon across the bars and employing a curb chain, is far more complex, its construction allowing pressure to be brought to bear on no less than four of the seven parts involved in the bitting principles.

When the bit in response to the feel on the rein assumes an angle of 45° in the mouth, a downward pressure is exerted on the *poll,* which is encouraged to flex, by the eye of the bit moving forwards and downwards and thus transmitting pressure via the cheek and headpiece.

Simultaneously, there is a corresponding action on the curb groove, the curb chain tightening to induce a relaxation (flexing) of the lower jaw and a retraction of the nose.

The degree of leverage possible is governed by the length of the cheek above and below the mouthpiece. The longer the cheek

A selection of snaffle bits and a conventional Weymouth comprising the curb bit, curb chain and a light bradoon.

SADDLE AND BRIDLE

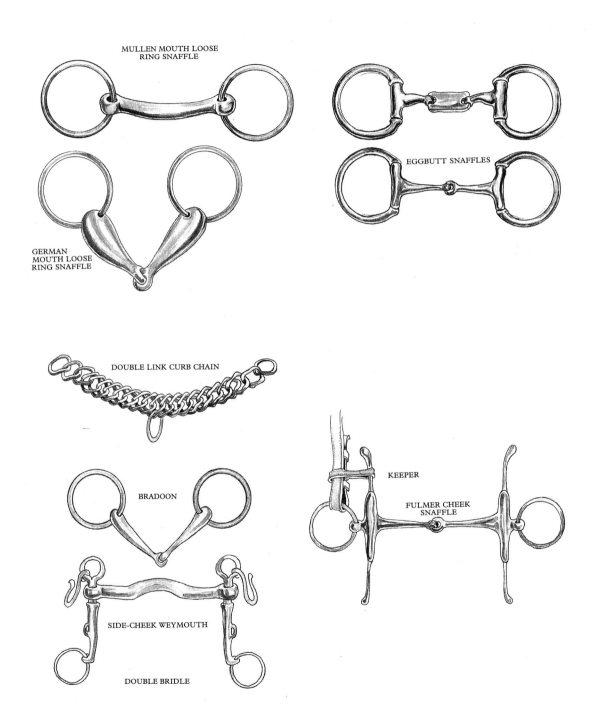

MULLEN MOUTH LOOSE
RING SNAFFLE

EGGBUTT SNAFFLES

GERMAN
MOUTH LOOSE
RING SNAFFLE

DOUBLE LINK CURB CHAIN

BRADOON

KEEPER

FULMER CHEEK
SNAFFLE

SIDE-CHEEK WEYMOUTH

DOUBLE BRIDLE

MULLEN MOUTH
PELHAM

HARTWELL MOUTH
PELHAM

KIMBLEWICK